R.D.Weaver
1998

CORE Lectures

Simulation-Based Econometric Methods

The "CORE Foundation" was set up in 1987 with
the goal of stimulating new initiatives and research
activities at CORE.
One of these initiatives is the creation of
CORE LECTURES,
a series of books based on the lectures delivered each
year by an internationally renowned scientist invited
to give a series of lectures in one of the research areas
of CORE.

CORE Lectures

SIMULATION-BASED ECONOMETRIC METHODS

CHRISTIAN GOURIÉROUX
and
ALAIN MONFORT

OXFORD UNIVERSITY PRESS
1996

Oxford University Press, Great Clarendon Street, Oxford OX2 6DP

Oxford New York

Athens Auckland Bangkok Bogota Bombay
Buenos Aires Calcutta Cape Town Dar es Salaam
Delhi Florence Hong Kong Istanbul Karachi
Kuala Lumpur Madras Madrid Melbourne
Mexico City Nairobi Paris Singapore
Taipei Tokyo Toronto
and associated companies in
Berlin Ibadan

Oxford is a trade mark of Oxford University Press

Published in the United States by
Oxford University Press Inc., New York

British Library Cataloguing in Publication Data
Data available

Library of Congress Cataloging in Publication Data
Gouriéroux, Christian, 1949–   .
Simulation-based econometric methods / Christian Gouriéroux and
Alain Monfort.
p.   cm.—(OUP / CORE lecture series)
Includes bibliographical references.
1. Econometric models.   I. Monfort, Alain, 1943–   .   II. Title.
III. Series.
HB141   330'.01'5195—dc20   96–18570
ISBN 0–19–877475–3

Typeset by Focal Image Ltd.
Printed in Great Britain
on acid-free paper by
Biddles Ltd, Guildford and King's Lynn

We are especially grateful to L. Broze and B. Salanié for checking
the presentation and the proofs. They are not responsible
for remaining errors.

We also thank E. Garcia and F. Traore who carefully typed this text
and F. Henry who helped with the layout.

Contents

1

Introduction and Motivations

1.1   Introduction

The development of theoretical and applied econometrics has been widely influenced by the availability of powerful and cheap computers. Numerical calculations have become progressively less burdensome with the increasing speed of computers while, at the same time, it has been possible to use larger data sets. We may distinguish three main periods in the history of statistical econometrics.

Before the 1960s, models and estimation methods were assumed to lead to analytical expressions of the estimators. This is the period of the linear model, with the associated least squares approach, of the multivariate linear simultaneous equations, with the associated instrumental variable approaches, and of the exponential families for which the maximum likelihood techniques are suitable.

The introduction of numerical optimization algorithms characterized the second period (1970s and 1980s). It then became possible to derive the estimations and their estimated precisions without knowing the analytical form of the estimators. This was the period of nonlinear models for micro data (limited dependent variable models, duration models, etc.), for macro data (e.g. disequilibrium models, models with cycles), for time series (ARCH models, etc.), and of nonlinear statistical inference. This inference was based on the optimization of some nonquadratic criterion functions: a log likelihood function for the maximum likelihood approaches, a pseudo-log likelihood function for the pseudo-maximum likelihood approaches, or some functions of conditional moments for GMM (Generalized Method of Moments). However, these different approaches require a tractable form of the criterion function.

This book is concerned with the third generation of problems in which the econometric models and the associated inference approaches lead to criterion functions without simple analytical expression. In such problems the difficulty often comes from the presence of integrals of large dimensions in the probability density function or in the moments. The idea is to circumvent this numerical difficulty by an approach based on simulations. Therefore, even if the model is rather complicated, it will be assumed to be sufficiently simple to allow for simulations of the data, for given values of the parameters, and of the exogenous variables.

In Section 1.2 we briefly review the classical parametric and semi-parametric nonlinear estimation methods, such as maximum likelihood methods, pseudo-maximum likelihood methods, and GMM, since we will discuss their simulated counterparts in the next chapters.

In Section 1.3, we describe different problems for either individual data, time series, or panel data, in which the usual criterion functions contain integrals.

Finally, in Section 1.4 we give general forms for the models we are interested in, i.e. models for which it is possible to simulate the observations.

1.2   A Review of Nonlinear Estimation Methods

1.2.1   Parametric conditional models

To simplify the presentation, we assume that the observations are compatible with a parametric model. Let us introduce different kinds of variable. The endogenous variables y_t, $t = 1, \ldots, T$ are the variables whose values have to be explained. y_t may be uni- or multidimensional. We denote by z_t, $t = 1, \ldots, T$, a set of exogenous variables, in the sense that we are interested in the conditional distribution of $y_1, \ldots, y_T$ given $z_1, \ldots, z_T$ and initial conditions $\underline{y_0}$: $f_0(y_1, \ldots, y_T / z_1, \ldots, z_T, \underline{y_0})$. This p.d.f. (probability distribution function) may be decomposed into:

$$f_0(y_1, \ldots, y_T / z_1, \ldots, z_T, \underline{y_0})$$

$$= \prod_{t=1}^{T} f_0(y_t / z_1, \ldots, z_T, \underline{y_0}, y_1, \ldots, y_{t-1})$$

$$= \prod_{t=1}^{T} f_0(y_t / z_1, \ldots, z_T, \underline{y_{t-1}}) \text{ with } \underline{y_t} = (\underline{y_0}, y_1, \ldots, y_t).$$

In the following sections we assume that there is no feedback between the y and the z variables. More precisely, we impose:

$$f_0(y_t / z_1, \ldots, z_T, \underline{y_{t-1}}) = f_0(y_t / \underline{z_t}, \underline{y_{t-1}}) = f_0(y_t / x_t), \qquad (1.1)$$

where x_t denotes $(\underline{z_t}, \underline{y_{t-1}})$. The equality

$$f_0(y_t / z_1, \ldots, z_T, \underline{y_{t-1}}) = f_0(y_t / z_1, \ldots, z_t, \underline{y_{t-1}})$$

is a condition for Sims or Granger noncausality of (y_t), on (z_t). In other words, the z_t are strongly exogenous variables.

Under condition (1.1), we get:

$$f_0(y_1, \ldots, y_T / z_1, \ldots, z_T, \underline{y_0}) = \prod_{t=1}^{T} f_0(y_t / x_t), \qquad (1.2)$$

and, therefore, it is equivalent to consider the links between $z_1, \ldots, z_T$ and $y_t, \ldots, y_T$ or the links between x_t and y_t, for any t.

Note that we have assumed that the conditional p.d.f. $f_0(y_t/x_t)$ does not depend on t; more precisely, we assume that the process (y_t, z_t) is stationary. Also note that, in cross sections or panel data models, the index t will be replaced by i and the y_is will be independent conditionally to the z_is.

To summarize, we are essentially interested in a part (1.2) of the true unknown distribution of all the observations, since the whole distribution consists of $f_0(y_1, \ldots, y_T/z_1, \ldots, z_T, \underline{y_0})$ and of the true unknown marginal distributions $f_0(z_1, \ldots, z_T, \underline{y_0})$ of $z_1, \ldots, z_T, \underline{y_0}$.

In order to make an inference about the conditional distribution, i.e. $f_0(y_t/x_t)$, we introduce a conditional parametric model. This model M is a set of conditional distributions indexed by a parameter θ, whose dimension is p:

$$M = \{f(y_t/x_t; \theta), \theta \in \Theta\}, \tag{1.3}$$

where $\Theta \subset R^p$ is the parameter set. This model is assumed to be well-specified; i.e.

$$f_0(y_t/x_t) \text{ belongs to } M, \tag{1.4}$$

and identifiable; i.e., there exists a unique (unknown) value θ_0 such that:

$$f_0(y_t/x_t) = f(y_t/x_t; \theta_0). \tag{1.5}$$

θ_0 is called the **true value** of the parameter.

In such a framework, the determination of the unknown conditional distribution is equivalent to the determination of the true value of the parameter.

1.2.2 Estimators defined by the optimization of a criterion function

The usual estimation approaches consist in optimizing with respect to the parameter a criterion depending on the observations $y_t, z_t, t = 1, \ldots, T$. The estimator is defined by:

$$\widehat{\theta}_T = \arg\max_\theta \Psi_T(y_1, \ldots, y_T, z_1, \ldots, z_T; \theta)$$
$$= \arg\max_\theta \Psi_T(\theta) \quad \text{(say)}. \tag{1.6}$$

In practice, the function Ψ_T is generally differentiable and the estimator is deduced from the p-dimensional system of first order conditions:

$$\frac{\partial \Psi_T}{\partial \theta}(\widehat{\theta}_T) = 0 \iff \frac{\partial \Psi_T}{\partial \theta_j}(\widehat{\theta}_T) = 0, \qquad j = 1, \ldots, p. \tag{1.7}$$

With few exceptions, this system does not admit an analytical solution and the estimation is obtained via a numerical algorithm. The most usual ones are based on the Gauss–Newton approach. The initial system is replaced by an approximated one deduced from (1.7) by considering a first order expansion around some value θ_q:

$$\frac{\partial \Psi_T}{\partial \theta}(\theta) \simeq \frac{\partial \Psi_T}{\partial \theta}(\theta_q) + \frac{\partial^2 \Psi_T(\theta_q)}{\partial \theta \, \partial \theta'}(\theta - \theta_q),$$

where $\frac{\partial^2 \Psi_T}{\partial \theta \, \partial \theta'}$ is the Hessian matrix. The condition $\frac{\partial \Psi_T}{\partial \theta}(\theta) = 0$ is approximately the same as the condition

$$\theta = \theta_q - \left[\frac{\partial^2 \Psi_T(\theta_q)}{\partial \theta \, \partial \theta'}\right]^{-1} \frac{\partial \Psi_T}{\partial \theta}(\theta_q). \tag{1.8}$$

The Newton–Raphson algorithm is based on the corresponding recursive formula:

$$\widehat{\theta}_{q+1} = \widehat{\theta}_q - \left[\frac{\partial^2 \Psi_T}{\partial \theta \, \partial \theta'}(\widehat{\theta}_q)\right]^{-1} \frac{\partial \Psi_T}{\partial \theta}(\widehat{\theta}_q). \tag{1.9}$$

As soon as the sequence $\widehat{\theta}_q$ converges, the limit is a solution $\widehat{\theta}_T$ of the first order conditions.

The criterion function may be chosen in various ways depending on the properties that are wanted for the estimator in terms of efficiency, robustness to some misspecifications and computability. We describe below some of the usual estimation methods included in this framework.

Example 1.1   (Conditional) maximum likelihood

The criterion function is the (conditional) log likelihood function:

$$\Psi_T(\theta) = \sum_{t=1}^{T} \log f(y_t/x_t; \theta).$$

Example 1.2   (Conditional) pseudo-maximum likelihood (PML) (Gouriéroux, Monfort, and Trognon 1984b, c)

In some applications it may be interesting for robustness properties to introduce a family of distributions which does not necessarily contain the true distribution. Let us introduce such a family $f^*(y_t/x_t; \theta)$. The PML estimator of θ based on the family f^* is defined by:

$$\widetilde{\theta}_T = \arg \max_{\theta} \sum_{t=1}^{T} \log f^*(y_t/x_t; \theta). \tag{1.10}$$

Such pseudo-models are often based on the normal family of distributions. Let us consider a well-specified form of the first and second order conditional moments:

$$\begin{cases} E(y_t/x_t) = m(x_t; \theta) \\ V(y_t/x_t) = \sigma^2(x_t, \theta) \quad \text{(say)}. \end{cases}$$

We may introduce the pseudo-family of distributions $N\left[m(x_t;\theta), \sigma^2(x_t;\theta)\right], \theta \in \Theta$, even if the true distribution is nonnormal. In such a case the criterion function is:

$$\Psi_T(\theta) = \sum_{t=1}^{T}\left[-\frac{1}{2}\log 2\pi - \frac{1}{2}\log \sigma^2(x_t;\theta) - \frac{1}{2}\frac{(y_t - m(x_t;\theta))^2}{\sigma^2(x_t;\theta)}\right]. \quad (1.11)$$

Example 1.3   Nonlinear least squares   (Jennrich 1969, Malinvaud 1970)

The estimator of θ is obtained by minimizing the prediction errors. With the same notation as before, it is given by:

$$\widehat{\theta}_T = \arg\min_{\theta} \sum_{t=1}^{T}[y_t - m(x_t;\theta)]^2. \quad (1.12)$$

It is easily checked that this procedure may be considered as a PML approach based on the family $\{N\left[m(x_t;\theta), 1\right], \theta \in \Theta\}$.

Example 1.4   Generalized method of moments   (Hansen 1982, Hansen and Singleton 1982)

Let us introduce some q-dimensional function $K(y_t, x_t)$ of the observable variables and let us assume that we have a well-specified expression for the conditional moment:

$$E_\theta[K(y_t, x_t)/x_t] = k(x_t;\theta). \quad (1.13)$$

This equality defines some estimating constraints. Indeed, it yields:

$$E_\theta[K(y_t; x_t) - k(x_t;\theta)/x_t] = 0,$$

which implies:

$$E_\theta a'(x_t)\left[K(y_t, x_t) - k(x_t;\theta)\right] = 0, \quad (1.14)$$

for any function a. The idea of the GMM is to look for a value $\widetilde{\theta}_T$, such that the empirical counterparts of the constraints (1.14) are approximately satisfied. More precisely, let us introduce r q-dimensional functions $a_j, j = 1, \ldots, r$, and denote $A = (a_1, \ldots, a_r)$. Let us also introduce a nonnegative symmetric matrix Ω of size $(r \times r)$. Then the estimator is:

$$\widetilde{\theta}_T = \arg\min_{\theta}\left\{\sum_{t=1}^{T} A'(x_t)\left[K(y_t, x_t) - k(x_t;\theta)\right]\right\}'$$

$$\times \Omega\left\{\sum_{t=1}^{T} A'(x_t)\left[K(y_t, x_t) - k(x_t;\theta)\right]\right\}. \quad (1.15)$$

The elements of matrix $A(x_t)$ are instrumental variables (with respect to the constraints).

Example 1.5   Extended methods

It is possible to extend all the previous examples in the following way. Even if we are interested in the parameters θ, we may introduce in the criterion function some additional (nuisance) parameters α. Then we can consider the solutions $\widetilde{\theta}_T$, $\widetilde{\alpha}_T$ of a program of the form:

$$(\widetilde{\theta}_T, \widetilde{\alpha}_T) = \arg\max_{\theta,\alpha} \Psi_T^*(\theta, \alpha).$$

Equivalently, we have:

$$\widetilde{\theta}_T = \arg\max_{\theta} \Psi_T(\theta),$$

where $\Psi_T(\theta) = \max_\alpha \Psi_T^*(\theta, \alpha)$ is the concentrated criterion. Such an approach is for instance the basis for the adjusted PML method (Broze and Gouriéroux 1993).

1.2.3   Properties of optimization estimators

As usual, two kinds of asymptotic properties have to be considered: the consistency of the estimator, and the form of its asymptotic distribution.

Consistency.   If the well normalized criterion function uniformly converges to some limit function:

$$\lim_{T\to\infty} \frac{1}{h_T} \Psi_T(\theta) = \Psi_\infty(\theta),$$

and if this limit function has a unique maximum θ_0^∞, then the estimator $\widehat{\theta}_T = \arg\max_\theta \Psi_T(\theta)$ converges to this value. Therefore in practice three conditions have to be fulfilled:

  (i)   the uniform convergence of the normalized criterion function;

 (ii)   the uniqueness of θ_0^∞ (identifiability condition of θ with respect to the criterion function);

(iii)   the equality between this solution θ_0^∞ (often called **pseudo-true value**) and the true value θ_0.

Asymptotic normality.   Whenever the estimator is consistent, we may expand the first order conditions around the true-value θ_0. We get:

$$\frac{\partial \Psi_T}{\partial \theta}(\theta_0) + \frac{\partial^2 \Psi_T}{\partial \theta\, \partial \theta'}(\theta_0)(\widehat{\theta}_T - \theta_0) \simeq 0$$

$$\Longleftrightarrow \widehat{\theta}_T - \theta_0 \simeq \left[-\frac{\partial^2 \Psi_T}{\partial \theta\, \partial \theta'}(\theta_0)\right]^{-1} \frac{\partial \Psi_T}{\partial \theta}(\theta_0).$$

The criterion function is often such that there exist normalizing factors h_T, h_T^*, with:

$$\lim_{T \to \infty} \left[-\frac{1}{h_T} \frac{\partial^2 \Psi_T}{\partial \theta \, \partial \theta'} (\theta_0) \right] = J(\theta_0), \text{ where } J(\theta_0) \text{ is invertible;} \quad (1.16)$$

$$\frac{1}{h_T^*} \frac{\partial \Psi_T}{\partial \theta} (\theta_0) \xrightarrow{d} N[0, I(\theta_0)], \text{ where } I(\theta_0) \text{ is invertible.} \quad (1.17)$$

Therefore we get:

$$\frac{h_T}{h_T^*} \left(\widehat{\theta}_T - \theta_0 \right) \simeq \left[-\frac{1}{h_T} \frac{\partial^2 \Psi_T}{\partial \theta \, \partial \theta'} (\theta_0) \right]^{-1} \frac{1}{h_T^*} \frac{\partial \Psi_T}{\partial \theta} (\theta_0)$$

$$\simeq J(\theta_0)^{-1} \frac{1}{h_T^*} \frac{\partial \Psi_T}{\partial \theta} (\theta_0).$$

We deduce that:

$$\frac{h_T}{h_T^*} \left(\widehat{\theta}_T - \theta_0 \right) \xrightarrow{d} N\left[0, J(\theta_0)^{-1} I(\theta_0) J(\theta_0)^{-1} \right]. \quad (1.18)$$

Under stationarity conditions, we generally have: $h_T = T$, $h_T^* = \sqrt{T}$, $h_T / h_T^* = \sqrt{T}$.

Optimal choice of the criterion function. Some estimation approaches naturally lead to a class of estimators. For instance, in the GMM approach we can choose in different ways the instrumental variables A and the distance matrix Ω. Therefore the estimators $\widehat{\theta}_T(A, \Omega)$ and their asymptotic variance–covariance matrices,

$$V_{as} \left[\sqrt{T} \left(\widehat{\theta}_T(A, \Omega) - \theta_0) \right) \right] = \Sigma(A, \Omega),$$

are naturally indexed by A and Ω. So, one may look for the existence of an optimal choice for this couple, A, Ω, i.e. for a couple A^*, Ω^* such that:

$$\Sigma(A^*, \Omega^*) \ll \Sigma(A, \Omega), \quad \forall A, \Omega,$$

where $\ll$ is the usual ordering on symmetric matrices. For the usual estimation methods, such optimal estimators generally exist.

1.3 Potential Applications of Simulated Methods

In this section we present some parametric problems for which the likelihood function $f(y_t / x_t; \theta)$, and the conditional moments $m(x_t; \theta)$, $\sigma^2(x_t; \theta)$, $k(x_t; \theta)$, ..., do not admit a tractable form. In such a framework the optimization algorithms, such as the Newton–Raphson algorithms, cannot be used directly since they require a closed form of the criterion function Ψ. Generally this difficulty arises because of the partial observability of some endogenous variables; this lack of observability will introduce some multidimensional integrals in the expression of the different functions and these integrals could be replaced by approximations based on simulations. In such models it is usual to distinguish the underlying endogenous variables (called the **latent variables**), which are not totally observable, and the observable variables. The latent variables will be denoted with an asterisk.

As can be clearly seen from the examples below, this computational problem appears for a large variety of applications concerning either individual data, time series, or panel data models, in microeconomics, macroeconomics, insurance, finance, etc.

1.3.1   Limited dependent variable models

Example 1.6   Multinomial probit model   (McFadden 1976)

This is one of the first applications that has been proposed for the simulated estimation methods we are interested in (McFadden 1989, Pakes and Pollard 1989). It concerns qualitative choices of an individual among a set of M alternatives. If the individual i is a utility maximizer, and if U_{ij} is the utility level of alternative j, the selection is defined by:

$$j \text{ is the retained alternative if and only if } U_{ij} > U_{il} \quad \forall l \neq j.$$

The selection model is obtained in two steps. We first describe the latent variables (i.e. the utility levels) as functions of explanatory variables z, using a linear Gaussian specification:

$$U_{ij} = z_{ij}b_j + \upsilon_{ij}, \qquad j = 1, \ldots, M, i = 1, \ldots, n,$$
$$U_i = z_i b + \upsilon_i, \qquad i = 1, \ldots, n,$$

where $U_i = (U_{i1}, \ldots, U_{iM})'$, $\upsilon_i = (\upsilon_{i1}, \ldots, \upsilon_{iM})'$, and $\upsilon_i \sim N(0, \Omega)$.

Then in a second step we express the observable choices in term of the utility levels:

$$y_{ij} = \mathbb{1}_{j \text{ is retained by } i} = \mathbb{1}_{(U_{ij} > U_{il}, \forall \ell \neq j)}.$$

In such a framework the endogenous observable variable is a set of dichotomous qualitative variables. It admits a discrete distribution, whose probabilities are:

$$
\begin{aligned}
p_{ij} &= P\big[j \text{ is retained by } i/z_i\big] \\
&= P\big(U_{ij} > U_{il}, \forall l \neq j/z_i\big) \\
&= P\big(z_{ij}b_j + \upsilon_{ij} > z_{il}b_l + \upsilon_{il}, \forall l \neq j/z_i\big) \\
&= \int \cdots \int \mathbb{1}_{\prod_{l \neq j} [z_{il}b_l - z_{ij}b_j, +\infty]} (w_1, \ldots, w_{M-1}) \, dw_1 \cdots dw_{M-1},
\end{aligned}
$$

where g is the p.d.f. of the $M-1$ dimensional normal distribution associated with the variables $v_{ij} - v_{il}, l \neq j$.

Therefore the distribution of the endogenous observable variables has an expression containing integrals whose dimension is equal to the number of alternatives minus one. These integrals may be analytically approximated when J is not too large ($J \leq 3$ or 4), but for a number of applications, such as transportation choice, this number may be larger.

Example 1.7   Sequential choices and discrete duration models

In structural duration models, the value of the duration may often be considered as the result of a sequence of choices. For instance, in job search models (Lancaster 1990, Chesher and Lancaster 1983, Lippman and McCall 1976, Nickell 1979, Kiefer and Neumann 1979), under some stationarity assumptions each choice is based on a comparison between the potential supplied wage and a reservation wage, i.e. a minimal wage above which the job is accepted. Let us denote by y_{1it}^*, y_{2it}^* the potential and reservation wages for individual i at time t.

If we consider a sample of individuals becoming unemployed at date zero, the length of the unemployment spell for individual i is:

$$D_i = \inf \left\{ t : y_{1it}^* > y_{2it}^* \right\}.$$

If the latent bivariate model associated with the two underlying wages is a dynamic linear model, for instance with values of the wages:

$$\begin{cases} y_{1it}^* = a_1 y_{1i,t-1}^* + b_1 y_{2i,t-1}^* + z_{it} c_1 + u_{1,it}, \\ y_{2it}^* = a_2 y_{1i,t-1}^* + b_2 y_{2i,t-1}^* + z_{it} c_2 + u_{2,it}, \end{cases}$$

where $(u_{1,it}, u_{2,it})$ are i.i.d. normal $N(0, \Omega)$, it is directly seen that the distribution of the duration has probabilities defined by the multidimensional integrals:

$$P[D_i = d] = P\left\{ y_{1,i,1}^* < y_{2,i,1}^*, \ldots, y_{1,i,d-1}^* < y_{2,i,d-1}^*, y_{1,i,d}^* > y_{2,i,d}^* \right\}.$$

The maximal dimension of these integrals may be very large; since the probabilities appearing in the likelihood function correspond to the observed values of the durations, this dimension is equal to $\max_{i=1,\ldots,n} d_i$, where n is the number of individuals.

The same remark applies for the other examples of sequential choices, in particular for prepayment analysis (see Frachot and Gouriéroux 1994). In this framework the latent variables are an observed interest rate and a reservation interest rate.

1.3.2   Aggregation effect

The introduction of integrals in the expression of the distribution of the observable variables may also be the consequence of some aggregation phenomenon with respect to either individuals or time.

Example 1.8   Disequilibrium models with micro markets (Laroque and Salanié 1989, 1993)

Let us consider some micro markets $n = 1, \ldots, N$, characterized by the micro demand and supply:

$$
\begin{cases}
D_n(t) = \dfrac{1}{N} D(z_t, \varepsilon_{td}, \varepsilon_d^n, \theta), \\[2mm]
S_n(t) = \dfrac{1}{N} S(z_t, \varepsilon_{ts}, \varepsilon_s^n, \theta),
\end{cases}
$$

where z_t are some exogenous factors, $\varepsilon_{td}, \varepsilon_{ts}$ some macroeconomic error terms, which are the same for the different markets, and $\varepsilon_d^n, \varepsilon_s^n$ some error terms specific to each market. We assume that $(\varepsilon_d^n, \varepsilon_s^n)$ are i.i.d., independent of $z_t, \varepsilon_{td}, \varepsilon_{ts}$.

We now consider some observations of the exchanged quantity at a macro level. If N is large, we get:

$$
\begin{aligned}
Q_t &= \lim_{N \to \infty} \frac{1}{N} \sum_{n=1}^{N} \min(D_n(t), S_n(t)) \\
&= E_{\varepsilon_d, \varepsilon_s} \left[\min(D(z_t, \varepsilon_{td}, \varepsilon_d; \theta), S(z_t, \varepsilon_{ts}, \varepsilon_s; \theta)) \right].
\end{aligned}
$$

Therefore the expression of the observable variable Q_t in terms of the exogenous variable z_t and of the macroeconomic error terms appears as an expectation with respect to the specific error terms.

Example 1.9   Estimation of continuous time models from discrete time observations (Duffie and Singleton 1993, Gouriéroux *et al.* 1993)

In financial applications the evolution of prices is generally described by a diffusion equation, such as:

$$
dy_t = \mu(y_t, \theta)\, dt + \sigma(y_t, \theta)\, dW_t, \tag{1.19}
$$

where W_t is a Brownian motion. $\mu(y_t, \theta)$ is the drift term, and $\sigma(y_t, \theta)$ is the volatility term. However, the available observations correspond to discrete dates; they are denoted by $y_1, y_2, \ldots, y_t, y_{t+1}, \ldots$. The distribution of these observable variables generally does not admit an explicit analytical form (see Chapter 6), but appears as the solution of some integral equation. This difficulty may be seen in another way. Let us approximate the continuous time model (1.19) by its discrete time counterpart with a small time unit $1/n$. We introduce the **Euler approximation** $y^{(n)}$ of the process y.

This process is defined for dates $t = k/n$ and satisfies the recursive equation:

$$y_{(k+1)/n}^{(n)} = y_{k/n}^{(n)} + \frac{1}{n}\mu\left[y_{k/n}^{(n)}; \theta\right] + \frac{1}{\sqrt{n}}\sigma\left(y_{k/n}^{(n)}; \theta\right)\varepsilon_k, \qquad (1.20)$$

where (ε_k) is a standard Gaussian white noise. The distribution of $y_1, y_2, \ldots, y_t,$ $y_{t+1}, \ldots$ may be approximated by the distribution of $y_1^{(n)}, y_2^{(n)}, \ldots, y_t^{(n)}, y_{t+1}^{(n)}, \ldots$. We note that the process $y^{(n)}$ is Markovian of order one and we deduce that it is sufficient to determine the distribution of $y_{t+1}^{(n)}$ conditional on $y_t^{(n)}$ to deduce the distribution we are looking for. Let us introduce the conditional distribution of $y_{(k+1)/n}^{(n)}$ given $y_{k/n}^{(n)}$: $f\left(y_{(k+1)/n}^{(n)}/y_{k/n}^{(n)}\right)$ say. From (1.20), this distribution is normal with mean $y_{k/n}^{(n)} + \frac{1}{n}\mu\left[y_{k/n}^{(n)}; \theta\right]$, and variance $\frac{1}{n}\sigma^2\left(y_{k/n}^{(n)}; \theta\right)$. The conditional distribution of $y_{t+1}^{(n)}$ given $y_t^{(n)}$ is given by:

$$f\left(y_{t+1}^{(n)}/y_t^{(n)}\right) = \int \cdots \int \prod_{k=0}^{n-1} f\left(y_{t+(k+1)/n}^{(n)}/y_{t+k/n}^{(n)}\right) \prod_{k=1}^{n-1} dy_{t+k/n}^{(n)},$$

and requires the computation of an $(n-1)$-dimensional integral since we have to integrate out all the missing values $y_{t+1/n}^{(n)}, \ldots, y_{t+(n-1)/n}^{(n)}$.

1.3.3 Unobserved heterogeneity[1]

The introduction of unobserved heterogeneity in nonlinear models also creates multiple integrals.

Example 1.10   Random parameter model

A nonlinear regression model such as:

$$\begin{cases} y_i = m(z_i'\theta) + \sigma w_i, & i = 1, \ldots, n \\ w_i \sim \text{IIN}(0, 1), \end{cases}$$

may be extended by allowing parameter θ to depend on the individuals. To avoid identification problems, the usual practice consists in writing

$$y_i = m(z_i'\theta_i) + \sigma w_i, \quad i = 1, \ldots, n,$$

where $\theta_i, i = 1, \ldots, n$, are i.i.d. variables, for instance distributed as $N(\theta, \Omega)$, and independent of the error terms w_i. Then the conditional probability distribution function (p.d.f.) of the endogenous variable y_i, given the exogenous variables z_i, is:

$$f(y_i/z_i) = \frac{1}{\sigma}\int \varphi\left[\frac{y_i - m[z_i'(\theta + \Omega^{1/2}u)]}{\sigma}\right]\prod_{k=1}^{K}\varphi(u_k)\,du_k,$$

where K is the number of explanatory variables and φ the p.d.f. of the standard normal distribution.

---

[1] See Gouriéroux and Monfort (1991, 1993a).

Example 1.11   *Heterogeneity factor*

The modelling of qualitative variables, count data, duration data, etc., is generally based on conditional specifications of the form

$$l(y_i/z_i) = f(y_i; z_i\theta),$$

where f is a well-chosen distribution, such as logistic, Poisson, or exponential, depending on the kind of endogenous variable. Therefore the whole influence of the explanatory variables is driven by the scoring function $z_i\theta$. It is important to take into account the possibility of omitted explanatory variables independent of the retained ones. It is known that in a linear Gaussian model the OLS estimators of the θ parameter remain unbiased in the case of such an omission, but this property is no longer valid for nonlinear specifications. This heterogeneity will be introduced by adding an error term to the scoring function:

$$l(y_i/z_i, u_i) = f(y_i; z_i\theta + \sigma u_i),$$

where for instance the u_i' are i.i.d. variables, with given p.d.f. g. Then the conditional distribution of y_i given z_i is:

$$l(y_i/z_i) = \int f(y_i; z_i\theta + \sigma u)g(u)\, du.$$

Except for some very special and unrealistic choices of the couple of distributions (f, g) (for instance Poisson–gamma for count data, exponential–gamma for duration data), the integral cannot be computed analytically.

Two remarks are in order. First, the dimension of the integral is equal to the number of underlying scoring functions and is not very large in practice. The numerical problems arise from the large number of such integrals that have to be evaluated, since this number, which is equal to the number of individuals, may attain 100 000–1 000 000 in insurance problems, for instance.

Second, a model with unobserved heterogeneity may be considered a random parameter model, in which only the constant term coefficient has been considered random.

1.3.4 Nonlinear dynamic models with unobservable factors

The typical form of such models is:

$$\begin{cases} y_t = r_1(\underline{z_t}, \underline{y_{t-1}}, y_t^*, \varepsilon_{1t}; \theta), \\ y_t^* = r_2(\underline{z_t}, \underline{y_{t-1}}, y_{t-1}^*, \varepsilon_{2t}; \theta), \end{cases}$$

where (ε_{1t}), (ε_{2t}) are independent i.i.d. error terms the distributions of which are known (see 1.4.2), and (z_t) depicts an observable process of exogenous variables.

The process (z_t) is assumed to be independent of the process $(\varepsilon_{1t}, \varepsilon_{2t})$. $\underline{y_{t-1}}$ denotes the set of past values $y_{t-1}, y_{t-2}, \ldots$ of the process y. (y_t) is the observable endogenous process and (y_t^*) is the endogenous unobservable latent factor.

If the functions $r_1(\underline{z_t}, \underline{y_{t-1}}, y_t^*, \cdot; \theta)$ and $r_2(\underline{z_t}, \underline{y_{t-1}}, y_{t-1}^*, \cdot; \theta)$ are one to one, the previous equations define the conditional p.d.f. $f(y_t/\underline{z_t}, \underline{y_{t-1}}, y_t^*; \theta)$ and $f(y_t^*/\underline{z_t}, \underline{y_{t-1}}, y_{t-1}^*; \theta)$. Therefore the p.d.f. of $\underline{y_T}, y_T^*$ given $\underline{z_T}$ (and some initial values) is $\prod_{t=1}^{T} f(y_t/\underline{z_t}, \underline{y_{t-1}}, y_t^*; \theta) f(y_t^*/\underline{z_t}, \underline{y_{t-1}}, y_{t-1}^*; \theta)$, and the likelihood function, i.e. the p.d.f. of $\underline{y_T}$, appears as the multivariate integral

$$\int \prod_{t=1}^{T} f(y_t/\underline{z_t}, \underline{y_{t-1}}, y_t^*; \theta) f(y_t^*/\underline{z_t}, \underline{y_{t-1}}, y_{t-1}^*; \theta) \prod_{t=1}^{T} d\mu(y_t^*)$$

where $\mu(y_t^*)$ denotes the dominating measure.

Example 1.12   Factor ARCH model (Diebold and Nerlove 1989, Engle *et al.* 1990)

The relationship between the factors and the observable variables corresponds to a linear specification:

$$y_t = \lambda y_t^* + C\varepsilon_{1t}, \quad (\varepsilon_{1t}) \sim \text{IIN}(0, Id_m),$$

where y_t, λ are m-dimensional vectors and C is a lower triangular $(m \times m)$ matrix. We introduce here a single factor y^*, which is assumed to satisfy an ARCH evolution:

$$y_t^* = \left(\alpha_1 + \alpha_2 y_{t-1}^{*2}\right)^{1/2} \varepsilon_{2t}, \quad (\varepsilon_{2t}) \sim \text{IIN}(0, 1), \text{ independent of } (\varepsilon_{1t}).$$

Example 1.13   Stochastic volatility model (Harvey *et al.* 1994, Danielsson and Richard 1993, Danielsson 1994)

The simplest model of this kind is

$$y_t = \exp\left(\frac{1}{2} y_t^*\right) \varepsilon_{1t}$$
$$y_t^* = a + b y_{t-1}^* + \sigma \varepsilon_{2t},$$

where $(\varepsilon_{1t}, \varepsilon_{2t})$ is a standard bivariate Gaussian white noise. In this kind of model the conditional distribution of y_t given y_t^* is $N(0, \exp y_t^*)$ and the latent factor y_t^* is an AR(1) process.

Example 1.14   Switching state space models (Shephard 1994, Kim 1994, Billio and Monfort 1995)

These models are:

$$y_t = \mu(y_{2t}^*, \underline{y_{t-1}}) + A(y_{2t}^*, \underline{y_{t-1}}) y_{1t}^* + B(y_{2t}^*, \underline{y_{t-1}}) \varepsilon_t$$
$$y_{1t}^* = \nu(y_{2t}^*, \underline{y_{t-1}}) + C(y_{2t}^*, \underline{y_{t-1}}) y_{1t-1}^* + D(y_{2t}^*, \underline{y_{t-1}}) \eta_t$$
$$y_{2t}^* = 1\!\!1_{\{0\}}(y_{2t-1}^*) 1\!\!1_{[\pi_0(y_{t-1}),1]}(u_t) + 1\!\!1_{\{1\}}(y_{2t-1}^*) 1\!\!1_{[0,\pi_1(y_{t-1})]}(u_t)$$

where $\{\varepsilon_t\}$, $\{n_t\}$ are independent standard Gaussian white noises and $\{u_t\}$ is a white noise, independent of $\{\varepsilon_t\}\{n_t\}$ and whose marginal distribution is $\mathcal{U}_{[0,1]}$, the uniform distribution on $[0, 1]$.

In this model the first factor y_{1t}^* is a quantitative state variable whereas y_{2t}^* is a binary regime indicator. (The case of more than two regimes is a straightforward generalization.) This general framework contains many particular cases: switching ARMA models, switching factor models, dynamic switching regressions, deformed time models, models with endogenously missing data, etc.

Example 1.15 Dynamic disequilibrium models (Laroque and Salanié 1993, Lee 1995)

In this kind of model the latent factors are demand and supply, whereas the observed variable y_t is the minimum of the demand and the supply. Such a model is:

$$D_t = r_{2D}(z_t, D_{t-1}, S_{t-1}, \varepsilon_{Dt}; \theta)$$
$$S_t = r_{2S}(z_t, D_{t-1}, S_{t-1}, \varepsilon_{St}; \theta)$$
$$Q_t = \min(D_t, S_t) \quad (= r_1(D_t, S_t))$$

Note that no random error appears in r_1; this implies that the model is, in some way, degenerated and that the general formula given above for the likelihood function is not valid. However, it is easily shown (see Chapter 7) that the likelihood function appears as a sum of 2^T T-dimensional integrals.

1.3.5   Specification resulting from the optimization of some expected criterion

An example of this kind appears in a paper by Laffont *et al.* (1991). The authors derive from economic theory a first price auction model. For an auction with J bidders, the winning bid has the form

$$y = E[\max(v_{(J-1)}; p_0)/v_{(J)}],$$

where v_j, $j = 1, \ldots, J$ are the underlying private values, p_0 is a reservation price, independent of the v_js, and $v_{(j)}$ is the order statistic associated with the v_js.

In this example the function linking the latent variables v_j, $j = 1, \ldots, J$, p_0, and the observed bid y has a directly integral form. Note that, by taking the expectation, we eliminate the conditioning effect and arrive at:

$$Ey = E(\max(v_{(J-1)}, p_0)),$$

but some integrals remain because of the max and the ordering of the bids.

1.4 Simulation

1.4.1 Two kinds of simulation

For a given parametric model, it is possible to define the distribution of $y_1, \ldots, y_T$ conditional on $z_1, \ldots, z_T, \underline{y_0}$, $f(\cdot/z_1, \ldots, z_T, \underline{y_0}; \theta)$, say, and the distribution of y_t conditional on $x_t = (\underline{z_t}, \underline{y_{t-1}})$, $f(\cdot/x_t; \theta)$, say. It is particularly important in the sequel to distinguish two kinds of simulation.

Path simulations correspond to a set of artificial values $(y_t^s(\theta), t = 1, \ldots, T)$ such that the distribution of $y_1^s(\theta), \ldots, y_T^s(\theta)$ conditional on $z_1, \ldots, z_T, \underline{y_0}$ is equal to $f(\cdot/z_1, \ldots, z_T, \underline{y_0}; \theta)$.

Conditional simulations correspond to a set of artificial values $(y_t^s(\theta), t = 1, \ldots, T)$ such that the distribution of $y_t^s(\theta)$ conditional on $x_t = (\underline{z_t}, \underline{y_{t-1}})$ is equal to $f(\cdot/x_t; \theta)$, and this for any t.

It is important to note that these simulations may be performed for different values of the parameter, and that the conditional distributions of the simulations will depend on these values.

Moreover, it is possible to perform several independent replications of such a set of simulations. More precisely, for path simulations we can build several sets $y^s(\theta) = (y_t^s(\theta), t = 1, \ldots, T), s = 1, \ldots, S$, such that the variables $y^s(\theta)$ are independent conditionally on $z_1, \ldots, z_T, \underline{y_0}$ and $y_1, \ldots, y_T$. This possibility is the basis of simulated techniques using path simulations, since the empirical distribution of the $y^s(\theta), s = 1, \ldots, S$ will provide for large S a good approximation of the untractable conditional distribution $f(\cdot/z_1, \ldots, z_T, \underline{y_0}; \theta)$.

Similarly, for conditional simulations we can build several sets $y^s(\theta) = (y_t^s(\theta), t = 1, \ldots, T), s = 1, \ldots, S$, such that the variables $y_t^s(\theta), t = 1, \ldots, T, s = 1, \ldots, S$, are independent conditionally on $z_1, \ldots, z_T, \underline{y_0}$. This possibility is the basis of simulated techniques using conditional simulations, since the empirical distribution of $y_t^s(\theta), s = 1, \ldots, S$ will provide for large S a good approximation of the untractable conditional distribution $f(\cdot/\underline{z_t}, \underline{y_{t-1}}; \theta)$, and this for any t.

1.4.2 How to simulate?

A preliminary transformation of the error terms

The usual software packages provide either independent random numbers uniformly distributed on [0,1], or independent drawings from the standard normal distribution. The use of these packages requires a preliminary transformation of the error terms, in order to separate the effect of the parameters and to obtain, after transformation, the basic distribution.

Example 1.16   Gaussian error terms

If the initial model contains Gaussian error terms ε_t^* independently following $N(0, \Omega)$, where Ω depends on the unknown parameter θ, it is possible to use the transformation $\varepsilon_t^* = A\varepsilon_t$, where $AA' = \Omega$, and where ε_t has the fixed distribution $N(0, Id)$.

We may simulate $\varepsilon_t^{*s}(\theta)$ for a given value of the matricial parameter $A(\theta)$ by first drawing independently the components of ε_t from the standard normal (ε_t^s is the corresponding simulated vector) and then computing $\varepsilon_t^{*s}(\theta) = A(\theta)\varepsilon_t^s$. When θ changes it is possible to keep the same drawing ε_t^s of ε_t in order to get the different drawings of ε_t^*. In fact, we shall see later that it is *necessary* to keep these basic drawings fixed when θ changes, in order to have good numerical and statistical properties of the estimators based on these simulations.

Example 1.17   Inversion technique

If ε_t^* is an error term with a unidimensional distribution whose cumulative distribution function (c.d.f.) $F_\theta(\cdot)$, parameterized by θ, is continuous and strictly increasing, we know that the variable

$$\varepsilon_t = F_\theta(\varepsilon_t^*)$$

follows a uniform distribution on $[0, 1]$. We may draw a simulated value ε_t^s in this known distribution, and $\varepsilon_t^{*s}(\theta) = F_\theta^{-1}(\varepsilon_t^s)$, obtained by applying the quantile function, is a simulated value in F_θ.

Particular cases are:

- Exponential distribution:

$$F_\theta(x) = 1 - \exp(-\theta x), \qquad x \geq 0, \theta > 0,$$

$$\varepsilon_t^* = -\frac{1}{\theta} \log(1 - \varepsilon_t), \qquad \text{where } \varepsilon_t \sim U_{[0,1]},$$

$$\varepsilon_t^* = -\frac{1}{\theta} \log \tilde{\varepsilon}_t, \qquad \text{where } \tilde{\varepsilon}_t \sim U_{[0,1]}.$$

- Weibull distribution:

$$F_\theta(x) = 1 - \exp(-x^\theta), \qquad x \geq 0, \theta > 0,$$

$$\varepsilon_t^* = \left[-\log(1 - \varepsilon_t) \right]^{1/\theta}$$

$$\varepsilon_t^* = \left[-\log \tilde{\varepsilon}_t \right]^{1/\theta}, \qquad \text{where } \tilde{\varepsilon}_t \sim U_{[0,1]}.$$

- Cauchy distribution:

$$F_\theta(x) = \frac{1}{2} + \frac{1}{\pi} \arctan\left[\frac{x}{\theta} \right]$$

$$\varepsilon_t^* = \theta \tan\left[\pi\left(\varepsilon_t - \frac{1}{2} \right) \right], \qquad \text{where } \varepsilon_t \sim U_{[0,1]}.$$

Path simulations

The models of the previous subsections are often defined in several steps from some latent variables with structural interpretations. We may jointly simulate the latent and the observable endogenous variables—for instance demand, supply, and exchanged quantity—in the dynamic disequilibrium model (example 1.15), the underlying factor and the observed vector in the ARCH model (example 1.12), the utility levels and the observed alternatives in the multivariate probit model (example 1.6).

After the preliminary transformation of the error terms, the models have the following structure:

$$(M^*) \begin{cases} y_t = r_1(\underline{z_t}, \underline{y_{t-1}}, y_t^*, \varepsilon_t; \theta), \\ y_t^* = r_2(\underline{z_t}, \underline{y_{t-1}}, \underline{y_{t-1}^*}, \varepsilon_t; \theta), \qquad t = 1, \dots, T, \end{cases} \tag{1.21}$$

where (ε_t) is a white noise whose distribution is known.

The simulated paths of both latent and observable processes are obtained in a recursive way, from some given value θ of the parameter, some initial values $\underline{y_0}, y_0^*$, the observed exogenous path (z_t), and simulations of the normalized error terms (ε_t). The recursive formulas are:

$$\begin{cases} \underline{y_0^{*s}}(\theta) = \underline{y_0^*}, \underline{y_0^s}(\theta) = \underline{y_0}, \\ y_t^{*s}(\theta) = r_2\big[\underline{z_t}, \underline{y_{t-1}^s}(\theta), \underline{y_{t-1}^{*s}}(\theta), \varepsilon_t^s; \theta\big], \\ y_t^s(\theta) = r_1\big[\underline{z_t}, \underline{y_{t-1}^s}(\theta), \underline{y_t^{*s}}(\theta), \varepsilon_t^s; \theta\big]. \end{cases}$$

Conditional simulations

For a general dynamic model with unobservable latent variables such as (1.21), it is not in general possible to draw in the conditional distribution of y_t given $z_1, \dots, z_T, \underline{y_{t-1}}$. However, this possibility exists if the model admits a reduced form of the kind:

$$(M) \ y_t = r(\underline{z_t}, \underline{y_{t-1}}, \varepsilon_t; \theta) \qquad t = 1, \dots, T, \tag{1.22}$$

where (ε_t) is a white noise with a known distribution. The conditional simulations are defined by:

$$y_t^s(\theta) = r(\underline{z_t}, \underline{y_{t-1}}, \varepsilon_t^s; \theta), \tag{1.23}$$

where the ε_t^s are independent drawings in the distribution of ε_t.

These conditional simulations are different from the path simulations given by:

$$\tilde{y}_t^s(\theta) = r(\underline{z_t}, \underline{\tilde{y}_{t-1}^s}(\theta), \varepsilon_t^s; \theta),$$

which are computed conditionally to the simulated values and not to the observed ones.

1.4.3 Partial path simulations

Finally, we may note that the untractability of the likelihood function is often due to the introduction of some additional error terms. More precisely, if some error terms were known, the form of the likelihood function would be easily derived. Let us partition the vector of errors

$$\varepsilon_t = \begin{pmatrix} u_t \\ w_t \end{pmatrix}$$

into two subvectors such that the p.d.f. conditional to a path (z_t, u_t) has a closed form. This means that the integration with respect to the remaining errors w_t is simple. We have:

$$l((y_t)/(z_t); \theta) = E_{(u_t)} l((y_t)/(z_t), (u_t); \theta),$$

for any fixed path (y_t). Therefore we can approximate the unknown conditional p.d.f. by:

$$l((y_t)/(z_t); \theta) \simeq \frac{1}{S} \sum_{s=1}^{S} l((y_t)/(z_t), (u_t^s); \theta),$$

i.e. by using simulations only of the u error terms.

Example 1.18 Factor ARCH models

Let us consider example (1.12). When the process (ε_{2t}) is known, the factors are also known. The conditional distribution $l((y_t)/(\varepsilon_{2t}))$ is equal to the conditional distribution of (y_t) given (y_t^*); i.e., it corresponds to an independent Gaussian process, with mean λy_t^* and variance–covariance matrix CC'.

Example 1.19 Random parameter models

In the model:

$$y_i = m(z_i'(\theta + \Omega^{1/2} u_i)) + \sigma w_i, \quad w_i \sim \text{IIN}(0, 1), \quad u_i \sim \text{IIN}(0, Id),$$

introduced in example 1.10, we may easily integrate out w_i conditionally to u_i.

2

The Method of Simulated Moments (MSM)

2.1 Path Calibration or Moments Calibration

The basic idea of simulated estimation methods is to adjust the parameter of interest θ in order to get similar properties for the observed endogenous variables (y_t) and for their simulated counterparts $(y_t^s(\theta))$. However, the choice of an adequate calibration criterion is important to provide consistency of the associated estimators. In particular, two criteria may seem natural: the first one measures the difference between the two paths $(y_t, t$ varying) and $(y_t^s(\theta), t$ varying); the second one measures the difference between some empirical moments computed on (y_t) and $(y_t^s(\theta))$ respectively. It will be seen in this subsection that the first criterion does not necessarily provide consistent estimators. To illustrate this point, we consider a static model without exogenous variables. The observable variables satisfy:

$$y_i = r(u_i; \theta_0), \qquad i = 1, \dots, n, \tag{2.1}$$

where θ_0 is the unknown true value of a scalar parameter, (u_i) are i.i.d. variables with known p.d.f. $g(u)$, and r is a given function.

We introduce the first order moment of the endogenous variable:

$$E y_i = \int r(u; \theta_0) g(u)\, du = k(\theta_0) \qquad \text{(say)}, \tag{2.2}$$

and assume that the function k does not have a closed form.

Now we can replace the unobservable errors by simulations drawn independently from the distribution g. If $u_i^s, i = 1, \dots, n$, are such simulations, we deduce simulated values of the endogenous variables associated with a value θ of the parameter by computing

$$y_i^s(\theta) = r(u_i^s; \theta). \tag{2.3}$$

2.1.1   Path calibration

Let us introduce the path calibrated estimator of θ as:

$$\tilde{\theta}_n = \arg\min_{\theta} \sum_{i=1}^{n} \left(y_i^s(\theta) - y_i\right)^2. \tag{2.4}$$

Under usual regularity conditions, this estimator tends asymptotically to the solution $\tilde{\theta}_\infty$ of the limit problem:

$$
\begin{aligned}
\tilde{\theta}_\infty &= \arg\min_{\theta} \lim_{n} \frac{1}{n} \sum_{i=1}^{n} \left(y_i^s(\theta) - y_i\right)^2 \\
&= \arg\min_{\theta} E_{u,u^s} \left[r(u^s; \theta) - r(u; \theta_0)\right]^2 \\
&= \arg\min_{\theta} \left\{ Vr(u^s; \theta) + Vr(u; \theta_0) \right. \\
&\quad \left. + \left[Er(u^s; \theta) - Er(u; \theta_0)\right]^2 \right\}.
\end{aligned}
\tag{2.5}
$$

where $\tilde{\theta}_\infty$ satisfies the asymptotic first order conditions:

$$\frac{\partial}{\partial \theta} Vr(u; \tilde{\theta}_\infty) + 2\frac{\partial}{\partial \theta} Er(u; \tilde{\theta}_\infty)[Er(u; \tilde{\theta}_\infty) - Er(u; \theta_0)] = 0.$$

We note that the path calibrated estimator is consistent if and only if $\tilde{\theta}_\infty = \theta_0$ is a solution, i.e. if and only if $\frac{\partial}{\partial \theta} Vr(u; \theta_0) = 0$, a condition that is not satisfied in general. For instance, if we have $Ey_i = \theta_0$, $Vy_i = \theta_0^2$, we get:

$$\tilde{\theta}_\infty = \arg\min_{\theta} \left[\theta^2 + \theta_0^2 + (\theta - \theta_0)^2\right]$$

$$\iff \tilde{\theta}_\infty = \theta_0/2 \neq \theta_0.$$

2.1.2   Moment calibration

Alternatively, we may look for a moment calibrated estimator. Let us consider the empirical first order moments computed from the observations and from the simulations. The estimator is defined by:

$$\hat{\theta}_n = \arg\min_{\theta} \left[\frac{1}{n} \sum_{i=1}^{n} y_i - \frac{1}{n} \sum_{i=1}^{n} y_i^s(\theta)\right]^2. \tag{2.6}$$

It converges to the solution θ_∞ of the limit problem:

$$
\begin{aligned}
\theta_\infty &= \arg\min_{\theta}[Ey_i - Ey_i^s(\theta)]^2 \\
&= \arg\min_{\theta}[Er(u; \theta_0) - Er(u^s; \theta)]^2 \\
&= \arg\min_{\theta}[k(\theta_0) - k(\theta)]^2.
\end{aligned}
\tag{2.7}
$$

As soon as k is one to one, this limit problem has the unique solution $\theta_\infty = \theta_0$, and the estimator $\hat{\theta}_n$ is consistent.

2.2 The Generalized Method of Moments (GMM)

This estimation method has already been introduced in Chapter 1. Here we briefly recall its main properties, making a distinction between the static and the dynamic case. The GMM will be approximated by the method of simulated moments (MSM). In particular, the expression of the asymptotic variance–covariance matrix of the GMM estimator will serve as a benchmark for measuring the efficiency loss arising from simulations.

2.2.1 The static case

Let us consider i.i.d. observations (y_i, z_i), $i = 1, \ldots, n$, on endogenous and exogenous variables. We introduce some functions $K(y_i, z_i)$ of these observations, where K is of size q, and we assume that the conditional expectation of $K(y_i, z_i)$ given z_i has a well-specified form:

$$E_0[K(y_i, z_i)/z_i] = k(z_i; \theta_0), \tag{2.8}$$

where E_0 is the expectation for the true distribution of (y, z), and θ_0 is the true value of the parameter whose size is p.

Now let Z_i be a matrix function of z_i with size (K, q), where $K \geq p$. The elements of Z_i may be seen as intrumental variables, since they satisfy the orthogonality conditions:

$$E_0 Z_i[K(y_i, z_i) - k(z_i, \theta_0)] = 0. \tag{2.9}$$

The GMM estimators are based on the empirical counterpart of the above orthogonality conditions. If Ω is a (K, K) symmetric positive semi-definite matrix, the estimator is defined by:

$$\hat{\theta}_n(\Omega)$$
$$= \arg\min_\theta \left(\sum_{i=1}^n Z_i[K(y_i, z_i) - k(z_i; \theta)] \right)' \Omega \left(\sum_{i=1}^n Z_i[K(y_i, z_i) - k(z_i; \theta)] \right). \tag{2.10}$$

Proposition 2.1 $\bigm|$ Under regularity conditions (see Hansen 1982),

(i) $\hat{\theta}_n(\Omega)$ is a consistent estimator of the true value θ_0.

(ii) The GMM estimator is asymptotically normal:

$$\sqrt{n}(\hat{\theta}_n(\Omega) - \theta_0) \xrightarrow{d} N(0, \Sigma_1^{-1}\Sigma_2\Sigma_1^{-1}),$$

where: $\Sigma_1 = D'\Omega D$,

$$\Sigma_2 = D'\Omega V_0 \{Z[K(y, z) - k(z, \theta_0)]\} \Omega D,$$

$$D = E_0 \left[Z \frac{\partial k}{\partial \theta'}(z; \theta_0) \right].$$

This asymptotic variance–covariance matrix depends on Ω, and it is possible to choose this matrix in an optimal way, i.e. to select Ω^* such that:

$$V_{as} \left[\sqrt{n} \left(\hat{\theta}_n(\Omega) - \theta_0 \right) \right] \gg V_{as} \left[\sqrt{n} \left(\hat{\theta}_n(\Omega^*) - \theta_0 \right) \right], \quad \forall \Omega.$$

Proposition 2.2 $\bigm|$ An optimal choice of the matrix Ω is:

$$\Omega^* = \left(V_0 \{Z [K(y, z) - k(z; \theta_0)]\} \right)^{-1}$$
$$= \left(E_z \{Z V_0 [K(y, z)/z] Z'\} \right)^{-1}.$$

Then $\Sigma_1 = \Sigma_2$, and:

$$V_{as} \left[\sqrt{n} \left(\hat{\theta}_n(\Omega^*) - \theta_0 \right) \right] = [D'\Omega^* D]^{-1}.$$

The optimal Ω^* matrix depends on the unknown distribution of the observations. It has to be consistently estimated. It is easily checked that the replacement of Ω^* by a consistent estimator does not change the asymptotic properties. Such an estimator is:

$$\left\{ \frac{1}{n} \sum_{i=1}^{n} Z_i \left[K(y_i, z_i) - k(z_i; \tilde{\theta}_n) \right] \left[K(y_i, z_i) - k(z_i; \tilde{\theta}_n) \right] Z_i' \right\}^{-1},$$

where $\tilde{\theta}_n$ is any consistent estimator of θ_0, for instance the GMM estimator with $\Omega = Id$.

2.2.2   The dynamic case

When lagged endogenous variables are present in the model, we have to distinguish two cases.

GMM based on dynamic conditional moments

Let us denote (y_{t-1}, z_t) by x_t and let us consider a well-specified form for the conditional moment of $K(y_t, x_t)$ given x_t:

$$E_0\left[K(y_t, x_t)/x_t\right] = E_0\left[K(y_t, y_{t-1}, z_t)/y_{t-1}, z_t\right] = k(x_t; \theta_0), \qquad (2.11)$$

and instrumental variables depending on x_t:

$$Z(x_t) = Z(y_{t-1}, z_t).$$

The GMM estimator is defined as before by:

$$\hat{\theta}_T(\Omega)$$
$$= \arg\min_{\theta} \left\{\sum_{t=1}^{T} Z_t\left[K(y_t, x_t) - k(x_t; \theta)\right]\right\}' \Omega \left\{\sum_{t=1}^{T} Z_t\left[K(y_t, x_t) - k(x_t, \theta)\right]\right\},$$

and has the same asymptotic properties as in the static case after replacing z_t by x_t.

GMM based on static conditional moments

Let us now introduce estimating constraints based on static moments, i.e. conditional only on the current and lagged exogenous variables z_t:

$$E_0\left[K(y_t, z_t)/z_t\right] = k(z_t; \theta_0). \qquad (2.12)$$

Then the instrumental variables have also to depend only on $z_t : Z_t = Z(z_t)$.

The estimator solution of

$$\hat{\theta}_T(\Omega)$$
$$= \arg\min_{\theta} \left\{\sum_{t=1}^{T} Z_t\left[K(y_t, z_t) - k(z_t; \theta)\right]\right\}' \Omega \left\{\sum_{t=1}^{T} Z_t\left[K(y_t, z_t) - k(z_t, \theta)\right]\right\}$$

is also consistent, asymptotically normal, but the form of the asymptotic variance–covariance matrix, and of the optimal Ω matrix are modified. We simply have to replace in the formulas given in propositions (2.1) and (2.2) $V_0\{Z[K(y, x) - k(x; \theta_0)]\}$, with:

$$\lim_T V_0\left\{\frac{1}{\sqrt{T}}\sum_{t=1}^{T} Z_t\left[K(y_t, z_t) - k(z_t; \theta_0)\right]\right\} = \Gamma_0 + \sum_{h=1}^{\infty}\left[\Gamma_h + \Gamma_h'\right], (2.13)$$

where

$$\Gamma_h = \mathrm{cov}_0\left[Z_t(K(y_t, z_t) - k(z_t; \theta_0)), Z_{t-h}(K(y_{t-h}, z_{t-h}) - k(z_{t-h}; \theta_0))\right].$$

In practice, the choice between dynamic and static conditional moments will be based on the type of models considered. It is clear that more information is contained in the dynamic conditional moments than in the static conditional moments, but static conditional moments may be easier to compute, for instance in models of type (M^*) (see 1.21) where unobservable endogenous variables are present. The distinction is particularly important for pure time series models, i.e. when exogenous variables z are absent. Introducing as endogenous variable

$$Y_t = \left[\begin{array}{c} y_{t+1} \\ y_t \end{array} \right],$$

for instance, we may consider GMM based on conditional moments: $E(y_t/y_{t-1})$, $E\left(y_t^2/y_{t-1}\right)$, $E(y_t y_{t+1}/y_{t-1})$ (dynamic conditional moments in our terminology), or GMM based on marginal moments: $E(y_t)$, $E\left(y_t^2\right)$, $E(y_t y_{t+1})$ (static conditional moments in our terminology).

2.3   The Method of Simulated Moments (MSM)[1]

2.3.1   Simulators

The application of GMM requires a closed form for the specification of the moments. In the examples described in Chapter 1, such a closed form does not exist and the function k will be replaced by an approximation based on simulations. Such an approximation $\tilde{k}$ is called a **simulator**. Even if it is natural to build such simulators by following the structural form of the model, it may often be preferable for precision or regularity reasons to introduce some other simulators. Let us, for instance, consider a static model defined by the reduced form

$$y_i = r(z_i, \varepsilon_i; \theta_0), \tag{2.14}$$

where (ε_i) has a known distribution; then we deduce from the definition of the conditional moment,

$$E_0\left[K(y_i, z_i)/z_i\right] = k(z_i; \theta_0),$$

that

$$E_0\left\{K\left[r(z_i, \varepsilon_i, \theta_0), z_i\right]/z_i\right\} = k(z_i; \theta_0). \tag{2.15}$$

We say that $\tilde{k}\left[z_i, \varepsilon_i^s; \theta\right] = K\left[r(z_i, \varepsilon_i^s, \theta), z_i\right]$, where ε_i^s, drawn from the distribution of ε_i, is a (conditionally) **unbiased simulator** of $k(z_i; \theta)$. This natural simulator may have drawbacks in terms of precision or in terms of discontinuity

---

[1]McFadden 1989, Pakes and Pollard 1989.

with respect to θ (see example 2.2), so it may be useful to look for other unbiased simulators $\tilde{k}(z_i, u_i; \theta)$, where u_i has a known distribution such that:

$$E[\tilde{k}(z_i, u_i; \theta)/z_i] = k(z_i, \theta), \tag{2.16}$$

the expectation being taken with respect to u_i.

Example 2.1   Models with a closed form for the distribution of the latent variables

As seen in Chapter 1, the structural models are generally defined in two steps, by using some latent variables. Moreover, the latent model is often tractable, and it is essentially the nonlinear transformation between the latent variables y_i^* and the observable ones y_i which creates the difficulties. Let us consider such a case, where the conditional distribution of y_i^* given z_i has a tractable form: $f^*(y^*/z; \theta)$, and let us denote by $y = a(y^*)$ the link between latent and observable variables. We have:

$$E_\theta [K(y_i, z_i)/z_i]$$
$$= E_\theta \left\{ K \left[a(y_i^*), z_i \right] /z_i \right\}$$
$$= \int K \left[a(y^*), z_i \right] f^*(y^*/z_i; \theta) \, dy^*.$$

If the conditional distributions $f^*(\cdot/z_i; \theta)$ have a fixed support (i.e. independent of θ), and if $\varphi(\cdot)$ is a nonnegative function with the same support and such that $\int \varphi(u) \, du = 1$, we get:

$$E_\theta [K(y_i, z_i)/z_i]$$
$$= \int K [a(u), z_i] f^*(u/z_i; \theta) \, du$$
$$= \int K [a(u), z_i] \frac{f^*(u/z_i; \theta)}{\varphi(u)} \varphi(u) \, du.$$

Therefore:

$$\tilde{k}(z_i, u_i; \theta) = K [a(u_i), z_i] \frac{f^*(u_i/z_i; \theta)}{\varphi(u_i)},$$

where u_i, drawn from the distribution with p.d.f. φ, is a (conditionally) unbiased simulator. As a matter of fact we have exhibited a class of simulators, depending on the choice of function φ, called an **importance function**. The precision of the MSM estimators defined below will depend on the choice of the simulator—i.e., in the previous framework, of function φ.

Finally we can note that such a choice may depend on the value of the conditioning variable: we may introduce a conditional known distribution $\varphi(u_i/z_i)$, and the associated simulator:

$$\tilde{k}(z_i, u_i : \theta) = K[a(u_i), z_i] \frac{f^*(u_i/z_i; \theta)}{\varphi(u_i/z_i)}.$$

Example 2.2   Smooth simulators for the multinomial probit model

As an example of the previous class of simulators, let us consider the multinomial probit model (see example 1.6).

In the multinomial probit model, we have:

$$y_i = (y_{i1}, \ldots, y_{iJ})',$$

where:

$$y_{ij} = \mathbb{1}_{(U_{ij} > U_{i\ell}, \forall \ell \neq j)},$$
$$U_{ij} = z_{ij}b_j + A_j u_i, \quad \text{where } u_i \sim \text{IIN}(0, Id),$$

and A_j is the jth row of a matrix A satisfying $AA' = \Omega$. If we are interested in the conditional moments associated with the selection probabilities

$$K_j(y_i, z_i) = \mathbb{1}_{(y_{ij}=1)},$$
$$k_j(z_i; \theta_0) = E_0[K_j(y_i, z_i)/z_i] = P_0[y_{ij} = 1/z_i],$$

a natural simulator is:

$$\tilde{k}_j(z_i, u; \theta) = K_j[r(u_i, z_i; \theta), z_i]$$
$$= \mathbb{1}_{(z_{ijb_j} + A_j u_i > z_{i\ell}b_\ell + A_\ell u_i, \ \forall \ell \neq j)}.$$

However, this simulator, called the **frequency simulator**, is not differentiable (and not even continuous) with respect to the parameters b_j, A_j. It may be replaced by another simulator based on importance functions. Indeed, let us consider the variables

$$v_{j\ell} = U_{ij} - U_{i\ell},$$

measuring the differences between the utility levels.   The distribution of $v_{j1}, \ldots, v_{j,j-1}, v_{j,j+1}, \ldots, v_{j,J}$ is a normal distribution.   Let us denote $f_j(v_j/z_i, \theta)$ the associated p.d.f. We have:

$$k_j(z_i; \theta) = \int f_j(v_j/z_i; \theta) \mathbb{1}_{(v_{j\ell}>o, \forall \ell \neq j)} \, dv_j$$
$$= \int \frac{f_j(v_j/z_i; \theta) \mathbb{1}_{(v_{j\ell}>o, \forall \ell \neq j)} \varphi(v_j/z_i)}{\varphi(v_j/z_i)} \, dv_j.$$

Therefore, we may use the simulator

$$\tilde{k}_j(z_i, v_j; \theta) = \frac{f_j(v_j/z_i; \theta)}{\varphi(v_j/z_i)},$$

where v_j is drawn from a known distribution $\varphi(v_j/z_i)$ whose support is $(\mathbb{R}^+)^{J-1}$. For instance, φ might correspond to a product of exponential distributions, to a product of truncated normal distributions, and so on. This kind of simulator is clearly differentiable with respect to θ as soon as f_j is.

2.3.2 Definition of the MSM estimators

The estimator is derived by calibrating some empirical moments based on observations and simulations.

Static case

Let $\tilde{k}(z_i, u_i; \theta)$, where u_i has a known conditional distribution, be an unbiased simulator of $k(z_i; \theta)$. The MSM is defined as the solution of:

$$\hat{\theta}_{Sn}(\Omega) = \arg \min_{\theta} \psi_{Sn}(\theta), \qquad (2.17)$$

where:

$$\psi_{Sn}(\theta) = \left\{ \sum_{i=1}^{n} Z_i \left[K(y_i, z_i) - \frac{1}{S} \sum_{s=1}^{S} \tilde{k}(z_i, u_i^s; \theta) \right] \right\}' \Omega$$

$$\times \left\{ \sum_{i=1}^{n} Z_i \left[K(y_i, z_i) - \frac{1}{S} \sum_{s=1}^{S} \tilde{k}(z_i, u_i^s; \theta) \right] \right\}.$$

Such estimators depend on the moments K that are retained, on the instruments, on the matrix Ω, on the choice of the simulator, and on the number S of replications. When S tends to infinity, $\frac{1}{S} \sum_{s=1}^{S} \tilde{k}(z_i, u_i^s; \theta)$ tends to $E[\tilde{k}(z_i, u; \theta)/z_i] = k(z_i; \theta)$, and the estimator coincides with the GMM estimator.

Dynamic case

As before, we distinguish the cases of dynamic and static conditional moments, even if the objective functions are similar.

Dynamic conditional moment   Let us consider the dynamic moment condition:

$$E_0 \left[K(y_t, x_t)/x_t \right] = E_0 \left[K(y_t, \underline{y_{t-1}}, \underline{z_t})/\underline{y_{t-1}}, \underline{z_t} \right] = k(x_t; \theta_0),$$

and an unbiased simulator of $k(x_t; \theta)$; this simulator $\tilde{k}(x_t, u; \theta)$ is such that $E[\tilde{k}(x_t, u; \theta)/x_t] = k(x_t; \theta)$, where the distribution of u given x_t is known. Then the simulated moment estimator is defined by:

$$\hat{\theta}_{ST}(\Omega) = \arg \min_{\theta} \psi_{ST}(\theta), \qquad (2.18)$$

where:

$$\psi_{ST}(\theta) = \left\{ \sum_{t=1}^{T} Z(x_t) \left[K(y_t, x_t) - \frac{1}{S} \sum_{s=1}^{S} \tilde{k}(x_t, u_t^s; \theta) \right] \right\}' \Omega$$

$$\times \left\{ \sum_{t=1}^{T} Z(x_t) \left[K(y_t, x_t) - \frac{1}{S} \sum_{s=1}^{S} \tilde{k}(x_t, u_t^s; \theta) \right] \right\},$$

and u_t^s is drawn in the known conditional distribution of u given x_t.

Static conditional moment   Let us consider the static moment condition:

$$E_0\left[K(y_t, \underline{z_t})/\underline{z_t}\right] = k(\underline{z_t}; \theta_0),$$

and an unbiased simulator $\tilde{k}$ such that:

$$E_0\left[\tilde{k}(\underline{z_t}, u; \theta)/\underline{z_t}\right] = k(\underline{z_t}; \theta_0),$$

where the conditional distribution of u given $\underline{z_t}$ is known. Then the simulated moment estimator is defined by:

$$\hat{\theta}_{ST}(\Omega) = \arg\min_{\theta} \psi_{ST}(\theta), \tag{2.19}$$

where:

$$\psi_{ST}(\theta) = \left\{\sum_{t=1}^{T} Z(\underline{z_t})\left[K(y_t, \underline{z_t}) - \frac{1}{S}\sum_{s=1}^{S}\tilde{k}(\underline{z_t}, u_t^s; \theta)\right]\right\}' \Omega$$

$$\times \left\{\sum_{t=1}^{T} Z(\underline{z_t})\left[K(y_t, \underline{z_t}) - \frac{1}{S}\sum_{s=1}^{S}\tilde{k}(\underline{z_t}, u_t^s; \theta)\right]\right\},$$

and u_t^s is drawn in the conditional distribution of u given $\underline{z_t}$.

It is clear that formulas (2.18) and (2.19) are similar, but, as already mentioned, it is important to distinguish the two cases for the following reason. If we consider the simulators introduced in the two cases, they are defined differently, the first one being conditioned by x_t, the second one by $\underline{z_t}$. More precisely, if the model has a well-defined reduced form, i.e. if it is of the (M) type (see (1.22)), i.e.

$$y_t = r(\underline{y_{t-1}}, \underline{z_t}, u; \theta),$$

where u has a known distribution:

$$\tilde{k}(x_t, u_t; \theta) = K\left[r(\underline{y_{t-1}}, \underline{z_t}, u_t; \theta), x_t\right]$$

is an unbiased simulator of the dynamic conditional moment. Note that in this case y_t^s is simulated (through u) conditionally to the observed lagged values $\underline{y_{t-1}}$, i.e. we use conditional simulations.

Let us now consider a static conditional moment.   The function $K[r(\underline{y_{t-1}}, \underline{z_t}, u; \theta), \underline{z_t}]$ with fixed $\underline{y_{t-1}}$ cannot be used as an unbiased simulator conditional on the variables $\underline{z_t}$ alone. Before defining the simulator, it is first necessary to replace the recursive form of the model, $y_t = r(\underline{y_{t-1}}, z_t, u_t; \theta)$, by a final form in which the lagged values of y are replaced by functions of past exogenous variables and past innovations: $y_t = r_f(\underline{z_t}, \underline{u_t}; \theta)$. Then $K[r_f(\underline{z_t}, \underline{u_t}; \theta), \underline{z_t}]$ is an unbiased simulator conditional on $\underline{z_t}$. In this case it is necessary to draw the whole path $\underline{u_t}$ or the whole path $\underline{y_t}$. Therefore the simulations of the endogenous variables are performed unconditionally on the observed values of these variables.

It is important to note that if the model has no well-defined reduced form—for instance in the (M^*) case (see (1.22))—only the MSM based on static conditional moments is available.

Drawings and Gauss–Newton algorithms

As noted before, the optimization of the criterion function ψ is generally solved by a numerical algorithm, which requires the computation of the objective function for different values $\theta_1, \ldots, \theta_p$ of θ. It is important to insist on the fact that the drawings u^s are made at the beginning of the procedure and kept fixed during the execution of the algorithm. If some new drawings were made at each iteration of the algorithm, this would then introduce some new randomness at each step; it would then not be possible to obtain the numerical convergence of the algorithm, and the asymptotic statistical properties would no longer be valid.

2.3.3 Asymptotic properties of the MSM

Static case

Proposition 2.3 When n tends to infinity and S is fixed,

(i) $\hat{\theta}_{Sn}(\Omega)$ is strongly consistent;

(ii) $\sqrt{n}\left[\hat{\theta}_{Sn}(\Omega) - \theta_0\right] \xrightarrow[n \to \infty]{d} N\left[0; Q_S(\Omega)\right]$, where:

$$
\begin{aligned}
Q_S(\Omega) &= \Sigma_1^{-1}\Sigma_2\Sigma_1^{-1} + \frac{1}{S}\Sigma_1^{-1}D'\Omega E_0 V(Z\tilde{k}/z)\Omega D\Sigma_1^{-1} \\
&= \Sigma_1^{-1}\Sigma_2\Sigma_1^{-1} + \frac{1}{S}\Sigma_1^{-1}D'\Omega V_0[Z(\tilde{k} - k)]\Omega D\Sigma_1^{-1} \\
&= \Sigma_1^{-1}\Sigma_2\Sigma_1^{-1} + \frac{1}{S}\Sigma_1^{-1}D'\Omega E_0[ZV(\tilde{k}/z)Z']\Omega D\Sigma_1^{-1},
\end{aligned}
$$

with:

$$
\Sigma_2 = D'\Omega V_0\left[Z(K - k)\right]\Omega D,
$$

$$
D = E_0\left[Z\frac{\partial k}{\partial \theta'}\right],
$$

$$
\Sigma_1 = D'\Omega D,
$$

and where $\tilde{k}$ and K are simplified notations for $\tilde{k}(z, u; \theta_0)$ and $K(y, z)$ respectively.

Proof. This is given in Appendix 2A.

The asymptotic variance–covariance matrix is decomposed into two terms: the first one $\Sigma_1^{-1}\Sigma_2\Sigma_1^{-1}$ is the asymptotic covariance matrix of the GMM estimator, and the second one summarizes the effect of simulations. It is nonnegative and decreases with the number of simulations; in the limit, when $S \to \infty$, the MSM and GMM estimators are asymptotically equivalent.

Corollary 2.1 $V_{as}\left[\hat{\theta}_{Sn}(\Omega)\right] \gg \Sigma_1^{-1}\Sigma_2\Sigma_1^{-1}$, where $\Sigma_1^{-1}\Sigma_2\Sigma_1^{-1}$ is the asymptotic covariance matrix of the GMM estimator.

Moreover, this additional effect of the simulation depends on the quality of the simulator $V(\tilde{k}/z)$. For instance, if we consider a simulator with two random generators—$\tilde{k}(z, u_1, u_2; \theta)$, and the simulator obtained by integrating out u_2 : $\tilde{\tilde{k}}(z, u_1; \theta) = E[\tilde{k}(z, u_1, u_2, ; \theta)/u_1]$—we have:

$$V(\tilde{k}/z) = V\left[E(\tilde{k}/u_1, z)/z\right] + E\left[V(\tilde{k}/u_1, z)/z\right] \gg V(\tilde{\tilde{k}}/z).$$

Therefore, whenever possible, we have to decrease the number of random terms appearing in the simulator.

Corollary 2.2 | Let us assume that $y = r(z, \varepsilon; \theta)$.
(i) If u is a subvector of ε, and if the simulator is of the form: $\tilde{k}(u, z : \theta) = E_\theta\left[K(y, z)/z, u\right]$, then:

$$Q_S(\Omega) = \left(1 + \frac{1}{S}\right) \Sigma_1^{-1} \Sigma_2 \Sigma_1^{-1}$$
$$-\frac{1}{S} \Sigma_1^{-1} D' \Omega V_0\left[Z(K - \tilde{k})\right] \Omega D' \Sigma_1^{-1}.$$

(ii) In particular, $Q_S(\Omega) \ll \left(1 + \frac{1}{S}\right) \Sigma_1^{-1} \Sigma_2 \Sigma_1^{-1}$, and the upper bound is reached for the simulator $\tilde{k}(z, \varepsilon; \theta) = K\left[r(z, \varepsilon; \theta), z\right]$ corresponding to $u = \varepsilon$.

Proof. (i) We have:

$$V_0\left[Z(\tilde{k} - k)\right] = V_0\{Z\left[E(K/z, u) - E(K/z)\right]\}$$
$$= V_0\{Z[(K\left[r(z, \varepsilon, ; \theta_0), z\right] - E(K/z)) - (K\left[r(z, \varepsilon; \theta_0), z\right]$$
$$-E(K/z, u)])\}$$
$$= V_0\{Z\left[K - E(K/z)\right]\} - V_0\{Z\left[K - E(K/z, u)\right]\}$$
$$= V_0[Z(K - k)] - V_0\left[Z(K - \tilde{k})\right].$$

Therefore the result directly follows by replacing $V_0\left[Z(\tilde{k} - k)\right]$ by this decomposition in the second expression of $Q_S(\Omega)$ given in Proposition 2.3.

(ii)
$$Q_S(\Omega) = \left(1 + \frac{1}{S}\right) \Sigma_1^{-1} \Sigma_2 \Sigma_1^{-1}$$
$$-\frac{1}{S} \Sigma_1^{-1} D' \Omega V_0\left[Z(K - \tilde{k})\right] \Omega D' \Sigma_1^{-1}$$
$$\ll \left(1 + \frac{1}{S}\right) \Sigma_1^{-1} \Sigma_2 \Sigma_1^{-1},$$

since the second term in the decomposition of $Q_s(\Omega)$ is nonpositive. Moreover, this term vanishes when

$$K\left[r(z, \varepsilon; \theta), z\right] = k(z, u, \theta). \qquad \text{(QED)}$$

TABLE 2.1: Efficiency

Number S of replications	1	2	3	9
Lower bound of the asymptotic relative efficiency	50 %	66.6 %	75 %	90 %
Maximal relative increase of confidence intervals	141 %	122 %	115 %	102 %

In this case, the asymptotic relative efficiency of the MSM estimator defined as the smallest eigenvalue of

$$Q_S(\Omega)^{-1}\Sigma_1^{-1}\Sigma_2\Sigma_1^{-1},$$

is, under the condition of Corollary 2.2, larger than $(1 + \frac{1}{S})^{-1}$. It is interesting to note that the efficiency loss is not large even with a small number of replications. We give in Table 2.1 the values of $(1+\frac{1}{S})^{-1}$ (lower bound of the asymptotic relative efficiency) and of $(1 + \frac{1}{S})^{+1/2}$ corresponding to the maximal relative increase in the length of confidence intervals.

Dynamic case

For the MSM based on dynamic conditional moments, the results are identical to the previous ones, and we do not repeat them.

For static conditional moments (or unconditional moments for pure time series), the results are modified. More precisely, if $(y_t^s(\theta))$ is a simulated path of the endogenous process, and if the simulator used for $E_\theta[K(y_t, z_t)/z_t]$ is $K[y_t^s(\theta), z_t]$, then the asymptotic variance–covariance matrix of the MSM estimator is $(1 + \frac{1}{S})$ times that of the GMM estimator (see Duffie and Singleton 1993).

2.3.4   Optimal MSM

In the previous subsection, and for a given set of conditional moments, we get a class of MSM estimators, since the matrix Ω and the set of instruments Z may be chosen in various ways. In this section we discuss the choices of Ω and Z for the static case (or, equivalently, for the dynamic conditional moment case).

Optimal choice of Ω

The asymptotic variance–covariance matrix of the MSM estimator is:

$$Q_S(\Omega) = \Sigma_1^{-1} D'\Omega \left\{ V_0[Z(K - k)] + \frac{1}{S} V_0[Z(\tilde{k} - k)] \right\} \Omega D \Sigma_1^{-1}$$

$$= (D'\Omega D)^{-1} D'\Omega \left\{ V_0[Z(K-k)] + \frac{1}{S} V_0[Z(\tilde{k}-k)] \right\} \Omega D (D'\Omega D)^{-1}.$$

From the Gauss–Markov theorem, we know that the nonnegative symmetric matrix $(D'\Omega D)^{-1}D'\Omega\Sigma_0\Omega D(D'\Omega D)^{-1}$ is minimized for $\Omega = \Sigma_0^{-1}$. We deduce the following result.

Proposition 2.4 We have: $Q_S(\Omega) \gg Q_S(\Omega^*)$, where the optimal choice of the matrix is:

$$\Omega^* = \left\{ V_0[Z(K - k)] + \frac{1}{S}V_0[Z(\tilde{k} - k)] \right\}^{-1}.$$

The asymptotic variance–covariance matrix corresponding to this choice is:

$$Q_S(\Omega^*) = \left(D'\Omega^* D\right)^{-1}, \tag{2.20}$$

where

$$D = E_0 \left(Z \frac{\partial k}{\partial \theta'} \right).$$

As usual, the optimal matrix depends on the unknown distribution and has to be consistently estimated. Let us consider the first term, for instance. We have:

$$V_0[Z(K - k)] = E_0 \left\{ [Z(K - k)][Z(K - k)]' \right\}$$
$$\simeq \frac{1}{n} \sum_{i=1}^{n} Z_i \left[K(y_i, z_i) - k(z_i, \tilde{\theta}_n) \right] \left[K(y_i, z_i) - k(z_i, \tilde{\theta}_n) \right]' Z_i',$$

where $\tilde{\theta}_n$ is a consistent estimator of θ_0.

This approximation is consistent; since k does not have a closed form, it has to be approximated using the simulator $\tilde{k}$. To get a good approximation of k, it is necessary to have a large number of replications S_2. Let us denote by $u_{i,2}^s$, $s = 1, \ldots S_2$, some other simulated values of the random term with known distribution, the matrix

$$\hat{\Omega}^* = \left\{ \frac{1}{n} \sum_{i=1}^{n} Z_i \left[K(y_i, z_i) - \frac{1}{S_2} \sum_{s=1}^{S_2} \tilde{k}(z_i, u_{i,2}^s; \tilde{\theta}_n) \right] \right.$$
$$\times \left[K(y_i, z_i) - \frac{1}{S_2} \sum_{s=1}^{S_2} \tilde{k}(z_i, u_{i,2}^s; \tilde{\theta}_n) \right]' Z_i'$$
$$+ \frac{1}{S}\frac{1}{n} \sum_{i=1}^{n} Z_i \left[\tilde{k}(z_i, u_i^{s_1}; \tilde{\theta}_n) - \frac{1}{S_2} \sum_{s=1}^{S_2} \tilde{k}(z_i, u_{i,2}^s; \tilde{\theta}_n) \right]$$
$$\left. \times \left[\tilde{k}(z_i, u_i^{s_1}; \tilde{\theta}_n) - \frac{1}{S_2} \sum_{s=1}^{S_2} \tilde{k}(z_i, u_{i,2}^s; \tilde{\theta}_n) \right]' Z_i' \right\}^{-1}, \tag{2.21}$$

where $u_i^{s_1}$ is a simulated value of u, is a consistent estimator of the optimal matrix Ω^*, when n and S_2 tend to infinity. So, whereas the derivation of the estimation of

θ by MSM requires only a small number of simulated values, the determination of the optimal matrix and of the associated precision require a much larger set of other simulated values; however, these simulations are used only once.

Finally, we may compare the optimal asymptotic variance–covariance matrix of the MSM with the optimal asymptotic variance–covariance matrix of the GMM. The latter corresponds to another choice of the matrix $\Omega^{**} = (V_0\,[Z(K-k)])^{-1}$ is given by:

$$Q^* = \left(D'\Omega^{**}D\right)^{-1}.$$

We directly note that $\Omega^{**} \gg \Omega^*$, which implies:

$$Q_S(\Omega^*) \gg Q^*.$$

It is also clear that:

$$Q^* = \lim_{S \to \infty} Q_S(\Omega^*).$$

Selection of the instruments

When the optimal matrix is retained, the asymptotic variance–covariance matrix is:

$$Q_S(\Omega^*) = \left\{ E_0\left(\frac{\partial k'}{\partial \theta}Z'\right)\left\{ V_0[Z(K-k)] + \frac{1}{S}V_0[Z(\tilde{k}-k)]\right\}^{-1} E_0\left(Z\frac{\partial k}{\partial \theta'}\right)\right\}^{-1}$$

$$= \left\{ E_0\left(\frac{\partial k'}{\partial \theta}Z'\right)\left\{ E_0\left(Z\left[V_0(K/z) + \frac{1}{S}V(\tilde{k}/z)\right]Z'\right)\right\}^{-1} E_0\left(Z\frac{\partial k}{\partial \theta}\right)\right\}^{-1}.$$

Then we can use a classical result on optimal instruments. If A and C are random matrices of suitable dimensions, are functions of z, and are such that C is square and positive definite, then the matrix

$$E_0(A'Z')[E_0(ZCZ')]^{-1}E_0(ZA)$$

is maximized for $Z = A'C^{-1}$ and the maximum is $E_0(A'C^{-1}A)$.

Proposition 2.5: The optimal instruments are:

$$Z_S^* = \frac{\partial k'}{\partial \theta}[V_0(K/z) + \frac{1}{S}V(\tilde{k}/z)]^{-1},$$

where the different functions k, $\tilde{k}$ are evaluated at the true value θ_0. With this choice the asymptotic variance–covariance matrix is:

$$Q_S^* = \left\{ E_0\left[\frac{\partial k'}{\partial \theta}\left(V_0(K/z) + \frac{1}{S}V(\tilde{k}/z)\right)^{-1}\frac{\partial k}{\partial \theta'}\right]\right\}^{-1}.$$

When S goes to infinity, we find the well-known optimal instruments for the GMM:

$$Z^* = \frac{\partial k'}{\partial \theta} [V_0(K/z)]^{-1},$$

and the associated asymptotic variance–covariance matrix:

$$Q^* = \left\{ E_0 \left[\frac{\partial k'}{\partial \theta} V_0(K/z) \frac{\partial k}{\partial \theta'} \right] \right\}^{-1}.$$

Also note that when $\tilde{k} = K$, i.e. when the frequency simulator is used, we have:

$$Z_S^* = \left(1 + \frac{1}{S} \right)^{-1} Z^*,$$

and, therefore, the optimal instruments are identical in the MSM and the GMM.

2.3.5   An extension of the MSM

In the usual presentation of the GMM (see Hansen 1982), the true value of the parameter is defined by a set of estimating constraints of the form:

$$E_0[g(y_i, z_i; \theta_0)/z_i] = 0, \tag{2.22}$$

where g is a given function of size q; we consider the static case for notational convenience. It is important to note that in the previous sections we have considered a specific form of these estimating constraints, i.e.

$$g(y_i, z_i; \theta_0) = K(y_i, z_i) - k(z_i; \theta_0) \qquad \text{(see (2.8)).}$$

What happens if we now consider the general form (2.22)? As before, we may introduce an unbiased simulator of $g(y_i, z_i; \theta)$. This simulator $\tilde{g}(y_i, z_i, u_i; \theta)$, which depends on an auxiliary random term u_i with a known and fixed distribution conditional on y_i, z_i, is based on a function $\tilde{g}$ with a tractable form and satisfies the unbiasedness condition:

$$E[\tilde{g}(y_i, z_i, u_i; \theta)/y_i, z_i] = g(y_i, z_i; \theta). \tag{2.23}$$

Then we can define an MSM estimator as a solution of the optimization problem:

$$\hat{\theta}_{Sn}(\Omega) = \arg\min_\theta \left[\sum_{i=1}^{n} Z_i \frac{1}{S} \sum_{s=1}^{S} \tilde{g}(y_i, z_i, u_i^s; \theta) \right]'$$

$$\times \Omega \left[\sum_{i=1}^{n} Z_i \frac{1}{S} \sum_{s=1}^{S} \tilde{g}(y_i, z_i, u_i^s; \theta) \right], \tag{2.24}$$

where $u_i^s, i = 1, \ldots, n, s = 1, \ldots, S$, are independent drawings in the distribution of u, and Z_i are instrumental variable functions of z_i.

Proposition 2.6 | When n goes to infinity and S is fixed, the estimator $\hat{\theta}_{Sn}(\Omega)$ defined by (2.24)

(i) is consistent, and

(ii) is such that $\sqrt{n}[\hat{\theta}_{Sn}(\Omega) - \theta_o] \xrightarrow[n \to \infty]{d} N[0; Q_S(\Omega)]$ where

$$Q_S(\Omega) = \Sigma_1^{-1} \Sigma_2 \Sigma_1^{-1} + \frac{1}{S} \Sigma_1^{-1} D' \Omega E_0[ZV(\tilde{g}/y, z)Z']$$
$$\times \Omega D \Sigma^{-1}$$
$$\Sigma_2 = D' \Omega V_0(Zg) \Omega D$$
$$D = E_0[Z \frac{\partial g}{\partial \theta'}]$$
$$\Sigma_1 = D' \Omega D.$$

Proof. See Appendix 2A.

Example 2.3   Simulated score

It is well known that the maximum likelihood method may be considered a GMM. More precisely, let us consider the i.i.d. case and let us denote by $f(y_i/z_i; \theta)$ the conditional p.d.f. of y_i given z_i. The ML estimator satisfies the likelihood equations

$$\sum_{i=1}^{n} \frac{\partial \log f}{\partial \theta}(y_i/z_i; \hat{\theta}_n) = 0,$$

and is a GMM estimator based on the estimating constraints associated with the score function:

$$E_0 \left[\frac{\partial \log f}{\partial \theta}(y_i/z_i; \theta_0)/z_i \right] = 0. \tag{2.25}$$

If the p.d.f. has an untractable form, and if $\tilde{g}(y_i, z_i, u_i; \theta)$ is an unbiased simulator of the score; that is, if

$$E[\tilde{g}(y_i, z_i, u_i; \theta)/y_i, z_i] = \frac{\partial \log f}{\partial \theta}(y_i/z_i; \theta) \tag{2.26}$$

then a consistent estimator of θ is the MSM estimator based on $\tilde{g}$.

Example 2.4   An unbiased simulator of the score function for latent variable models

Let us consider a latent model with i.i.d. variables $(y_i^*, z_i), i = 1, \ldots, n$, and let us denote by $f^*(y_i^*/z_i; \theta)$ the conditional p.d.f. of y_i^* given z_i. If the endogenous observable variable is a known function of y_i^* : $y_i = a(y_i^*)$, we know that the score function is such that:

$$E_\theta \left[\frac{\partial \log f^*}{\partial \theta} (y_i^*/z_i; \theta)/y_i, z_i \right] = \frac{\partial \log f}{\partial \theta} (y_i/z_i; \theta).$$

Therefore it is natural to consider the previous equality as an unbiasedness condition and to propose the unbiased simulator $(\partial \log f^*/\partial \theta)(y_i^{*s}/z_i; \theta)$, where y_i^{*s} is drawn in the conditional distribution of y_i^* given y_i, z_i. If this drawing can be summarized by a relation (in distribution), i.e.

$$y_i^* = b(y_i, z_i, u_i; \theta),$$

where u_i has a fixed known distribution, the unbiased simulator is:

$$\tilde{g}(y_i, z_i, u_i; \theta) = \frac{\partial \log f^*}{\partial \theta} [b(y_i, z_i, u_i; \theta)/z_i; \theta]. \tag{2.27}$$

In practice such a simulator will be used only if the function b has a simple form. This is the case for some limited dependent variable models (see Chapter 5).

Example 2.5   Derivation of the asymptotic variance–covariance matrix for a simulated score estimator

In the special case of the simulated score, the size of $\tilde{g}$ is equal to the size of the parameter and D is a square matrix. Therefore the asymptotic variance–covariance matrix given in Proposition 2.6 does not depend on Ω and is equal to:

$$V_{as} \left[V_n \left(\hat{\theta}_{Sn} - \theta_0 \right) \right] = \left[E_0 \left(Z \frac{\partial g}{\partial \theta'} \right) \right]^{-1} V_0(Zg) \left[E_0 \left(\frac{\partial g'}{\partial \theta} Z' \right) \right]^{-1}$$

$$+ \frac{1}{S} \left[E_0 \left(Z \frac{\partial g}{\partial \theta'} \right) \right]^{-1} E_0[ZV (\tilde{g}/y, z) Z'] \left[E_0 \left(\frac{\partial g'}{\partial \theta} Z' \right) \right]^{-1}$$

and, since $g = \partial \log f/\partial \theta$, $\partial g/\partial \theta' = \partial^2 \log f/\partial \theta \partial \theta'$, and $\tilde{g} = \partial \log f^*/\partial \theta$, we get:

$$E_0 \left[Z \frac{\partial^2 \log f}{\partial \theta \partial \theta'} (y/z; \theta_0) \right]^{-1} \left\{ V_0 \left[Z \frac{\partial \log f}{\partial \theta} (y/z; \theta_0) \right] \right.$$

$$\left. + \frac{1}{S} E_0 \left[ZV[\tilde{g}(y, z, u; \theta_0)/y, z]Z' \right] \right\} E_0 \left[\frac{\partial^2 \log f}{\partial \theta \partial \theta'} (y/z; \theta_0)Z' \right]^{-1}.$$

In particular, if the instruments are $Z = Id$ (these are the optimal instruments for the GMM based on the score function), and if the simulator is based on the latent score (see (2.27)), we get:

$$V_{as}[\sqrt{n}(\hat{\theta}_{Sn} - \theta_0)] = I^{-1} \left\{ I + \frac{1}{S} E_0 V[\tilde{g}(y, z, u; \theta_0)/y, z] \right\} I^{-1}$$

$$= I^{-1} \left\{ I + \frac{1}{S} (I^* - I) \right\} I^{-1}$$

$$= I^{-1} + \frac{1}{S} I^{-1} (I^* - I) I^{-1}$$

where I and I^* are respectively the information matrix of the observable model,

$$I = E_0 \left[-\frac{\partial^2 \log f}{\partial \theta \, \partial \theta'} (y/z; \theta_0) \right] = E_0 V_0 \left[\frac{\partial \log f}{\partial \theta} (y/z; \theta_0)/z \right],$$

and the information matrix of the latent model:

$$I^* = E_0 \left[-\frac{\partial^2 \log f^*}{\partial \theta \partial \theta'} (y^*/z; \theta_0) \right] = E_0 V_0 \left[\frac{\partial \log f^*}{\partial \theta} (y^*/z; \theta_0)/z \right].$$

The price that must be paid for the simulations is $\frac{1}{S} I^{-1} (I^* - I) I^{-1}$; as usual it decreases as $\frac{1}{S}$ when S increases and, moreover, it is proportional to the information difference $I^* - I$ between the latent model and the observable model.

Appendix 2A: Proofs of the Asymptotic Properties of the MSM Estimator

2A.1 Consistency

Let us consider the general form of the MSM estimator defined by (2.24):

$$\hat{\theta}_{Sn}(\Omega) = \arg \min_\theta \left[\sum_{i=1}^n Z_i \frac{1}{S} \sum_{s=1}^S \tilde{g}(y_i, z_i, u_i^s; \theta) \right]' \Omega$$

$$\times \left[\sum_{i=1}^n Z_i \frac{1}{S} \sum_{s=1}^S \tilde{g}(y_i, z_i, u_i^s; \theta) \right]$$

$$= \arg \min_\theta M_{Sn}(\theta) \quad \text{(say)}.$$

When S is fixed and n goes to infinity, $\frac{1}{n^2} M_{Sn}(\theta)$ converges almost surely to:

$$\left[E_z(Z E_y^0 E_u \tilde{g}(y, z, u^s; \theta)) \right]' \Omega E_z[Z E(E_z^0 E_u \tilde{g}(y, z, u^s; \theta))],$$

where E_u is the conditional expectation with respect to the distribution of u^s given (y, z) (i.e. with respect to the marginal distribution of u since u^s and (y, z) are independent), E_y^0 is the conditional expectation with respect to the true conditional distribution of y given z, and E_z is the expectation with respect to the distribution of z.

Since $E_u \tilde{g}(y, z, u^s; \theta) = g(y, z; \theta)$ and $E_y^0 g(y, z; \theta_0) = 0$, it is clear that this limit is equal to zero and, therefore, minimal for $\theta = \theta_0$. Assuming that the previous almost sure convergence is uniform in $\theta \in \Theta$ compact and that θ_0 is the unique minimum, we obtain the strong consistency of $\hat{\theta}_{Sn}(\Omega)$. Taking $\tilde{g}(y_i, z_i, u_i^s; \theta) = K(y_i, z_i) - k(z_i, u_i^s; \theta)$, we get part (i) of Proposition 2.3.

2A.2 Asymptotic normality

The first order conditions of the minimization defining $\hat{\theta}_{Sn}(\Omega)$ (denoted $\hat{\theta}_{Sn}$ for the sake of simplicity) are:

$$0 = \frac{1}{n\sqrt{n}} \sum_{i=1}^{n} \frac{1}{S} \sum_{s=1}^{S} \frac{\partial \tilde{g}'}{\partial \theta}(y_i, z_i, u_i^s; \hat{\theta}_{Sn}) Z_i' \Omega$$

$$\times \sum_{i=1}^{n} Z_i \frac{1}{S} \sum_{s=1}^{S} \tilde{g}(y_i, z_i, u_i^s; \hat{\theta}_{Sn}).$$

An expansion around θ_0 gives:

$$0 \# \frac{1}{n} \sum_{i=1}^{n} \frac{1}{S} \sum_{s=1}^{S} \frac{\partial \tilde{g}'}{\partial \theta}(y_i, z_i, u_i^s; \theta_0) Z_i' \Omega$$

$$\times \frac{1}{\sqrt{n}} \sum_{i=1}^{n} Z_i \frac{1}{S} \sum_{s=1}^{S} \tilde{g}(y_i, z_i, u_i^s; \theta_0)$$

$$+ \frac{1}{n} \sum_{i=1}^{n} \frac{1}{S} \sum_{s=1}^{S} \frac{\partial \tilde{g}'}{\partial \theta}(y_i, z_i, u_i^s; \theta_0) Z_i' \Omega$$

$$\times \frac{1}{n} \sum_{i=1}^{n} Z_i \frac{1}{S} \sum_{s=1}^{S} \frac{\partial \tilde{g}}{\partial \theta'}(y_i, z_i, u_i^s; \theta_0) \sqrt{n}(\hat{\theta}_{Sn} - \theta_0)$$

$$+ \frac{1}{n} \sum_{j=1}^{q} \frac{1}{S} \sum_{s=1}^{S} \frac{\partial^2 \tilde{g}_j}{\partial \theta \partial \theta'}(y_i, z_i, u_i^s; \theta_0)$$

$$\times \left\{ Z_i' \Omega \frac{1}{n} \sum_{i=1}^{n} Z_i \frac{1}{S} \sum_{s=1}^{S} \tilde{g}(y_i, z_i, u_i^s; \theta_0) \right\}_j \sqrt{n}(\hat{\theta}_{Sn} - \theta_0),$$

where j denotes the jth component.

When n goes to infinity, the last term goes to zero because:

$$E\left[Z\tilde{g}(y, z, u^s; \theta_0)\right] = E_z\left[Z E_0\left[g(y, z; \theta_0)/z\right]\right] = 0.$$

It follows that:

$$0 \# D'\Omega \frac{1}{\sqrt{n}} \sum_{i=1}^{n} Z_i \frac{1}{S} \sum_{s=1}^{S} \tilde{g}(y_i, z_i, u_i^s; \theta_0) + D'\Omega D\sqrt{n}(\hat{\theta}_{Sn} - \theta_0)$$

with $D = E_0[Z \frac{\partial g}{\partial \theta'}(y, z; \theta_0)]$, where E_0 is the expectation with respect to the true distribution of (y, z).

When n goes to infinity:

$$\frac{1}{\sqrt{n}} \sum_{i=1}^{n} Z_i \frac{1}{S} \sum_{s=1}^{S} \tilde{g}(y_i, z_i, u_i^s; \theta_0)$$

converges in distribution to $N(0, \Sigma_g)$, with:

$$\begin{aligned}
\Sigma_g &= V \left[Z \frac{1}{S} \sum_{s=1}^{S} \tilde{g}(y, z, u^s; \theta_0) \right] \\
&= V_0 E_u \left[Z \frac{1}{S} \sum_{s=1}^{S} \tilde{g}(y, z, u^s; \theta_0) \right] \\
&\quad + E_0 V_u \left[Z \frac{1}{S} \sum_{s=1}^{S} \tilde{g}(y, z, u^s; \theta_0) \right] \\
&= V_0 [Z g(y, z, \theta_0)] + \frac{1}{S} E_0 \left[Z V_u \tilde{g}(y, z, u^s; \theta_0) Z' \right].
\end{aligned}$$

This implies that $\sqrt{n}(\hat{\theta}_{Sn} - \theta)$ converges in distribution to:

$$\begin{aligned}
Q_S(\Omega) &= (D'\Omega D)^{-1} D'\Omega \Sigma_g \Omega D (D'\Omega D)^{-1} \\
&= \Sigma_1^{-1} \Sigma_2 \Sigma_1^{-1} + \frac{1}{S} \Sigma_1^{-1} D'\Omega E_0(Z V_u \tilde{g} Z') \Omega D \Sigma_1^{-1}
\end{aligned}$$

with

$$\begin{aligned}
\Sigma_1 &= D'\Omega D \\
\Sigma_2 &= D'\Omega V_0(Zg) \Omega D.
\end{aligned}$$

Particular case

In the particular case where

$$\tilde{g}(y, z, u^s; \theta) = K(y, z) - \tilde{k}(z, u^s; \theta)$$

and $\quad g(y, z; \theta) = K(y, z) - k(z; \theta),$

we get the results of Proposition 2.3. Since the general form of $Q_S(\Omega)$ directly reduces to the third form given in this proposition with $D = E_0 \left[Z \frac{\partial k}{\partial \theta'}(z, \theta_0) \right]$, the two other forms are obtained immediately.

3

Simulated Maximum Likelihood, Pseudo-Maximum Likelihood, and Nonlinear Least Squares Methods

In the previous chapter we discussed the simulated analogues of the method of moments. We are now considering simulated versions of other estimation methods such as maximum likelihood, pseudo-maximum likelihood or nonlinear least squares. The main characteristic of the associated estimators is their non consistency when the number S of replications is fixed. Therefore theoretical consistency may only be obtained either by performing a large number S ($S \to +\infty$) of replications, or by introducing some correction to eliminate the asymptotic bias; however, this theoretical problem may not be so important in practice.

3.1 Simulated Maximum Likelihood Estimators (SML)

The maximum likelihood estimator of a parameter θ is defined as:

$$\hat{\theta}_T = \arg \max_{\theta} \log f(\underline{y_T}/\underline{z_T}; \theta), \qquad (3.1)$$

where $f(\underline{y_T}/\underline{z_T}; \theta)$ is the conditional p.d.f. of $\underline{y_T} = (y_1, \ldots, y_T)$, given $\underline{z_T} = (z_1, \ldots, z_T)$ and some initial conditions.

We are interested in problems where this p.d.f. has an untractable form, and it is important to distinguish two cases. In the first case it is possible to find unbiased simulators of each conditional p.d.f. $f(y_t/\underline{y_{t-1}}, \underline{z_t}; \theta)$, also denoted $f(y_t/x_t; \theta)$, appearing in the decomposition:

$$\log f(\underline{y_T}/\underline{z_T}; \theta) = \sum_{t=1}^{T} \log f(y_t/x_t; \theta).$$

This first case often occurs if the model has a well-defined reduced form (see (1.22)):

$$(M) \ y_t = r(z_t, \underline{y_{t-1}}, \varepsilon_t; \theta).$$

However, such simulators do not generally exist in dynamic models with unobservable factors (see Section 1.3.4), defined as

$$(M^*) \ y_t = r_1(\underline{z_t}, \underline{y_{t-1}}, y_t^*, \varepsilon_{1t}; \theta)$$
$$y_t^* = r_2(\underline{z_t}, \underline{y_{t-1}}, \underline{y_{t-1}^*}, \varepsilon_{2t}; \theta).$$

In this second case other approaches must be found (see Section 3.1.5).

3.1.1   Estimator based on simulators of the conditional density functions

Let us denote by $\tilde{f}(y_t, x_t, u; \theta)$ an unbiased simulator of $f(y_t/x_t; \theta)$, i.e. such that

$$E(\tilde{f}(y_t, x_t, u; \theta)/x_t, y_t) = f(y_t/x_t; \theta), \tag{3.2}$$

and where the conditional distribution of u given x_t, y_t is known. In practice this distribution is often independent of x_t, y_t.

Then we may draw independently, for each index t, S simulated values u_t^s, $s = 1, \ldots, S$, of the auxiliary random term u.

Definition 3.1 | A simulated maximum likelihood estimator of θ is:

$$\hat{\theta}_{ST} = \arg\max_\theta \sum_{t=1}^T \log \left[\frac{1}{S} \sum_{s=1}^S \tilde{f}(y_t, x_t, u_t^s; \theta) \right].$$

It is obtained after replacement of the untractable conditional p.d.f. with an unbiased approximation based on the simulator.

3.1.2   Asymptotic properties

Let us first study the consistency properties of such estimators. We distinguish two cases: S fixed and S tending to infinity with T.

S fixed

If $S = 1$, the objective function,

$$\frac{1}{T} \sum_{t=1}^T \log \tilde{f}(y_t, x_t, u_t^s; \theta),$$

tends asymptotically to the limit function:

$$\psi_\infty(\theta) = E_0 \int \log \tilde{f}(y, x, u; \theta) g(u) \, du, \tag{3.3}$$

where g is the p.d.f. of u. We know that the true value of the parameter θ_0 is the solution of $\max_\theta E_0 \log f(y/x; \theta)$, but it is not in general a solution of the maximization of (3.3), since the log and the integral do not commute, and $\hat{\theta}_{ST}$ is not consistent. This inconsistency comes from the choice of the simulator $\tilde{f}$ as an unbiased simulator of f. If $\log \tilde{f}(y_t, x_t, u; \theta)$ were an unbiased simulator of $\log f(y_t/x_t; \theta)$, the limit function ψ_∞ would have been

$$\psi_\infty(\theta) = E_0 \int \log \tilde{f}(y, x, u; \theta) g(u) \, du$$
$$= E_0 \log f(y/x; \theta),$$

and would have a maximum at θ_0. However, in practice it is often possible to exhibit unbiased simulators of f, but it is difficult to exhibit unbiased simulators of $\log f$.

S tending to infinity

If S tends to infinity, the limit objective function is:

$$\lim_{T,S \to \infty} \frac{1}{T} \sum_{t=1}^{T} \log \left[\frac{1}{S} \sum_{s=1}^{S} \tilde{f}(y_t, x_t, u_t^s; \theta) \right]$$
$$= \lim_{T \to \infty} \frac{1}{T} \sum_{t=1}^{T} \log \left[\int \tilde{f}(y_t, x_t, u; \theta) g(u) \, du \right]$$
$$= E_0 \log \left[\int \tilde{f}(y_t, x_t, u; \theta) g(u) \, du \right]$$
$$= E_0 \log f(y_t, x_t; \theta), \text{ since } \tilde{f} \text{ is an unbiased simulator of } f.$$

It is the same limit problem as for usual maximum likelihood estimation, and the estimator is consistent.

Proposition 3.1 | (i) The SML estimator is consistent, if T and S tend to infinity.
| (ii) It is inconsistent if S is fixed and T tends to infinity.

When we compare Proposition 3.1 with the property of consistency of MSM valid even for fixed S, the SML approaches may appear uninteresting. However:

(a) In practice it is sufficient to retain a number S of replications such that $\hat{\theta}_{ST} \simeq \lim_{S \to \infty} \hat{\theta}_{ST}$, and such a number often is of moderate size.

(b) The MSM also requires a large number of simulations in order to compute the standard errors of the estimator.

(c) In finite samples, what really matters is the relative magnitude of the square of the bias and of the variance of the estimator. As discussed below, the magnitude of the bias may be reduced by the choice of suitable simulators, or by the introduction of some correction terms, while the variance of an SML estimator (close to the variance of the efficient ML estimator) is generally smaller than the variance of an MSM estimator (close to the variance of an inefficient GMM estimator).

(d) Finally, whereas the GMM approach may be preferred to the ML approach since it requires less distributional assumptions (GMM is a semi-parametric approach), this argument fails for the MSM approach which requires the complete specification of the distribution for simulation purposes.

When the number of replications S tends to infinity, the simulation step may have an effect on the asymptotic covariance matrix of the simulated ML estimator, except if the speed of divergence of S is sufficiently large. The following result is proved in Gouriéroux and Monfort (1991).

Proposition 3.2   If $S, T \to \infty$ and $\sqrt{T}/S \to 0$, then the SML estimator is asymptotically equivalent to the ML estimator.

3.1.3   Study of the asymptotic bias

An expansion for the asymptotic bias

When S tends to infinity, the bias is of order $\frac{1}{S}$. More precisely, we have the following result (Gouriéroux and Monfort 1991):

Proposition 3.3 | When S tends to infinity, the asymptotic bias is equivalent to
$$B = E_0 \hat{\theta}_{ST} - \theta_0 \sim \frac{1}{S} I^{-1}(\theta_0) E_0[a(y, x; \theta)],$$
where $I(\theta_0)$ is the information matrix, and
$$a(y, x; \theta_0) = \frac{E_u \frac{\partial \tilde{f}}{\partial \theta} V_u \tilde{f}}{(E_u \tilde{f})^3} - \frac{\text{cov}_u\left(\frac{\partial \tilde{f}}{\partial \theta}, \tilde{f}\right)}{(E_u \tilde{f})^2}.$$

As expected, the bias depends on the choice of the simulator, and may be reduced by a sensible selection of $\tilde{f}$. Moreover, the square of the bias compared with the variance may be measured by:

$$B' I(\theta_0) B = \frac{1}{S^2} E_0[a(y, x; \theta_0)]' I^{-1}(\theta_0) E_0[a(y, x; \theta_0)].$$

Therefore it is small when the underlying ML estimator is precise, i.e. when $I^{-1}(\theta_0)$ is small.

A first order correction for the asymptotic bias

As noted before, the inconsistency comes from the choice of a simulator $\log \tilde{f}$ which is a biased simulator of $\log f$. How can we partially correct this effect if the bias is not too large? We have:

$$\log \tilde{f} = \log(f + \tilde{f} - f)$$

$$\simeq \log f + \frac{\tilde{f} - f}{f} - \frac{1}{2}\frac{(\tilde{f} - f)^2}{f^2}$$

and:

$$E_u \log \tilde{f} \simeq \log f + \frac{E_u \tilde{f} - f}{f} - \frac{1}{2}E_u\frac{(\tilde{f} - f)^2}{f^2}$$

$$= \log f - \frac{1}{2}E_u\frac{(\tilde{f} - f)^2}{f^2}.$$

Therefore $\log \tilde{f} + \frac{1}{2}[(\tilde{f} - f)^2/f^2]$ is a simulator of $\log f$ with a smaller bias than $\log \tilde{f}$ in general. A first order correction of the SML estimator consists in computing the corrected estimator:

$$\tilde{\theta}_{ST} = \arg\min_{\theta} \left\{ \sum_{t=1}^{T} \log\left[\frac{1}{S}\sum_{s=1}^{S}\tilde{f}(y_t, x_t, u_t^s; \theta)\right] \right.$$

$$\left. + \frac{S}{2}\sum_{t=1}^{T} \frac{\sum_{s=1}^{S}\left[\tilde{f}(y_t, x_t, u_t^s; \theta) - \frac{1}{S}\sum_{s=1}^{S}\tilde{f}(y_t, x_t, u_t^s; \theta)\right]^2}{\left[\sum_{s=1}^{S}\tilde{f}(y_t, x_t, u_t^s; \theta)\right]^2} \right\}.$$

$$(3.4)$$

3.1.4 Conditioning

In a number of examples described in Chapter 1, the conditional p.d.f. has an integral form:

$$f(y_t/x_t; \theta) = \int f^*(y_t/x_t; u; \theta)g(u)\,du, \qquad (3.5)$$

where u is a subvector of the error term ε appearing in the reduced form of the model. In such a case it is possible to introduce the simulator:

$$\tilde{f}(y, x, u; \theta) = f^*(y/x; u; \theta), \text{ where } u \text{ has a distribution with p.d.f. } g. (3.6)$$

It is also possible to introduce an importance function φ with the same support as g, such that $\varphi(u) > 0$, $\int \varphi(u)\, du = 1$, and to introduce the simulator:

$$\tilde{f}(y, x, u; \theta) = f^*(y/x; u; \theta) \frac{g(u)}{\varphi(u)}, \qquad (3.7)$$

where u has a distribution with p.d.f. φ.

We give below some examples where some conditioning naturally appears.

Example 3.1   Panel probit (or Tobit) model with individual effect

In this model the latent variables are indexed by individual and time and follow a linear model with individual random effect:

$$y_{it}^* = z_{it}b + \sigma_u u_i + \sigma_w w_{it},$$

where u_i, w_{it} are independent variables with standard normal distributions. The observable endogenous variables are either

$$y_{it} = \mathbb{1}_{(y_{it}^* > 0)} \text{ probit model } (\sigma_w \text{ may be constrained to 1}),$$

or $y_{it} = y_{it}^* \mathbb{1}_{(y_{it}^* > 0)}$ Tobit model.

The simulators may be based on the conditional distribution of y given z and the individual effect u, since it is easy to integrate out the other random terms w because the w_{it}, $t = 1, \ldots, T$ are independent. We get:

(a) probit model:

$$f^*(y_i/z_i, u_i; \theta) = \prod_{t:y_{it}=1} \Phi(z_{it}'b + \sigma_u u_i) \prod_{t:y_{it}=0} \Phi(-z_{it}'b - \sigma_u u_i).$$

(b) Tobit model:

$$f^*(y_i/z_i, u_i; \theta) = \prod_{t:y_{it}>0} \frac{1}{\sigma_w} \varphi\left(\frac{y_{it} - z_{it}'b - \sigma_u u_i}{\sigma_w}\right)$$
$$\times \prod_{t:y_{it}=0} \Phi\left(-\frac{z_{it}'b + \sigma_u u_i}{\sigma_w}\right).$$

Example 3.2   Panel probit (or Tobit) model with individual effect and serially correlated disturbances (Hajivassiliou and McFadden 1990, Keane 1990a, b, Stern 1992, Gouriéroux and Monfort 1993a)

The latent variables satisfy:

$$\begin{cases} y_{it}^* = z_{it}b + \sigma_u u_i + \varepsilon_{it}, \\ \varepsilon_{it} = \rho \varepsilon_{i,t-1} + \sigma_w w_{it}, \qquad t \geq 2, \\ \varepsilon_{i1} = \dfrac{\sigma_w}{(1-\rho^2)^{1/2}} w_{1t}, \end{cases}$$

where u_i, w_{it} are independent variables with standard normal distribution. The error term (ε_{it}) satisfies an autoregressive formulation and the initial value ε_{i1} is assumed to follow the marginal distribution associated with this autoregressive scheme. For a probit (or Tobit) model based on this latent variable, the p.d.f. of y conditional on z and u is no longer tractable (since the ε_{it}, $t = 1, \ldots, T$ are correlated), but another conditioning is available. Let us consider the global error term for individual i. It is a T-dimensional vector:

$$\xi_i = \sigma_u u_i e_T + \varepsilon_i, \tag{3.8}$$

where e_T is the vector whose components are equal to one. The variance–covariance matrix of this error term is:

$$V\xi_i = \sigma_u^2 J_T + \Omega, \tag{3.9}$$

where the entries of J_T are one, and the generic entry of Ω is $\omega_{ij} = [\sigma_w^2/(1 - \rho^2)]\rho^{|i-j|}$.

Lemma 3.1 | ε_{it} may be decomposed into:
$$\varepsilon_{it} = \varepsilon_{it}^{(1)} + \varepsilon_{it}^{(2)}, \qquad t = 1, \ldots, T,$$
where $(\varepsilon_{it}^{(1)})$, $(\varepsilon_{it}^{(2)})$ are independent, and $(\varepsilon_{it}^{(1)})$ is a Gaussian white noise with variance: $\sigma_w^2/(1 + |\rho|)^2 = \sigma_M^2$.

Proof. The spectral density function of $(\varepsilon_{it}, t \in \mathbb{Z})$ is equal to:

$$\frac{\sigma_w^2}{2\pi|1 - \rho \exp i\omega|^2} = \frac{\sigma_w^2}{2\pi(1 - 2\rho \cos \omega + \rho^2)}.$$

It has a monotonic form with a minimum value for $\sigma_w^2(1 + |\rho|)^{-2}$ and the result follows.

QED

Now we may consider another decomposition of the global error term:

$$\xi_i = \sigma_u u_i e_T + \varepsilon_i = \sigma_u u_i e_T + \varepsilon_i^{(1)} + \varepsilon_i^{(2)} = \varepsilon_i^{(1)} + v_i,$$

where $\varepsilon_i^{(1)}$ and v_i are independent, $v_i \sim N[0, \sigma_u^2 J_T + \Omega - \sigma_M^2 Id_T]$. Therefore we can write:

$$\xi_i = \varepsilon_i^{(1)} + Au_i^*,$$

where $AA' = \sigma_u^2 J_T + \Omega - \sigma_M^2 Id_T$ and $u_i^* \sim N(0, Id_T)$.

If we condition with respect to u_i^*, i.e. if we integrate out $\varepsilon_i^{(1)}$, we obtain the following conditional p.d.f.:

(*a*) probit model (we can take $\sigma_w^2 = 1$):

$$f^*(y_i/z_i, u_i^*; \theta) = \prod_{t:y_{it}=1} \Phi\left(\frac{z_{it}b + a_t u_i^*}{\sigma_M}\right)$$

$$\times \prod_{t:y_{it}=0} \Phi\left(\frac{-z_{it}b - a_t u_i^*}{\sigma_M}\right),$$

where a_t is the tth row of matrix A.

(*b*) Tobit model:

$$f^*(y_i/z_i, u_i^*; \theta) = \prod_{t:y_{it}>0} \frac{1}{\sigma_M} \varphi\left(\frac{y_{it} - z_{it}b - a_t u_i^*}{\sigma_M}\right)$$

$$\times \prod_{t:y_{it}=0} \Phi\left(\frac{-z_{it}b - a_t u_i^*}{\sigma_M}\right).$$

3.1.5   Estimators based on other simulators

In dynamic models where latent variables are present, it is often impossible to find unbiased simulators of the conditional p.d.f. $f(y_t/y_{t-1}, z_t; \theta)$, and the methods presented in the previous sections do not apply. In this kind of model the overall p.d.f. of the observable and latent endogenous variables $(\underline{y_T}, \underline{y_T^*})$ can be written:

$$f(\underline{y_T}, \underline{y_T^*}/\underline{z_T}, y_0, y_0^*; \theta)$$

$$= \prod_{t=1}^{T} f(y_t, y_t^*/\underline{z_t}, \underline{y_{t-1}}, \underline{y_{t-1}^*}; \theta)$$

$$= \prod_{t=1}^{T} f(y_t/\underline{z_t}, \underline{y_{t-1}}, \underline{y_t^*}; \theta) f(y_t^*/\underline{z_t}, \underline{y_{t-1}}, \underline{y_{t-1}^*}; \theta),$$

and the likelihood function is:

$$f(\underline{y_T}/\underline{z_T}, y_0, y_0^*; \theta)$$

$$= \int \prod_{t=1}^{T} f(y_t/\underline{z_t}, \underline{y_{t-1}}, \underline{y_t^*}; \theta) f(y_t^*/\underline{z_t}, \underline{y_{t-1}}, \underline{y_{t-1}^*}; \theta) \prod_{t=1}^{T} d\mu(y_t^*).$$

The likelihood function appears as a T-dimensional integral (if y_t^* is univariate) of a function which in general does not have a closed form.

Let us consider, for instance, the typical M^* model (see example 1.17):

$$y_t = r_1(z_t, \underline{y_{t-1}}, \underline{y_t^*}, \varepsilon_{1t}; \theta),$$

$$y_t^* = r_2(z_t, \underline{y_{t-1}}, \underline{y_{t-1}^*}, \varepsilon_{2t}; \theta),$$

where $\varepsilon_t = (\varepsilon'_{1t}, \varepsilon'_{2t})$ is a white noise whose distribution is known. If ε_{1t} and ε_{2t} are contemporaneously independent, the function $f(y_t/\underline{z_t}, \underline{y_{t-1}}, y_t^*; \theta)$ (resp. $f(y_t^*/\underline{z_t}, \underline{y_{t-1}}, y_{t-1}^*; \theta)$) appearing in the previous integral is the p.d.f. of the image distribution of the distribution of ε_{1t} (resp. ε_{2t}) by $r_1(\underline{z_t}, \underline{y_{t-1}}, y_t^*, \cdot; \theta)$ (resp. $r_2(\underline{z_t}, \underline{y_{t-1}}, y_{t-1}^*; \cdot; \theta)$).

For this kind of likelihood function the ML method is untractable; moreover, the previous SML methods do not apply either. In this context three kinds of solution have been proposed. The first one is based on numerical approximations and will not be described here (see Kitagawa 1987, and Chapter 6 below), the second one is based on simulations of the whole likelihood function using the importance sampling technique, and the third one is based on simulations of $E[\log f(\underline{y_T}, y_T^*/\underline{z_T}, \underline{y_0}, y_0^*; \theta)/\underline{y_T}]$ in the Expectation Maximization (EM) algorithm.

Importance sampling methods[1]

As previously seen, the likelihood function naturally appears as the expectation of the function $\prod_{t=1}^{T} f(y_t/\underline{z_t}, \underline{y_{t-1}}, y_t^*; \theta)$ with respect to the p.d.f. $\prod_{t=1}^{T} f(y_t^*/\underline{z_t}, \underline{y_{t-1}}, y_{t-1}^*; \theta)$, where $\underline{z_t}$ and $\underline{y_{t-1}}$ are observed values. It is important to note that this p.d.f. is neither $f(y_T^*/\underline{z_T}, \underline{y_0}, y_0^*; \theta)$ (except if $\underline{y_{t-1}}$ does not appear in $f(y_t^*/\underline{z_t}, \underline{y_{t-1}}, y_{t-1}^*; \theta)$, i.e. if (y_t) does not cause (y_t^*)), nor $f(y_T^*/\underline{y_T}, \underline{z_T}, \underline{y_0}, y_0^*; \theta)$. However, it may be easy to draw in this p.d.f.; for instance, in the M^* model such a drawing is recursively obtained by using the formula

$$y_t^{*s}(\theta) = r_2[\underline{z_t}, \underline{y_{t-1}}, y_{t-1}^{*s}(\theta), \varepsilon_{2t}^s; \theta],$$

where $\varepsilon_{2t}^s, t = 1, \ldots, T$, are independent drawings in the distribution of ε_2. Therefore an unbiased simulator of the whole likelihood function $f(\underline{y_T}/\underline{z_T}, \underline{y_0}, y_0^*; \theta)$ is:

$$\prod_{t=1}^{T} f[y_t/\underline{z_t}, \underline{y_{t-1}}, y_t^{*s}(\theta); \theta],$$

where the $y_t^s(\theta)$ are drawn in the auxiliary p.d.f. mentioned above. This method is clearly an importance sampling method.

This basic importance sampling method may be very slow, in the sense that the simulator may have a large variance; therefore accelerated versions of this method have been proposed, in particular the Accelerated Gaussian Importance Sampling method in the Gaussian case (see Danielsson and Richard 1993), and the Sequentially Optimal Sampling methods of various orders in the switching state space models (see Billio and Monfort 1995, and Chapter 7 below).

---

[1] See Danielsson and Richard (1993); Billio and Monfort (1995).

Simulated Expectation Maximization (SEM) algorithm[2]

The log likelihood function can be written:

$$\log f(\underline{y_T}/\underline{z_T}, \underline{y_0}, \underline{y_0^*}; \theta) = \log f(\underline{y_T}, \underline{y_T^*}/\underline{z_T}, \underline{y_0}, \underline{y_0^*}; \theta)$$
$$- \log f(\underline{y_T^*}, /\underline{y_T}, \underline{z_T}, \underline{y_0}, \underline{y_0^*}; \theta).$$

Since the LHS of the equation does not depend on $\underline{y_T^*}$, we have, for any values $\theta^{(i)}$ of the parameter,

$$\log f(\underline{y_T}/\underline{z_T}, \underline{y_0}, \underline{y_0^*}; \theta) = E_{\theta^{(i)}}[\log f(\underline{y_T}, \underline{y_T^*}/\underline{z_T}, \underline{y_0}, \underline{y_0^*}; \theta)/\underline{y_T}, \underline{z_T}, \underline{y_0}, \underline{y_0^*}]$$
$$- E_{\theta^{(i)}}[\log f(\underline{y_T^*}/\underline{y_T}, \underline{z_T}, \underline{y_0}, \underline{y_0^*}; \theta)/\underline{y_T}, \underline{z_T}, \underline{y_0}, \underline{y_0^*}].$$

Let us define $\theta^{(i+1)}$ as the value maximizing the first term of the RHS with respect to θ. Using the Kullback inequality, it is easily seen that the $\theta^{(i+1)}$ thus obtained is such that:

$$\log f(\underline{y_T}/\underline{z_T}, \underline{y_0}, \underline{y_0^*}; \theta^{(i+1)}) \geq \log f(\underline{y_T}/\underline{z_T}, \underline{y_0}, \underline{y_0^*}; \theta^{(i)}).$$

This is the principle of the EM algorithm, which is an increasing algorithm such that the sequence $\theta^{(i)}$ converges to the ML estimator. The problem with this algorithm is that, although $\log f(\underline{y_T}, \underline{y_T^*}/\underline{z_T}, \underline{y_0}, \underline{y_0^*}; \theta)$ has in general a closed form, the same is not true for its conditional expectation:

$$E_{\theta^{(i)}}[\log f(\underline{y_T}, \underline{y_T^*}/\underline{z_T}, \underline{y_0}, \underline{y_0^*}; \theta)/\underline{y_T}, \underline{z_T}, \underline{y_0}, \underline{y_0^*}],$$

which is the quantity to be maximized.

In the SEM algorithm, this expectation is replaced by an approximation based on simulations. So the problem is now to be able to draw in the conditional distribution of $\underline{y_T^*}$ given $\underline{y_T}, \underline{z_T}, \underline{y_0}, \underline{y_0^*}$ and θ. There is no general solution to this problem. Shephard (1993), in the context of a nonlinear state space time series model, has used the Metropolis–Hastings algorithm to solve this problem (see Appendix 3A).

3.2   Simulated Pseudo-Maximum Likelihood and Nonlinear Least Squares Methods

3.2.1   Pseudo-maximum likelihood (PML) methods[3]

These methods are semi-parametric methods. They require the specification of some parametric form for the conditional moments of interest, generally first order moments (PML of order 1), or first and second order moments (PML of order 2).

---

[2]See Shephard (1993).
[3]See Gouriéroux *et al.* (1984b, 1984c) and Gouriéroux and Monfort (1993b).

Pseudo-maximum likelihood of order 1

Let us introduce a parametric specification for the first order dynamic conditional moment:

$$E_\theta(y_t/x_t) = E_\theta(y_t/\underline{y_{t-1}}, \underline{z_t}) = m(x_t; \theta), \qquad (3.10)$$

where m is a tractable known function. We assume that there exists a unique value θ_0 of θ such that $m(x_t; \theta_0)$ is the true conditional expectation of y_t given x_t. In the PML approach we also introduce a family of p.d.f.s $\bar{f}(y; m)$ indexed by the mean. The PML1 estimator is the solution of:

$$\hat{\theta}_T = \arg\max_\theta \sum_{t=1}^T \log \bar{f}(y_t; m(x_t; \theta)). \qquad (3.11)$$

Therefore we proceed as if the conditional distribution of y_t given x_t were $\bar{f}(y_t; m(x_t; \theta))$, and as if $\hat{\theta}_T$ were the associated maximum likelihood estimator. But the family $\bar{f}$ is in general misspecified ($\bar{f}(y_t; m(x_t; \theta_0))$ is not the true conditional p.d.f. of y_t given x_t) and the interpretation of $\hat{\theta}_T$ as a maximum likelihood estimator is invalid. If the pseudo-family $\bar{f}(y; m)$ is chosen arbitrarily, the corresponding PML1 estimator is, in general, inconsistent. However, there exist pseudo-families which ensure the consistency of $\hat{\theta}_T$.

Proposition 3.4 | The PML1 estimator is consistent if and only if the family is such that:

$$\bar{f}(y; m) = \exp[A(m) + B(y) + C(m)y].$$

(see Gouriéroux *et al.* 1984*b*).

The p.d.f. has an exponential form with a cross term in m and y, which is linear in y. For this reason such families are called **linear exponential families**. For such a choice the criterion function becomes:

$$\hat{\theta}_T = \arg\max_\theta \sum_{t=1}^T \{A[m(x_t; \theta)] + C[m(x_t; \theta)]y_t\}. \qquad (3.12)$$

The estimator satisfies the first order conditions:

$$\sum_{t=1}^T \frac{\partial m'}{\partial \theta}(x_t; \hat{\theta}_T) \left\{ \frac{\partial A}{\partial m}[m(x_t; \hat{\theta}_T)] + \frac{\partial C}{\partial m}[m(x_t; \hat{\theta}_T)]y_t \right\} = 0,$$

or, since $m(x_t; \theta)$ is the conditional mean of y_t,

$$\sum_{t=1}^T \frac{\partial m'}{\partial \theta}(x_t; \hat{\theta}_T) \frac{\partial C}{\partial m}[m(x_t; \hat{\theta}_T)][y_t - m(x_t; \hat{\theta}_T)] = 0.$$

It is an orthogonality condition corresponding to the first order conditional moment, with instruments $\frac{\partial m'}{\partial \theta}(x_t; \theta_0) \frac{\partial C}{\partial m}[m(x_t; \theta_0)]$. Several classical families of distributions belong to the class of linear exponential families. Some examples are given below along with the associated criteria.

Example 3.3   Univariate normal family (with unit variance)

We have:

$$\bar{f}(y; m) = \frac{1}{\sqrt{2\pi}} \exp\left[-\frac{1}{2}(y - m)^2\right]$$
$$= \frac{1}{\sqrt{2\pi}} \exp\left(-\frac{m^2}{2} - \frac{y^2}{2} + ym\right).$$

The associated criterion is such that:

$$\hat{\theta}_T = \arg\min_\theta \sum_{t=1}^{T} [y_t - m(x_t; \theta)]^2,$$

and the PML1 method based on this normal family is the nonlinear least squares method.

Example 3.4   Multivariate normal family

This kind of family is suitable for multivariate endogenous variables. The p.d.f. associated with the normal distribution $N[m, \Sigma]$, Σ fixed, is:

$$\bar{f}(y; m) = \frac{1}{(2\pi)^{n/2}\sqrt{\det \Sigma}} \exp\left[-\frac{1}{2}(y - m)'\Sigma^{-1}(y - m)\right]$$
$$= \frac{1}{(2\pi)^{n/2}\sqrt{\det \Sigma}} \exp\left[-\frac{1}{2}y'\Sigma^{-1}y - \frac{1}{2}m'\Sigma^{-1}m + m'\Sigma^{-1}y\right].$$

The PML1 estimator is a weighted nonlinear least squares estimator:

$$\hat{\theta}_T = \arg\min_\theta [y_t - m(x_t; \theta)]'\Sigma^{-1}[y_t - m(x_t; \theta)].$$

Example 3.5   Poisson family

We have:

$$\bar{f}(y; m) = \exp(-m)\frac{m^y}{y!}$$
$$= \exp(-m - \log y! + y \log m).$$

The estimator is defined by:

$$\hat{\theta}_T = \arg\max_\theta \sum_{t=1}^{T} \{y_t \log m(x_t; \theta) - m(x_t; \theta)\},$$

and can be computed only if the conditional mean $m(x_t; \theta)$ is always strictly positive.

Some other linear exponential families include the binomial, negative binomial, multinomial, and gamma families.

Pseudo-maximum likelihood of order 2

A similar approach may be followed if we specify both first and second order dynamic conditional moments:

$$\begin{cases} E_\theta(y_t/x_t) = m(x_t; \theta), \\ V_\theta(y_t/x_t) = \Sigma(x_t; \theta). \end{cases} \tag{3.13}$$

We now introduce a pseudo-family indexed by its mean and its variance–covariance matrix. This pseudo-family is denoted by $\bar{f}(y; m, \Sigma)$, and the PML2 estimator is defined by:

$$\hat{\theta}_T = \arg \max_\theta \sum_{t=1}^T \log \bar{f}(y_t; m(x_t; \theta), \Sigma(x_t; \theta)). \tag{3.14}$$

The following proposition is the analogue of Proposition 3.4.

Proposition 3.5 | The PML2 estimator is consistent if and only if the family is **quadratic exponential**, i.e. has the form:

$$\bar{f}(y; m, \Sigma) = \exp\{A(m, \Sigma) + B(y) + C(m, \Sigma)y \\ + y'D(m, \Sigma)y\}.$$

Example 3.6   Multivariate normal family

This is the simplest example of a quadratic exponential family. The estimator is defined by:

$$\hat{\theta}_T = \arg \max_\theta \sum_{t=1}^T \left\{ -\frac{1}{2} \log \det \Sigma(x_t; \theta) \right.$$

$$\left. -\frac{1}{2}[y_t - m(x_t; \theta)]'\Sigma(x_t; \theta)^{-1}[y_t - m(x_t; \theta)] \right\}. \tag{3.15}$$

In the literature it is often called a **quasi-maximum likelihood estimator**, and is widely used for nonlinear simultaneous equation models and pure time series models.

Asymptotic properties of the PML method

Proposition 3.6 | As soon as the PML estimator is consistent, it is also asymptotically normal:

$$\sqrt{T}(\hat{\theta}_T - \theta_0) \xrightarrow{d} N[0, Q],$$

where :

$$Q = J^{-1}IJ^{-1},$$

$$J = -E_0\left[\frac{\partial^2 \log \bar{f}}{\partial\theta\,\partial\theta'}\right],$$

$$I = E_0\left[\frac{\partial \log \bar{f}}{\partial\theta}\frac{\partial \log \bar{f}}{\partial\theta'}\right].$$

Proof. see Gouriéroux *et al.* (1984*b*).

PML based on static conditional moments

Until now we have specified the form of some dynamic conditional moments, but in some problems it is the form of static conditional moments that is given (see Laroque and Salanié 1993):

$$\begin{cases} E_\theta(y_t/\underline{z_t}) = m(\underline{z_t};\theta), \\ V_\theta(y_t/\underline{z_t}) = \Sigma(\underline{z_t};\theta). \end{cases} \tag{3.16}$$

The PML1 and PML2 approaches may be applied as before; the condition for consistency, i.e. the choice of pseudo-family, remains the same, but the form of the asymptotic covariance matrix of the PML estimator has to take into account the serial correlation of the pseudo-score vector $\partial \log \bar{f}_t/\partial\theta$. We have:

$$V_{as}(\sqrt{T}(\hat{\theta}_T - \theta_0)) = J^{-1}IJ^{-1}, \tag{3.17}$$

where:

$$J = -E_0\left[\frac{\partial^2 \log \bar{f}_t}{\partial\theta\,\partial\theta'}\right],$$

$$I = \sum_{h=-\infty}^{+\infty} E_0\left[\frac{\partial \log \bar{f}_t}{\partial\theta}\frac{\partial \log \bar{f}_{t-h}}{\partial\theta'}\right],$$

$$\bar{f}_t = \bar{f}(y_t; m(\underline{z_t};\theta_0)) \text{ for PML1,}$$

$$\text{or } \bar{f}\left[y_t; m(\underline{z_t};\theta_0), \Sigma(\underline{z_t};\theta_0)\right] \text{ for PML2.}$$

3.2.2   Simulated PML approaches

Description of the methods

We are now interested in a parametric model whose likelihood function is untractable. When the likelihood function has no closed form, the same is likely to be true for dynamic or static conditional moments, and the exact PML methods cannot be used. In such a case we may extend the PML approaches by introducing approximations of first (and second) order conditional moments in the expression of the pseudo-log likelihood function. These approximations are based on simulations. The simulations will be conditional on $\underline{y_{t-1}}$, $\underline{z_t}$ in the case of dynamic conditional moments, and will be path simulations (conditional on $z_1, \ldots, z_T, \underline{y_0}$) in the case of static conditional moments.

Example 3.7   Simulated nonlinear least squares based on the dynamic conditional mean

We consider an unbiased simulator of the first order dynamic conditional moment $\tilde{m}(x_t, u; \theta)$, where u has a known distribution (conditionally on x_t), and such that:

$$E[\tilde{m}(x_t, u; \theta)/x_t] = m(x_t; \theta) = E_\theta(y_t/x_t).$$

The simulated nonlinear least squares estimator of θ is:

$$\hat{\theta}_{ST} = \arg\min_\theta \sum_{t=1}^{T} \left[y_t - \frac{1}{S} \sum_{s=1}^{S} \tilde{m}(x_t, u_t^s; \theta) \right]^2, \tag{3.18}$$

where the u_t^s are independent drawings of u.

Example 3.8   Simulated PML1 estimator based on the dynamic conditional mean

More generally, we may use any linear exponential family and define the SPML1 estimator:

$$\hat{\theta}_{ST} = \arg\max_\theta \sum_{t=1}^{T} \left\{ A\left[\frac{1}{S} \sum_{s=1}^{S} \tilde{m}(x_t; u_t^s; \theta) \right] + C\left[\frac{1}{S} \sum_{s=1}^{S} \tilde{m}(x_t; u_t^s; \theta) \right] y_t \right\}.$$

Example 3.9   Simulated PML2 estimator based on the static conditional moments

Let us introduce simulated paths $(y_t^s(\theta))$, for given values of $z_1, \ldots, z_T, \theta$ and initial values $\underline{y_0}$ of y. Then $\frac{1}{S} \sum_{s=1}^{S} y_t^s(\theta)$ is an unbiased simulator of:

$$E_\theta(y_t/\underline{z_t}) = m(\underline{z_t}; \theta),$$

and:

$$\frac{1}{S-1} \sum_{s=1}^{S} \left[y_t^s(\theta) - \frac{1}{S} \sum_{s=1}^{S} y_t^s(\theta) \right] \left[y_t^s(\theta) - \frac{1}{S} \sum_{s=1}^{S} y_t^s(\theta) \right]'$$

is an unbiased simulator of $V_\theta(y_t/\underline{z}_t) = \Sigma(\underline{z}_t; \theta)$.

The SPML2 estimator is obtained by solving the program (3.15) after replacement of $m(\underline{z}_t; \theta)$, $\Sigma(\underline{z}_t; \theta)$ by the previous approximations.

Asymptotic properties

These are similar to the properties of the SML method (Gouriéroux and Monfort 1991, Laroque and Salanié 1989, 1993, 1994).

Proposition 3.7 | (i) The SPML estimators are consistent if T and S tend to infinity. They are inconsistent if S is fixed and T tends to infinity.
(ii) They have the same asymptotic distribution as the associated PML estimators if $\sqrt{T}/S \to 0$.

3.3 Bias Corrections for Simulated Nonlinear Least Squares

We consider a static model $y_t = r(z_t, u_t; \theta)$, and simulated nonlinear least squares based on the complete simulator $\tilde{m}(z_t, u; \theta) = r(z_t, u; \theta)$. It would be easy to extend the approaches below to other kinds of simulator and PML approaches.

The SNLS estimator is:

$$\hat{\theta}_{ST} = \arg\min_\theta \sum_{t=1}^T \left[y_t - \frac{1}{S} \sum_{s=1}^S r(z_t, u_t^s; \theta) \right]^2. \qquad (3.19)$$

It satisfies the first order conditions:

$$\sum_{t=1}^T \left\{ \frac{1}{S} \sum_{s=1}^S \frac{\partial r}{\partial \theta}(z_t, u_t^s; \hat{\theta}_{ST}) \left[y_t - \frac{1}{S} \sum_{s=1}^S r(z_t, u_t^s; \hat{\theta}_{ST}) \right] \right\} = 0. \qquad (3.20)$$

3.3.1 Corrections based on the first order conditions

Asymptotically, i.e. when T tends to infinity, S fixed, the first order conditions are:

$$E_0 \left\{ \frac{1}{S} \sum_{s=1}^S \frac{\partial r}{\partial \theta}(z_t, u_t^s; \theta_{S\infty}) \left[y_t - \frac{1}{S} \sum_{s=1}^S r(z_t, u_t^s; \theta_{S\infty}) \right] \right\} = 0,$$

where $\theta_{S\infty} = \lim_T \hat{\theta}_{ST}$. Let us introduce the conditional mean $m(z_t; \theta) = E_\theta(y_t/z_t)$. We get:

$$E_0 \left\{ \frac{1}{S} \sum_{s=1}^S \frac{\partial r}{\partial \theta}(z_t, u_t^s; \theta_{S\infty}) [y_t - m(z_t; \theta_{S\infty})] \right\}$$

$$-E_0 \left\{ \frac{1}{S} \sum_{s=1}^S \frac{\partial r}{\partial \theta}(z_t, u_t^s; \theta_{S\infty}) \frac{1}{S} \sum_{s=1}^S [r(z_t, u_t^s; \theta_{S\infty}) - m(z_t; \theta_{S\infty})] \right\} = 0,$$

or:

$$E_0 \left\{ \frac{\partial m}{\partial \theta}(z_t : \theta_{S\infty}) \left[m(z_t; \theta_0) - m(z_t; \theta_{S\infty}) \right] \right\}$$
$$- \frac{1}{S} E_0 \operatorname{cov} \left[\frac{\partial r}{\partial \theta}(z_t, u; \theta_{S\infty}), r(z_t, u; \theta_{S\infty})/z_t \right] = 0.$$

We note that the solution $\theta_{S\infty}$ is different from the true value θ_0; therefore the SNLS estimator is inconsistent for fixed S. Moreover, we see that the asymptotic bias is of order $\frac{1}{S}$. This bias comes from the correlation introduced between the 'instruments' $\frac{\partial r}{\partial \theta}(z_t, u_t^s; \theta_{S\infty})$ and the residuals $y_t - r(z_t, u_t^s; \theta_{S\infty})$.

This correlation vanishes if different simulations are used for the instruments and for the moments, i.e. if the estimator is defined as a solution of:

$$\sum_{t=1}^{T} \left\{ \frac{1}{S^*} \sum_{s=1}^{S^*} \frac{\partial r}{\partial \theta}(z_t, \tilde{u}_t^s; \theta) \left[y_t - \frac{1}{S} \sum_{s=1}^{S} r(z_t, u_t^s; \theta) \right] \right\} = 0, \qquad (3.21)$$

where $\tilde{u}_t^s$ and u_t^s are independent drawings in the distribution of u. Note that this modified estimator is an MSM estimator, since we have the moment condition:

$$E(y_t/z_t, \tilde{u}_t^1, \ldots, \tilde{u}_t^{S^*}) = m(z_t; \theta),$$

and we may choose as conditioning variables $\tilde{z}_t = (z_t, \tilde{u}_t^1, \ldots, \tilde{u}_t^{S^*})$. Therefore the results of Chapter 2 apply.

This corrected estimator is consistent for S fixed and T tending to infinity, and its asymptotic variance–covariance matrix is (for $S^* = S$) given by:

$$\left\{ E_0 \left[\frac{\partial m}{\partial \theta}(z_t; \theta_0) \frac{\partial m}{\partial \theta'}(z_t; \theta_0) \right] \right\}^{-1} \left\{ E_0 \left[\frac{\partial m}{\partial \theta}(z_t; \theta_0) \frac{\partial m}{\partial \theta'}(z_t; \theta_0) V_0(y_t/z_t) \right] \right.$$
$$+ \frac{1}{S} E_0 \left[V_0(y_t/z_t) \left(\left(1 + \frac{1}{S}\right) V \left[\frac{\partial r}{\partial \theta}(z_t, u_t; \theta_0)/z_t \right] + \frac{\partial m}{\partial \theta}(z_t; \theta_0) \frac{\partial m}{\partial \theta'}(z_t; \theta_0) \right) \right] \right\}$$
$$\times \left\{ E_0 \left[\frac{\partial m}{\partial \theta}(z_t; \theta_0) \frac{\partial m}{\partial \theta'}(z_t; \theta_0) \right] \right\}^{-1}.$$

3.3.2   Corrections based on the objective function

This method is analogous to the one presented in Section 3.1.3 for the SML approach, but since the criterion function is quadratic it will provide an exact bias correction. Let us consider the limit of the criterion function:

$$\lim_{T \to \infty} \frac{1}{T} \sum_{t=1}^{T} \left[y_t - \frac{1}{S} \sum_{s=1}^{S} r(z_t, u_t^s; \theta) \right]^2$$

$$= E_0 \left[y_t - \frac{1}{S} \sum_{s=1}^{S} r(z_t, u_t^s; \theta) \right]^2$$

$$= E_0 \left\{ y_t - m(z_t; \theta) - \frac{1}{S} \sum_{s=1}^{S} \left[r(z_t, u_t^s; \theta) - m(z_t; \theta) \right] \right\}^2$$

$$= E_0 \left[y_t - m(z_t; \theta) \right]^2 + \frac{1}{S} E_0 V_0[r(z_t; u_t; \theta)/z_t]$$

$$= E_0 V_0(y_t/z_t) + E_0[m(z_t; \theta_0) - m(z_t; \theta)]^2 + \frac{1}{S} E_0 V_0[r(z_t, u_t; \theta)/z_t].$$

There are three terms in the previous decomposition. It is clear that $\theta = \theta_0$ gives the minimum of the sum of the two first terms and that the asymptotic bias is created by the third term. An idea proposed by Bierings and Sneek (1989) and Laffont *et al.* (1991) consists in modifying the criterion function in order to eliminate this term. Let us consider the following estimator:

$$\tilde{\theta}_{ST} = \arg \min_{\theta} \sum_{t=1}^{T} \left\{ \left[y_t - \frac{1}{S} \sum_{s=1}^{S} r(z_t, u_t^s; \theta) \right]^2 \right.$$

$$\left. - \frac{1}{S[S-1]} \sum_{s=1}^{S} \left[r(z_t, u_t^s; \theta) - \frac{1}{S} \sum_{s=1}^{S} r(z_t, u_t^s; \theta) \right]^2 \right\}, \quad (3.22)$$

with $S \geq 2$. The limit objective function is now $E_0 V_0(y_t/z_t) + E_0[m(z_t; \theta_0) - m(z_t; \theta)]^2$, and $\tilde{\theta}_{ST}$ is consistent for S fixed, T tending to infinity.

Appendix 3A: The Metropolis–Hastings (MH) Algorithm

3A.1 Definition of the algorithm

The aim of the Metropolis–Hastings algorithm is to simulate in a distribution P for which no direct simulation method is available and the p.d.f. of which, denoted by f, may only be known up to a multiplicative constant.

The MH algorithm is defined as follows (see Metropolis *et al.* 1953; Hastings 1970):

   (i) Choose any starting value $x^{(o)}$.

  (ii) At iteration $\tau + 1$, draw $y^{(\tau)}$ in a candidate (or instrumental) distribution defined by the p.d.f. $g(y/x^{(\tau)})$ and take

$x^{(\tau+1)} = y^{(\tau)}$ with probability $\rho(y^{(\tau)}, x^{(\tau)}) = \min\left[\dfrac{f(y^{(\tau)})g(x^{(\tau)}/y^{(\tau)})}{f(x^{(\tau)})g(y^{(\tau)}/x^{(\tau)})}, 1\right]$,

$x^{(\tau+1)} = x^{(\tau)}$ otherwise.

(iii) Change τ in $\tau + 1$, go to (ii).

It is important to note that, since f only appears in ρ through a ratio, the normalizing constant may be unknown. Also note that if $g(y/x) = g(x/y)$, the function g no longer appears in ρ. Finally, if the starting value $x^{(o)}$ is such that $f(x^{(o)}) > 0$, it is seen that $f(x^{(\tau+1)}) > 0$ for any τ, since a $y^{(\tau)}$ satisfying $f(y^{(\tau)}) = 0$ implies $\rho(y^{(\tau)}, x^{(\tau)}) = 0$ and is not chosen.

3A.2 Properties of the algorithm

A useful preliminary lemma is the following.

Lemma 3A.1 | Let us consider a Markov chain defined by the transition probabilities $dQ(y/x) = q(y/x)dy + \pi(x)d\varepsilon_x(y)$, where ε_x is the unit mass at x and $\pi(x) = 1 - \int q(y/x)dy$; if $f(x)q(y/x) = f(y)q(x/y)$, the distribution P defined by the p.d.f. f is an invariant distribution of the chain.

Proof. For any mesurable set A we have:

$$\int [\int_A dQ(y/x)]dP(x)$$

$$= \int [\int_A q(y/x)dy + \pi(x)\varepsilon_x(A)]f(x)dx$$

$$= \int [\int_A q(x/y)f(y)dy]dx + \int \pi(x)\mathbb{1}_A(x)f(x)dx$$

$$= \int_A [\int q(x/y)dx]f(y)dy + \int_A \pi(x)f(x)dx$$

$$= \int_A [1 - \pi(y)]f(y)dy + \int_A \pi(x)f(x)dx$$

$$= \int_A f(y)dy$$

$$= P(A).$$

QED

Using this lemma we can show the basic property of the MH algorithm.

Proposition 3A.1 | Consider a MH algorithm (in which the p.d.f.s $g(\cdot/x)$ have the same support as f). The MH algorithm defines a Markov chain admitting P as an invariant distribution.

Proof. The Markov chain defined by the MH algorithm is such that

$$q(y/x) = \rho(y, x)g(y/x).$$

Therefore, we have :

$$
\begin{aligned}
f(x)q(y/x) &= f(x)g(y/x) \min\left[\frac{f(y)g(x/y)}{f(x)g(y/x)}, 1 \right] \\
&= \min[f(y)g(x/y), f(x)g(y/x)] \\
&= f(y)q(x/y)
\end{aligned}
$$

and the previous lemma applies.

QED

Under additional assumptions, ergodicity results such as $\frac{1}{T}\sum_{\tau=1}^{T} h(x^{(\tau)}) \xrightarrow[T\to\infty]{} E_P h$ a.s. (for any P-integrable function h) can also be shown (see Tierney 1994; Robert 1996); in particular this result holds if f and g are strictly positive and continuous.

The MH algorithm is often used to draw in a conditional p.d.f. $f(x/z)$ when only the joint p.d.f. $f(x, z)$ is known, since $f(x/z)$ is proportional to $f(x, z)$.

The MH algorithm can also be used within the Gibbs algorithm in order to simulate in some conditional distributions. In this case it is important to note that the Markov chain obtained by using only one draw of the MH algorithms for each step of the Gibbs algorithm still has the correct invariant distribution, i.e. the one of the genuine Gibbs algorithm (see Robert 1996).

4

Indirect Inference

4.1 The Principle[1]

4.1.1 Instrumental model

When a model leads to a complicated structural or reduced form and to untractable likelihood functions, a usual practice consists in replacing the initial model (M) with an approximated one (M^a) which is easier to handle, and to replace the infeasible ML estimator of the initial model,

$$\hat{\hat{\theta}}_T = \arg\max_{\theta} \sum_{t=1}^{T} \log f(y_t/x_t; \theta),$$

by the ML estimator computed on the instrumental model:

$$\theta_T^a = \arg\max_{\theta} \sum_{t=1}^{T} \log f^a(y_t/x_t; \theta).$$

Since (M^a) and f^a are misspecified, the approximated ML estimator is generally inconsistent. The indirect inference will use simulations performed under the initial model to correct for the asymptotic bias of θ_T^a. To describe the approach, it is first important to distinguish the parameters of the two models (M) and (M^a). We denote by β the parameters of (M^a). The idea is as follows.

We first compute the PML estimator of β using model (M^a):

$$\hat{\beta}_T = \arg\max_{\beta} \sum_{t=1}^{T} \log f^a(y_t/x_t; \beta). \tag{4.1}$$

In parallel, we simulate values of the endogenous variables $y_t^s(\theta)$ using model (M) and a value θ of the parameter. As in previous chapters, we replicate S times such simulations. Then we estimate the parameter β of the instrumental model from these simulations. We get:

$$\hat{\beta}_{ST}(\theta) = \arg\max_{\beta} \sum_{s=1}^{S} \sum_{t=1}^{T} \log f^a(y_t^s(\theta)/\underline{y_{t-1}^s}(\theta), \underline{z_t}; \beta). \tag{4.2}$$

Note that for dynamic models we use path simulations.

---

[1] See Gouriéroux *et al.* (1993), Smith (1993), and Gallant and Tauchen (1996).

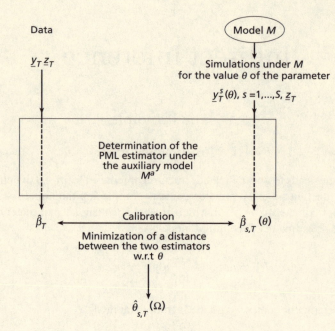

FIGURE 4.1: Indirect inference.

Finally, an indirect inference estimator of θ is defined by choosing a value $\hat{\theta}_{ST}$ for which $\hat{\beta}_T$ and $\hat{\beta}_{ST}(\theta)$ are as close as possible:

$$\hat{\theta}_{ST}(\Omega) = \arg\min_{\theta}[\hat{\beta}_T - \hat{\beta}_{ST}(\theta)]'\Omega[\hat{\beta}_T - \hat{\beta}_{ST}(\theta)], \tag{4.3}$$

where Ω is a symmetric nonnegative matrix, defining the metric. This procedure is summarized in Figure 4.1.

As usual, the estimation step is performed with a numerical algorithm, which computes $\hat{\theta}_{ST}(\Omega)$ as:

$$\hat{\theta}_{ST}(\Omega) = \lim_{p\to\infty}\theta^{(p)},$$

where:

$$\theta^{(p+1)} = h(\theta^{(p)}, \hat{\beta}_T, \hat{\beta}_{ST}(\theta^{(p)})),$$

and h is the updating function of the algorithm. Therefore a better diagram is given in Figure 4.2.

4.1.2   Estimation based on the score

Some other estimation criteria may be considered. For instance, instead of estimating θ through the PML estimators of β, we can consider directly the score

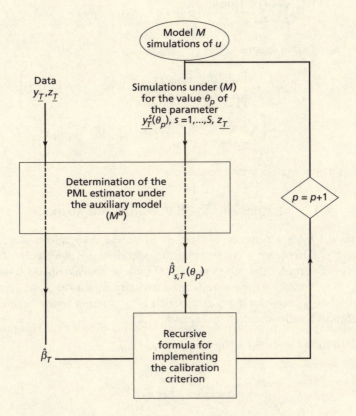

FIGURE 4.2: Numerical implementation of indirect inference.

function of the auxiliary, or instrumental, model. It is given by:

$$\sum_{t=1}^{T} \frac{\partial \log f^a}{\partial \beta}(y_t/\underline{y_{t-1}}, \underline{z_t}; \beta), \tag{4.4}$$

and is equal to zero for the PML estimator of β. An approach proposed by Gallant and Tauchen (1996) selects a value of θ such that:

$$\sum_{s=1}^{S}\sum_{t=1}^{T} \frac{\partial \log f^a}{\partial \beta}(y_t^s(\theta)/\underline{y_{t-1}^s}(\theta), \underline{z_t}; \hat{\beta}_T)$$

is as close as possible to zero:

$$\hat{\hat{\theta}}_{ST}(\Sigma) = \arg\min_{\theta} \left[\sum_{s=1}^{S}\sum_{t=1}^{T} \frac{\partial \log f^a}{\partial \beta}(y_t^s(\theta)/\underline{y_{t-1}^s}(\theta), \underline{z_t}; \hat{\beta}_T)\right]'$$

$$\times \Sigma \left[\sum_{s=1}^{S}\sum_{t=1}^{T} \frac{\partial \log f^a}{\partial \beta}(y_t^s(\theta)/\underline{y_{t-1}^s}(\theta), \underline{z_t}; \hat{\beta}_T)\right], \tag{4.5}$$

where Σ is a nonnegative symmetric matrix.

4.1.3   Extensions to other estimation methods

In Section 4.1.1 the estimation of θ is based on the comparison of PML estimators of β. However, it is possible to generalize this approach. In such extensions we consider the initial model (M) whose log likelihood function is $\sum_{t=1}^{T} \log f(y_t/\underline{y_{t-1}}, \underline{z_t}; \theta)$; we introduce an auxiliary parameter β and an estimation method of β based on the maximization of a criterion function (satisfying some technical conditions given in Appendix 4A):

$$\hat{\beta}_T = \arg\max_{\beta} \psi_T(\underline{y_T}, \underline{z_T}; \beta), \tag{4.6}$$

where:

$$\underline{z_T} = \{z_1, \dots, z_T\}.$$

Estimation based on auxiliary estimators

From simulated values of the endogenous variables $y_t^s(\theta)$, $t = 1, \dots, T$, $s = 1, \dots, S$, we can compute:

$$\hat{\beta}_{ST}(\theta) = \arg\max_{\beta} \sum_{s=1}^{S} \psi_T[\underline{y_T^s}(\theta), \underline{z_T}; \beta], \tag{4.7}$$

and the indirect inference estimator is defined by:

$$\hat{\theta}_{ST}(\Omega) = \arg\min_{\theta}[\hat{\beta}_T - \hat{\beta}_{ST}(\theta)]'\Omega[\hat{\beta}_T - \hat{\beta}_{ST}(\theta)], \tag{4.8}$$

where Ω is a symmetric nonnegative matrix.

Note that we obtain asymptotically equivalent indirect inference estimators of θ (see Appendix 4A) if, in the previous minimization, $\hat{\beta}_{ST}(\theta)$ is replaced by

- either $\frac{1}{S}\sum_{s=1}^{S}\hat{\beta}_T^s(\theta)$, with $\hat{\beta}_T^s(\theta) = \arg\max_\beta \psi_T[\underline{y}_T^s(\theta), \underline{z}_T; \beta]$,

- or $\tilde{\beta}_{ST}(\theta)$ with $\tilde{\beta}_{ST}(\theta) = \arg\max_\beta \psi_{ST}[y_{ST}^s(\theta), \underline{z}_{ST}; \beta]$, where the sequence of values for the exogenous variables is periodically repeated:

$$z_{kT+h} = z_h, \quad k = 0, \ldots, S - 1, h = 1, \ldots, T.$$

However, the last equivalence requires an additive decomposition for the derivative of the criterion function

$$\frac{\partial \psi_T}{\partial \beta}(\underline{y}_T, \underline{z}_T; \beta) = \frac{1}{T}\sum_{t=1}^{T}\frac{\partial \psi_1}{\partial \beta}(\underline{y}_t, \underline{z}_t; \beta),$$

which is the case if

$$\psi_T[\underline{y}_T, \underline{z}_T; \beta] = \frac{1}{T}\sum_{t=1}^{T}\psi_1(\underline{y}_t, \underline{z}_t; \beta)$$

(M-estimator type criterion), or if ψ_T is a moment criterion of the type

$$-\left[\frac{1}{T}\sum_{t=1}^{T}k(y_t, z_t) - \beta\right]'\left[\frac{1}{T}\sum_{t=1}^{T}k(y_t, z_t) - \beta\right],$$

(see example 4.1).

Estimation based on the score

In this approach the estimator is defined by:

$$\hat{\hat{\theta}}_{ST}(\Sigma) = \arg\min_\theta \left(\sum_{s=1}^{S}\frac{\partial \psi_T}{\partial \beta}[\underline{y}_T^s(\theta), \underline{z}_T; \hat{\beta}_T]\right)'$$

$$\times \Sigma \left(\sum_{s=1}^{S}\frac{\partial \psi_T}{\partial \beta}[\underline{y}_T^s(\theta), \underline{z}_T; \hat{\beta}_T]\right), \tag{4.9}$$

where Σ is a symmetric nonnegative matrix.

4.2   Properties of the Indirect Inference Estimators

4.2.1   The dimension of the auxiliary parameter

Even if we do not want to start a precise discussion of the identification issues at this stage (see Section 4.4.2), it is useful to make some remarks on the dimension of the auxiliary parameter β.

First, in order to get a unique solution $\hat{\theta}$ (or $\hat{\hat{\theta}}$) to the previous optimization problem, the dimension of the auxiliary parameter β must be larger than or equal to the dimension of the initial parameter θ. It is a kind of order identifiability condition.

Second, if the problem is just identified, i.e. if $\dim \beta = \dim \theta$, the different methods become simpler.

Proposition 4.1 | If $\dim \beta = \dim \theta$, we have, for T sufficiently large:
| (i) $\hat{\theta}_{ST}(\Omega) = \hat{\theta}_{ST}$ independent of Ω;
| (ii) $\hat{\hat{\theta}}_{ST}(\Sigma) = \hat{\hat{\theta}}_{ST}$ independent of Σ;
| (iii) $\hat{\theta}_{ST} = \hat{\hat{\theta}}_{ST}$.

Proof.

(i) In the just identified case, $\hat{\theta}_{ST}(\Omega)$ is the solution of the system

$$\hat{\beta}_T = \hat{\beta}_{ST}(\theta)$$

(since for such a choice the criterion function takes the minimal possible value 0 for T sufficiently large) and therefore it is independent of Ω.

(ii) Similarly, in the just identified case, $\hat{\hat{\theta}}_{ST}(\Sigma)$ is the solution of the system:

$$\sum_{s=1}^{S} \frac{\partial \psi_T}{\partial \beta} [\underline{y_T^s}(\theta), \underline{z_T}; \hat{\beta}_T] = 0$$

and is independent of Σ.

(iii) Finally, if

$$\sum_{s=1}^{S} \frac{\partial \psi_T}{\partial \beta} [\underline{y_T^s}(\hat{\hat{\theta}}_{ST}), \underline{z_T}; \beta_T] = 0$$

has a unique solution in β_T, we deduce that this solution is $\hat{\beta}_{ST}(\hat{\hat{\theta}}_{ST})$, and from (ii) that it is equal to $\hat{\beta}_T$. From (i) we know that $\hat{\beta}_T = \hat{\beta}_{ST}(\hat{\theta}_{ST})$, and therefore $\hat{\hat{\theta}}_{ST} = \hat{\theta}_{ST}$.

QED

4.2.2   Which moments to match?

The title of this subsection refers to the paper by Gallant and Tauchen (1996). The question is: What is the underlying parameter on which the estimation process is based?

This value may be specified only if we consider the asymptotic optimization problem. Let us consider for instance the PML methods used in Section 4.1.1. The criterion is asymptotically:

$$\lim_{T \to \infty} \frac{1}{T} \sum_{t=1}^{T} \log f^a(y_t/x_t; \beta) = E_\theta \log f^a(y_t/x_t; \beta).$$

The solution of this asymptotic problem is the function

$$b(\theta) = \arg \max_{\beta} E_\theta \log f^a(y_t/x_t; \beta), \tag{4.10}$$

called the **binding function**.

The estimation of θ is based on the pseudo-true value of β, i.e. the value of the binding function evaluated at the true value of θ_0: $b(\theta_0)$.

The indirect inference based on auxiliary PML estimators consists in:

(i)   determining $\hat{\beta}_T$, a direct consistent estimator of $b(\theta_0)$,

(ii)   determining $\hat{\beta}_{ST}(\cdot)$, a direct consistent estimator of function $b(\cdot)$ (when $T \to \infty$, S fixed),

(iii)   and then solving approximately $b(\theta_0) = b(\theta)$ to get an estimator of θ_0.

Note that the maximization of the criterion $E_\theta \log f^a(y_t/x_t; \beta)$ with respect to β is equivalent to the minimization of the Kullback–Leibler information criterion:

$$\text{KLIC} = E_\theta \log \frac{f(y_t/x_t; \theta)}{f^a(y_t/x_t; \beta)},$$

which gives the proximity between the two conditional distributions $f(y_t/x_t; \theta)$ and $f^a(y_t/x_t; \beta)$; $f^a(y_t/x_t; b(\theta))$ corresponds to the distribution of (M^a) that is the closest to $f(y_t/x_t; \theta)$.

In some specific cases the parameter $b(\theta)$ may admit an interpretation in terms of moments, but in general it has a much more complicated interpretation.

Moreover, as shown in the following example, MSM methods on static conditional moments are particular cases of indirect inference methods.

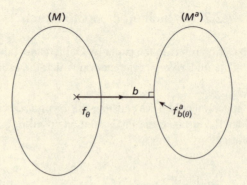

FIGURE 4.3: The binding function.

Example 4.1

If the criterion ψ_T is of the form:

$$\psi_T(\underline{y_T}, \underline{z_T}; \beta) = -\left[\frac{1}{T}\sum_{t=1}^{T}k(y_t, z_t) - \beta\right]'\left[\frac{1}{T}\sum_{t=1}^{T}k(y_t, z_t) - \beta\right],$$

the pseudo-true value of β is the marginal moment of $k(y_t, x_t)$:

$$b(\theta_0) = E_{\theta_0}k(y_t, z_t).$$

In this case, the indirect inference approach is asymptotically equivalent to an MSM approach. Indeed, we have:

$$\hat{\beta}_T = \frac{1}{T}\sum_{t=1}^{T}k(y_t, z_t)$$

$$\hat{\beta}_{ST}(\theta) = \arg\min_{\beta}\sum_{s=1}^{S}\left[\frac{1}{T}\sum_{t=1}^{T}k(y_t^s(\theta), z_t) - \beta\right]'\left[\frac{1}{T}\sum_{t=1}^{T}k(y_t^s(\theta), z_t) - \beta\right]$$

$$= \frac{1}{ST}\sum_{t=1}^{T}\sum_{s=1}^{S}k[y_t^s(\theta), z_t],$$

and:

$$\hat{\theta}_{ST}(\Omega) = \arg\min_{\theta}\left[\hat{\beta}_T - \hat{\beta}_{ST}(\theta)\right]'\Omega\left[\hat{\beta}_T - \hat{\beta}_{ST}(\theta)\right]$$

$$= \arg\min_{\theta}\left\{\frac{1}{T}\sum_{t=1}^{T}\left[k(y_t, z_t) - \frac{1}{S}\sum_{s=1}^{S}k(y_t^s(\theta), z_t)\right]\right\}'\Omega$$

$$\times\left\{\frac{1}{T}\sum_{t=1}^{T}\left[k(y_t, z_t) - \frac{1}{S}\sum_{s=1}^{S}k(y_t^s(\theta), z_t)\right]\right\}$$

is an MSM estimator based on the static conditional moment $E[k(y_t, z_t)/\underline{z_T}]$ and on the identity instrument matrix. In the pure time series case, i.e. when no exogenous variables are present, we find the MSM method proposed by Duffie and Singleton (1993).

4.2.3 Asymptotic properties

The asymptotic properties of the indirect inference estimators are given below for a general criterion function such that

$$\psi_T(\underline{y_T}, \underline{z_T}; \beta)$$

converges to a deterministic limit denoted by $\psi_\infty(\theta, \beta)$, and such that the binding function $b(\theta) = \arg\min_\beta \psi_\infty(\theta, \beta)$ is injective. We introduce the two matrices:

$$J_0 = p \lim_T -\frac{\partial^2 \psi_T}{\partial\beta\partial\beta'}[\underline{y_T}, \underline{z_T}; b(\theta_0)], \tag{4.11}$$

$$\bar{I}_0 = \lim_T V_0 \left\{ \sqrt{T} \frac{\partial \psi_T}{\partial\beta}(\underline{y_T}, \underline{z_T}; b(\theta_0)) - E_0\left[\sqrt{T} \frac{\partial \psi_T}{\partial\beta}(\underline{y_T}, \underline{z_T}; b(\theta_0))/\underline{z_T} \right] \right\}. \tag{4.12}$$

Proposition 4.2 The indirect inference estimator $\hat{\theta}_{ST}(\Omega)$ is consistent, asymptotically normal, when S is fixed and T goes to ∞: $\sqrt{T}(\hat{\theta}_{ST}(\Omega) - \theta_0) \xrightarrow{d} N[0, W(S, \Omega)]$, where:

$$W(S, \Omega) = \left(1 + \frac{1}{S}\right)\left[\frac{\partial b'}{\partial\theta}(\theta_0)\Omega\frac{\partial b}{\partial\theta'}(\theta_0)\right]^{-1}\frac{\partial b'}{\partial\theta}(\theta_0)$$

$$\times \Omega\Omega^{*-1}\Omega\frac{\partial b}{\partial\theta'}(\theta_0)\left[\frac{\partial b'}{\partial\theta}(\theta_0)\Omega\frac{\partial b}{\partial\theta'}(\theta_0)\right]^{-1},$$

$$\Omega^* = J_0\bar{I}_0^{-1}J_0.$$

Proof. See Appendix 4A.

As for the MSM, the effect of simulations is summarized by the multiplicative factor $1 + \frac{1}{S}$.

In the just identified case (dim β = dim θ) we have seen (Proposition 4.1) that the estimator and, therefore, its asymptotic precision are independent of Ω. Indeed since $\frac{\partial b}{\partial\theta'}(\theta_0)$ is invertible, the variance–covariance matrix reduces to:

$$W(S, \Omega) = \left(1 + \frac{1}{S}\right)\left[\frac{\partial b'}{\partial\theta}(\theta_0)\Omega^*\frac{\partial b}{\partial\theta'}(\theta_0)\right]^{-1}.$$

Similar results may be derived for estimators based on the score. They are direct consequences of the following result (see Appendix 4A).

Proposition 4.3 | The estimators $\hat{\hat{\theta}}_{ST}(\Sigma)$ and $\hat{\theta}_{ST}(J_0 \Sigma J_0)$ are asymptotically equivalent:

$$\sqrt{T}\left[\hat{\hat{\theta}}_{ST}(\Sigma) - \hat{\theta}_{ST}(J_0 \Sigma J_0)\right] = o_p(1).$$

The indirect inference estimators $\hat{\theta}_{ST}(\Omega)$ form a class of estimators indexed by the matrix Ω. The optimal choice of this matrix is $\Omega = \Omega^*$.

Proposition 4.4 | For the optimal matrix $\Omega^* = J_0 \bar{I}_0^{-1} J_0$, the asymptotic variance–covariance matrix of the indirect inference estimator is simplified in:

$$W(S, \Omega^*) = \left(1 + \frac{1}{S}\right)\left[\frac{\partial b'}{\partial \theta}(\theta_0) J_0 \bar{I}_0^{-1} J_0 \frac{\partial b}{\partial \theta'}(\theta_0)\right]^{-1}.$$

Of course, the optimal choice of Σ for estimators based on the score is $\Sigma^* = \bar{I}_0^{-1}$.

The expression of the asymptotic variance–covariance matrix contains the derivative of the binding function at the true value. It is possible to estimate this quantity consistently without determining the binding function and its derivative. $b(\theta)$ is the solution of:

$$b(\theta) = \arg\max_{\beta} p \lim \psi_T(y_T^s(\theta), \underline{z}_T; \beta)$$

$$= \arg\max_{\beta} \psi_\infty(\theta, \beta).$$

Equivalently, it satisfies the first order conditions:

$$\frac{\partial \psi_\infty}{\partial \beta}[\theta, b(\theta)] = 0, \quad \forall \theta.$$

A derivation of this relation with respect to θ gives:

$$\frac{\partial^2 \psi_\infty}{\partial \beta \, \partial \theta'}[\theta, b(\theta)] + \frac{\partial^2 \psi_\infty}{\partial \beta \, \partial \beta'}[\theta, b(\theta)]\frac{\partial b}{\partial \theta'}[\theta] = 0;$$

it implies:

$$\frac{\partial b}{\partial \theta'}(\theta_0) = \left(-\frac{\partial^2 \psi_\infty}{\partial \beta \, \partial \beta'}[\theta_0, b(\theta_0)]\right)^{-1}\frac{\partial^2 \psi_\infty}{\partial \beta \, \partial \theta'}[\theta_0, b(\theta_0)]$$

$$= J_0^{-1}\frac{\partial^2 \psi_\infty}{\partial \beta \, \partial \theta'}[\theta_0, b(\theta_0)].$$

We deduce an expression of the asymptotic variance–covariance matrix of the optimal indirect inference estimator which may be directly computed from the criterion function:

$$W(S, \Omega^*) = \left(1 + \frac{1}{S}\right) \left(\frac{\partial^2 \psi_\infty}{\partial \theta \, \partial \beta'} \bar{I}_0^{-1} \frac{\partial^2 \psi_\infty}{\partial \beta \, \partial \theta'}\right)^{-1}. \tag{4.13}$$

A consistent estimator of this matrix can be obtained by replacing ψ_∞ by ψ_T, $b(\theta_0)$ by $\hat{\beta}_T$, and $\bar{I}_0$ by a consistent estimator based on simulations (see Gouriéroux *et al.* 1993: Appendix 2). Significance and specification tests can also be based on the indirect inference method (see Gouriéroux *et al.* 1993).

4.2.4 Some consistent, but less efficient, procedures

Some symmetrical calibration procedures might also have been introduced. For instance, we might have considered:

$$\tilde{\theta}_{ST} = \arg\max_\theta \psi_T(\underline{y_T}, \underline{z_T}; \hat{\beta}_{ST}(\theta)), \tag{4.14}$$

or an estimator based on the score function (see Smith 1993):

$$\tilde{\tilde{\theta}}_{ST}(\Sigma) = \arg\min_\theta \left[\frac{\partial \psi_T}{\partial \beta}(\underline{y_T}, \underline{z_T}; \hat{\beta}_{ST}(\theta))\right]' \Sigma \left[\frac{\partial \psi_T}{\partial \beta}(\underline{y_T}, \underline{z_T}; \hat{\beta}_{ST}(\theta))\right]. \tag{4.15}$$

However, it can be checked that these methods, while consistent, are generally less efficient than the optimal ones we have described in the previous subsection.

4.3 Examples

The main step in the indirect inference approach is the determination of a good instrumental model (M^a) or a good auxiliary criterion ψ_T (which may be an approximation of the log likelihood function). We now give some examples of the determination of instrumental models in which the major part of the initial modelling has been kept. Some other examples, specific to limited dependent variable models and to financial problems, are given in Chapters 5 and 6 respectively.

4.3.1 Estimation of a moving average parameter[2]

The initial model

Let us consider a moving average process of order 1:

$$y_t = \varepsilon_t - \theta \varepsilon_{t-1}, \qquad t = 1, \ldots, T, \tag{4.16}$$

where (ε_t) is a Gaussian white noise with variance 1.

---

[2]See Gouriéroux *et al.* (1993) and Ghysels *et al.* (1994*b*).

The instrumental model

It is known that pure autoregressive formulations are easier to estimate than pure moving average formulations, since the pseudo-maximum likelihood method based on Gaussian errors coincides with ordinary least squares. So, the auxiliary model that is introduced is:

$$y_t = \beta_1 y_{t-1} + \cdots + \beta_r y_{t-r} + u_t, \tag{4.17}$$

where u_t is a Gaussian white noise. To get simple estimation procedures, we do not constrain the autoregressive parameters to be compatible with the truncated autoregressive version of the MA(1) formulation, i.e. such that $\beta_i = \beta^i$. Therefore we consider an unconstrained estimation of the autoregression coefficients. The associated pseudo-true values depend on the choice of the autoregressive order r; for instance, for $r = 1$,

$$b(\theta_0) = \lim_T \hat{\beta}_{1T} = \frac{\mathrm{cov}_{\theta_0}(y_t, y_{t-1})}{V_{\theta_0}(y_{t-1})} = \frac{-\theta_0}{(1 + \theta_0^2)};$$

and for $r = 2$:

$$b(\theta_0) = \lim_T \begin{pmatrix} \hat{\beta}_{1T} \\ \hat{\beta}_{2T} \end{pmatrix}$$

$$= \begin{bmatrix} V_{\theta_0} y_{t-1} & \mathrm{cov}_{\theta_0}(y_{t-1}, y_{t-2}) \\ \mathrm{cov}_{\theta_0}(y_{t-1}, y_{t-2}) & V_{\theta_0} y_{t-2} \end{bmatrix}^{-1} \begin{bmatrix} \mathrm{cov}_{\theta_0}(y_t, y_{t-1}) \\ \mathrm{cov}_{\theta_0}(y_t, y_{t-2}) \end{bmatrix}$$

$$= \begin{bmatrix} 1 + \theta_0^2 & -\theta_0 \\ -\theta_0 & 1 + \theta_0^2 \end{bmatrix}^{-1} \begin{bmatrix} -\theta_0 \\ 0 \end{bmatrix}.$$

Monte Carlo studies

We will compare different estimation methods of parameter θ: the direct maximum likelihood procedure applied to the MA(1) process, which gives an asymptotically efficient estimator (we used the Kalman filter), and three indirect inference methods using an AR(1), an AR(2), or an AR(3) model as the instrumental model.

The comparison is performed through a Monte Carlo study with $\theta_0 = 0.5$ and 200 replications. The number of observations is $T = 250$, and we use only one simulated path: $S = 1$. Moreover, we do not use the optimal indirect inference estimator, but only an estimator with $\Omega = Id$. In Figures 4.4, 4.5, and 4.6, we show the estimated finite sample p.d.f. of the ML estimator and of the three indirect inference estmators. Table 4.1 gives the empirical mean, the standard deviation, and the square root of the mean square error for each of these estimators. For all methods the finite sample bias is small. For one lag the efficiency loss is rather important, but the efficiency is almost reached for $r = 2$ and completely reached for $r = 3$. Furthermore, it is worth noting that in this experiment the computation of the indirect estimator based on $r = 3$ is about eighteen times faster than the computation of the ML estimator.

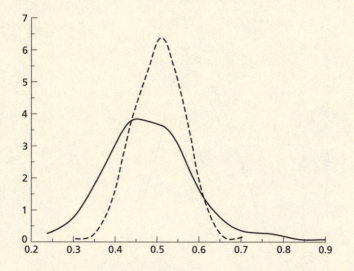

FIGURE 4.4: The p.d.f. of the ML estimator (– – –) and of the indirect inference estimator, $r = 1$ (———).

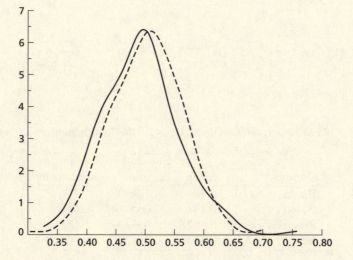

FIGURE 4.5: The p.d.f. of the ML estimator (– – –) and of the indirect inference estimator, $r = 2$ (———).

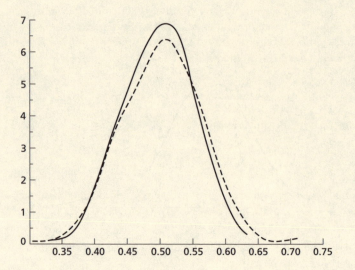

FIGURE 4.6: The p.d.f. of the ML estimator (−−−) and of the indirect inference estimator, $r = 3$ (———).

TABLE 4.1: Summary statistics for the four estimators

Estimator	Mean	Standard deviation	Root mean square error
Based on $r = 1$	0.481	0.105	0.106
Based on $r = 2$	0.491	0.065	0.066
Based on $r = 3$	0.497	0.053	0.053
ML	0.504	0.061	0.061

4.3.2 Application to macroeconometrics

Macroeconometrics is also a source of potential applications for indirect estimation methods. In this subsection we consider the practice of linearization in macroeconomic models without or with latent models. Some other examples are related to dynamic optimization problems. (The first application of indirect methods to such a problem is due to Smith (1993).)

Model without latent variables

We consider a dynamic model of the form:

$$y_t = g(y_{t-1}, z_t, u_t; \theta), \tag{4.18}$$

where y and u have the same dimension. If g is a complicated nonlinear function or if the u_t are correlated, (4.18) may be difficult to handle. It is often replaced by a linearized version with respect to u_t around zero:

$$y_t = g(y_{t-1}, x_t, 0; \beta) + \frac{\partial g}{\partial u'}(y_{t-1}, x_t, 0; \beta)u_t, \tag{4.19}$$

or, with respect to u_t and y_{t-1}, around zero and a long-run equilibrium value $\bar{y}$ (often taken equal to the historical average $\frac{1}{T}\sum_{t=1}^{T} y_t$ in practice):

$$y_t = g(\bar{y}, x_t, 0; \beta) + \frac{\partial g}{\partial y'}(\bar{y}, x_t; 0; \beta)(y_{t-1} - \bar{y}) + \frac{\partial g}{\partial u'}(\bar{y}, x_t, 0; \beta)u_t. \tag{4.20}$$

We may apply the indirect inference approach using either (4.19) or (4.20) as auxiliary model and β as auxiliary parameter. In such a case, the approach corrects for the linearization bias.

We may also apply indirect inference from (4.20) with the auxiliary parameter $(\beta', \bar{y}')'$. In this case we simultaneously estimate the 'implicit' long-run equilibrium associated with the linearized version.

Finally, there is no strong reason for expanding around $u = 0$ rather than around another point $\bar{u}$. This means that another approximated model is:

$$y_t = g(\bar{y}, x_t, \bar{u}; \beta) + \frac{\partial g}{\partial y'}(\bar{y}, x_t, \bar{u}; \beta)(y_{t-1} - \bar{y})$$

$$+ \frac{\partial g}{\partial u'}(\bar{y}, x_t, \bar{u}; \beta)(u_t - \bar{u}), \tag{4.21}$$

with auxiliary parameter $[\beta', \bar{y}', \bar{u}']'$.

Model with latent variables

Let us assume that the model can be put in the nonlinear state space form:

$$\begin{cases} y_t^* = g_{1t}(y_{t-1}^*) + g_{2t}(y_{t-1}^*)\eta_t, \\ y_t = g_{3t}(y_t^*)\varepsilon_t, \end{cases} \tag{4.22}$$

where y_t^* is a state vector which is in general (partially) unobserved and $(\varepsilon_t', \eta_t')'$ is a Gaussian white noise. The extended Kalman filter (Anderson and Moore 1979) could be used to compute an approximate log likelihood function, but this estimator is inconsistent. It could also be used as a first step estimator in the indirect estimation procedure, which in a second step provides a consistent and asymptotically normal estimator. In this example it is directly a criterion function (i.e. an algorithm) that is used, without looking for a tractable instrumental model.

4.3.3   The efficient method of moment

To get precise indirect inference estimators based on an instrumental model, it is intuitively possible to follow two kinds of approach. In the first one we select a simple auxiliary model, close to the initial model and containing a comparable number of parameters. In such a case this instrumental model often has a natural structural interpretation, and a number of examples of this kind are described in Chapters 5 and 6. Another approach consists in introducing an auxiliary model, essentially descriptive, with a large number of parameters, providing a good approximation for any distribution when the number of parameters tends to infinity. In such a framework the 'parameters' of this instrumental model do not have any structural interpretation, and are essentially used for calibration. This second approach has been applied with some semi-nonparametric models as an auxiliary model by Gallant and Tauchen (1996), and Gallant *et al.* (1994), and called the efficient method of moments, since the idea is to reach the asymptotic efficiency by increasing the number of auxiliary parameters.

For instance, when the observations correspond to a pure time series, they consider an auxiliary model where the p.d.f. is proportional to some polynomial times the p.d.f. of a normal distribution such as:

$$f^a(y_t/\underline{y_{t-1}}; \theta) = \frac{P^2(v_t; y_{t-1}^*, \ldots, y_{t-p}^*)\varphi(v_t)}{|r(y_{t-1}^*, \ldots, y_{t-p}^*)| \int P^2(u; y_{t-1}^*, \ldots, y_{t-p}^*)\varphi(u)\, du},$$

where:

$$v_t = [y_t - \mu(y_{t-1}^*, \ldots, y_{t-p}^*)]/r(y_{t-1}^*, \ldots, y_{t-p}^*),$$

$$\mu(y_{t-1}^*, \ldots, y_{t-p}^*) = b_o + \sum_{j=1}^{p} b_j y_{t-j}^*,$$

$$r(y^*_{t-1}, \ldots, y^*_{t-p}) = c_o + \sum_{j=1}^{p} c_j |y^*_{t-j}|$$

$$y^*_t = \ell \left(\frac{y_t - \bar{y}_T}{\hat{\sigma}_T} \right),$$

where $\bar{y}_T$ is the sample mean, $\hat{\sigma}_T$ the sample standard error, ℓ a logistic map, and P is a polynomial in v, whose coefficients are polynomial in $y^*_{t-1}, \ldots, y^*_{t-p}$.

4.4   Some Additional Properties of Indirect Inference Estimators

In this section we have gathered some additional theoretical results concerning the indirect inference approach. They concern the second order expansion of indirect inference estimators and particularly their ability to reduce the finite sample bias, and a definition of the indirect information on the parameter of interest contained in the auxiliary model.

4.4.1   Second order expansion

The form of the expansion

For notational convenience we consider an auxiliary parameter β with the same size as the parameter of interest θ. We assume that the first step estimator $\hat{\beta}_T$ admits the second order expansion:

$$\hat{\beta}_T = b(\theta_0) + \frac{A(v; \theta_0)}{\sqrt{T}} + \frac{B(v; \theta_0)}{T} + o\left(\frac{1}{T}\right), \tag{4.23}$$

where $A(v; \theta_0)$, $B(v; \theta_0)$ are random vectors, depending on some asymptotic random term v, and where the equality is in a distribution sense. We have previously seen that the first order term $A(v; \theta_0)$ follows a zero-mean normal distribution.

Considering, for the sake of simplicity, the pure time series framework, i.e. without explanatory variables, similar expansions are also valid for the first step estimators based on simulated data. We consider S replications and, for each index s, T simulated values $\{y^s_t(\theta), t = 1, \ldots, T\}$. The first step estimator associated with this set of simulated values $\hat{\beta}^s_T(\theta)$ (say) is such that:

$$\hat{\beta}^s_T(\theta) = b(\theta) + \frac{A(v_s; \theta)}{\sqrt{T}} + \frac{B(v_s; \theta)}{T} + o\left(\frac{1}{T}\right), \tag{4.24}$$

where the asymptotic random terms v, v_s, $s = 1, \ldots, S$, may be considered as i.i.d. by definition of the drawings.

Let us now consider an indirect inference estimator $\hat{\theta}_{ST}$ defined as the solution of the system:

$$\hat{\beta}_T = \frac{1}{S} \sum_{s=1}^{S} \hat{\beta}_T^s(\hat{\theta}_{ST}). \tag{4.25}$$

We shall discuss the second order expansion of $\hat{\theta}_{ST}$,

$$\hat{\theta}_{ST} = \theta_0 + \frac{a^*}{\sqrt{T}} + \frac{b^*}{T} + o\left(\frac{1}{T}\right), \tag{4.26}$$

in terms of functions A and B. From (4.25), we deduce:

$$b(\theta_0) + \frac{A(v; \theta_0)}{\sqrt{T}} + \frac{B(v; \theta_0)}{T}$$

$$= \frac{1}{S} \sum_{s=1}^{S} \left\{ b(\hat{\theta}_{ST}) + \frac{A(v_s; \hat{\theta}_{ST})}{\sqrt{T}} + \frac{B(v_s; \hat{\theta}_{ST})}{T} \right\} + o\left(\frac{1}{T}\right),$$

and, taking into account the expansion (4.26) of $\hat{\theta}_{ST}$:

$$b(\theta_0) + \frac{A(v; \theta_0)}{\sqrt{T}} + \frac{B(v; \theta_0)}{T}$$

$$= b(\theta_0) + \frac{\partial b}{\partial \theta'}(\theta_0) \frac{a^*}{\sqrt{T}} + \frac{\partial b}{\partial \theta'}(\theta_0) \frac{b^*}{T} + \frac{1}{2T} \left[a^{*\prime} \frac{\partial^2 b_j(\theta_0)}{\partial \theta \, \partial \theta'} a^* \right]_{j=1,\dots,p}$$

$$+ \frac{1}{S\sqrt{T}} \sum_{s=1}^{S} A(v_s; \theta_0) + \frac{1}{ST} \sum_{s=1}^{S} \frac{\partial A}{\partial \theta'}(v_s; \theta_0)a^*$$

$$+ \frac{1}{ST} \sum_{s=1}^{S} B(v_s; \theta_0) + o\left(\frac{1}{T}\right).$$

The identification of the first and second order terms of the two members of the equality provides the following terms in the expansion for $\hat{\theta}_{ST}$.

Proposition 4.5

$$a^* = \left[\frac{\partial b}{\partial \theta'}(\theta_0) \right]^{-1} \left[A(v; \theta_0) - \frac{1}{S} \sum_{s=1}^{S} A[v_s; \theta_0)] \right],$$

$$b^* = \left[\frac{\partial b}{\partial \theta'}(\theta_0) \right]^{-1} \left[B(v; \theta_0) - \frac{1}{S} \sum_{s=1}^{S} B[v_s; \theta_0)] \right]$$

$$- \left[\frac{\partial b}{\partial \theta'}(\theta_0) \right]^{-1} \left\{ \frac{1}{S} \sum_{s=1}^{S} \frac{\partial A}{\partial \theta'}(v_s; \theta_0)a^* \right.$$

$$+ \frac{1}{2} \left[a^{*\prime} \frac{\partial^2 b_j(\theta_0)}{\partial \theta \, \partial \theta'} a^* \right]_{j=1,\dots,p} \left. \right\}.$$

From these expressions, we can deduce the second order bias of the indirect inference estimator defined by (4.25). We have:

$$Ea^* = \left[\frac{\partial b}{\partial \theta'}(\theta_0)\right]^{-1}\left[EA(v; \theta_0) - \frac{1}{S}\sum_{s=1}^{S}EA(v_s; \theta_0)\right] = 0;$$

$$Eb^* = -\left[\frac{\partial b'}{\partial \theta'}(\theta_0)\right]^{-1}\left\{E\left[\frac{1}{S}\sum_{s=1}^{S}\frac{\partial A}{\partial \theta'}(v_s; \theta_0)a^*\right]\right.$$
$$\left.+\frac{1}{2}E\left[a^{*'}\frac{\partial^2 b_j}{\partial \theta \partial \theta'}(\theta_0)a^*\right]_{j=1,\dots,p}\right\}$$

$$= -\left[\frac{\partial b}{\partial \theta'}(\theta_0)\right]^{-1}\left\{E\sum_{j=1}^{p}\left[\frac{1}{S}\sum_{s=1}^{S}\frac{\partial A}{\partial \theta_j}(v_s; \theta_0)a_j^*\right]\right.$$
$$\left.+\frac{1}{2}\left[\text{Tr}\,E\frac{\partial^2 b_j}{\partial \theta \partial \theta'}(\theta_0)a^*a^{*'}\right]_{j=1,\dots,p}\right\}.$$

Since a^* is zero mean, and $A(v; \theta_0)$, $A(v_s; \theta_0)$, $s = 1, \dots, S$, are i.i.d., we deduce:

$$Eb^* = -\left[\frac{\partial b}{\partial \theta'}(\theta_0)\right]^{-1}\left\{\sum_{j=1}^{p}\text{cov}\left[\frac{1}{S}\sum_{s=1}^{S}\frac{\partial A}{\partial \theta_j}(v_s; \theta_0), a_j^*\right]\right.$$
$$\left.+\frac{1}{2}\left[\text{Tr}\left(\frac{\partial^2 b_j}{\partial \theta \partial \theta'}(\theta_0)Va^*\right)\right]_{j=1,\dots,p}\right\}$$

$$= -\left[\frac{\partial b}{\partial \theta'}(\theta_0)\right]^{-1}\left\{-\frac{1}{S}\sum_{j=1}^{p}\text{cov}\left[\frac{\partial A}{\partial \theta_j}(v; \theta_0), \left(\left[\frac{\partial b}{\partial \theta'}(\theta_0)\right]^{-1}A(v; \theta_0)\right)_j\right]\right.$$
$$+\frac{1}{2}\left(1 + \frac{1}{S}\right)$$
$$\left.\times\left[\text{Tr}\left(\frac{\partial^2 b_j}{\partial \theta \partial \theta'}(\theta_0)\left[\frac{\partial b}{\partial \theta'}(\theta_0)\right]^{-1}V(A(v; \theta_0))\left[\frac{\partial b'}{\partial \theta}(\theta_0)\right]^{-1}\right)\right]_{j=1,\dots,p}\right\}.$$

It may be noted that, whereas the initial second order bias of the first step estimator is:

$$E[\hat{\beta}_T] - b(\theta_0) = \frac{EB(v; \theta_0)}{T} + o\left(\frac{1}{T}\right), \tag{4.27}$$

the second order bias of the indirect inference estimator no longer depends on the second order terms $B(\cdot; \theta_0)$.

The case of a consistent first step estimator

Even if indirect inference is useful mainly when the initial model is untractable, it might also be used when a consistent estimator of θ is easily available, i.e. when there exists a consistent first step estimator $\hat{\beta}_T(\theta_0)$ such that $b(\theta_0) = \theta_0$. In such a framework we will see (as noted by Gouriéroux *et al.* (1994); McKinnon and Smith (1995)) that indirect inference is a possible approach for correcting for finite sample bias. In some sense the correction is similar to the one based on the median proposed by Andrews (1993), or to a kind of bootstrap approach.

By applying the previous proposition to this particular case, we obtain some simplifications on the second order expansion of the indirect inference estimator.

Proposition 4.6 | If $b(\theta) = \theta$, then

$$a^* = \left[A(v; \theta_0) - \frac{1}{S} \sum_{s=1}^{S} A(v_s; \theta_0) \right],$$

$$b^* = B(v; \theta_0) - \frac{1}{S} \sum_{s=1}^{S} B(v_s; \theta_0) - \frac{1}{S} \sum_{s=1}^{S} \frac{\partial A}{\partial \theta'}(v_s; \theta_0) a^*.$$

In particular, we deduce that, when S tends to infinity, we have:

$$\lim_{S \to \infty} \hat{\theta}_{ST} = \hat{\beta}_T - \frac{EB(v; \theta_0)}{T} + o\left(\frac{1}{T}\right). \tag{4.28}$$

The indirect inference estimator is simply equivalent to the initial estimator corrected for the second order bias. When the number of replications S is finite, the second order bias of the indirect inference estimator is smaller in absolute value than the one associated with the first step estimator as soon as:

$$\left| \frac{1}{S} \sum_{j=1}^{p} \text{cov}\left[\frac{\partial A}{\partial \theta_j}(v; \theta_0), A_j(v; \theta_0) \right] \right| \leq |EB(v; \theta_0)|, \tag{4.29}$$

which gives the limit number of replications providing this improvement.

Example 4.2

To illustrate the previous effect, let us consider the simple case of i.i.d. observations $y_1, \ldots, y_T$ with a normal distribution $N(m, \sigma^2)$. The true values m_0, σ_0^2 are unknown. If the first step estimator is the maximum likelihood estimator, we have:

$$\hat{m}_T = \frac{1}{T} \sum_{t=1}^{T} y_t = \bar{y}_T, \qquad \hat{\sigma}_T^2 = \frac{1}{T} \sum_{t=1}^{T} (y_t - \bar{y}_T)^2,$$

and we know that $\hat{\sigma}_T^2$ is second order biased . Now we have:

$$\hat{\sigma}_T^{2s}(\theta) = \frac{1}{T} \sum_{t=1}^{T} [y_t^s(\theta) - \bar{y}_T^s(\theta)]^2,$$

where $y_t^s(\theta) = m + \sigma u_t^s$, $u_t^s \sim \text{IIN}(0, 1)$. Therefore we have:

$$\hat{\sigma}_T^{2s}(\theta) = \sigma^2 \frac{1}{T} \sum_{t=1}^{T} (u_t^s - \bar{u}_T^s)^2.$$

Finally, the indirect inference estimator $\hat{\sigma}_{ST}^2$ of σ^2 is given by:

$$\hat{\sigma}_T^2 = \sigma_0^2 \frac{1}{T} \sum_{t=1}^{T} (u_t - \bar{u}_T)^2$$

$$= \frac{1}{S} \sum_{s=1}^{S} \hat{\sigma}_T^{2s}(\hat{\sigma}_{ST}^2)$$

$$= \hat{\sigma}_{ST}^2 \frac{1}{S} \sum_{s=1}^{S} \left[\frac{1}{T} \sum_{t=1}^{T} (u_t^s - \bar{u}_T^s)^2 \right],$$

or:

$$\hat{\sigma}_{ST}^2 = \sigma_0^2 \frac{\sum_{t=1}^{T} (u_t - \bar{u}_T)^2}{\frac{1}{S} \sum_{s=1}^{S} \sum_{t=1}^{T} (u_t^s - \bar{u}_T^s)^2}. \tag{4.30}$$

The finite sample distribution of $\hat{\sigma}_T^2$ is such that:

$$T \frac{\hat{\sigma}_T^2}{\sigma_0^2} \sim \chi^2(T - 1),$$

whereas the finite sample distribution of $\hat{\sigma}_{ST}^2$ is such that:

$$\frac{\hat{\sigma}_{ST}^2}{\sigma_0^2} \sim F[T - 1, S(T - 1)].$$

In Figure 4.7 we give the p.d.f. of $\hat{\sigma}_T^2/\sigma_0$ and of $\hat{\sigma}_{ST}^2/\sigma^2$ for $T = 20$ and $S = 10$. In the limit case, $S = +\infty$, we get $(T - 1)\hat{\sigma}_{\infty T}^2/\sigma_0^2 \sim \chi^2(T - 1)$, and $\hat{\sigma}_{\infty T}^2$ is unbiased.

Of course, when S is small the gain in the bias is balanced by a loss in the variance. In the example, the exact first and second order moments are:

$$E\hat{\sigma}_T^2 = \sigma_0^2 \frac{T - 1}{T}, \qquad V\hat{\sigma}_T^2 = \sigma_0^4 \frac{2(T - 1)}{T^2},$$

$$E[\hat{\sigma}_{ST}^2] = \sigma_0^2 \frac{S(T - 1)}{S(T - 1) - 2},$$

$$V[\hat{\sigma}_{ST}^2] = \sigma_0^4 \frac{2S^2(T - 1)[(S + 1)(T - 1) - 2]}{[S(T - 1) - 2]^2[S(T - 1) - 4]}.$$

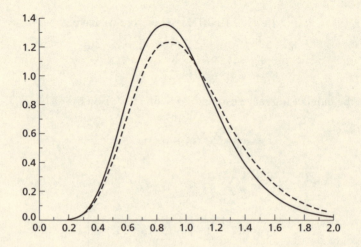

FIGURE 4.7: The p.d.f. of the estimator with and without correction by indirect inference $T = 20$, $S = 10$, (——): $\chi^2(T - 1)$, (---): $F[T - 1, S(T - 1)]$.

The mean square errors are:

$$
\begin{aligned}
\mathrm{MSE}_T &= (E\hat{\sigma}_T^2 - \sigma_0^2)^2 + V\hat{\sigma}_T^2 \\
&= \sigma_0^4 \left[\frac{1}{T^2} + \frac{2(T - 1)}{T^2} \right] \\
&= \sigma_0^4 \frac{2T - 1}{T^2}; \\
\mathrm{MSE}_{ST} &= (E\hat{\sigma}_{ST}^2 - \sigma_0^2)^2 + V\hat{\sigma}_{ST}^2 \\
&= \sigma_0^4 \left[\frac{4}{[S(T - 1) - 2]^2} + \frac{2S^2(T - 1)[(S + 1)(T - 1) - 2]}{[S(T - 1) - 2]^2[S(T - 1) - 4]} \right].
\end{aligned}
$$

For large T, we have:

$$
\mathrm{MSE}_T \sim \frac{2\sigma_0^4}{T}, \qquad \mathrm{MSE}_{ST} \sim \frac{2\sigma_0^4}{T} \frac{S + 1}{S}.
$$

4.4.2   Indirect information and indirect identification

Let us go back to the context of Sections 4.1.1 and 4.1.2, i.e. to the case where the criterion ψ_T is equal to:

$$
\frac{1}{T} \sum_{t=1}^{T} \log f^a(y_t/x_t; \beta),
$$

where $f^a(y_t/x_t; \beta) = f^a(y_t/\underline{y_{t-1}}, \underline{z_t}; \beta)$ is the conditional p.d.f. of some instrumental model (M^a); in other words, ψ_T is equal to $\frac{1}{T} L_T^a(\beta)$, where $L_T^a(\beta)$ is the log likelihood function of (M^a). We still assume that the true conditional p.d.f. belongs to the family $f(y_t/x_t; \theta)$ associated with model (M).

Let us introduce the usual Fisher information matrices of (M) and (M^a):

$$I(\theta) = V_\theta \left[\frac{\partial \log f(y_t/x_t; \theta)}{\partial \theta} \right] = V_\theta \left[\frac{1}{\sqrt{T}} \sum_{t=1}^{T} \frac{\partial \log f(y_t/x_t; \theta)}{\partial \theta} \right],$$

$$I^a(\beta) = V_\beta \left[\frac{\partial \log f^a(y_t/x_t; \beta)}{\partial \beta} \right] = V_\beta \left[\frac{1}{\sqrt{T}} \sum_{t=1}^{T} \frac{\partial \log f^a(y_t/x_t; \beta)}{\partial \beta} \right].$$

Note that in the expression of $I^a(\beta)$ the variance–covariance matrix is taken with respect to the distribution defined by the $f^a(y_t/x_t; \beta), t = 1, \ldots, T$.

We assume that both of them are invertible, which implies the local identifiability of both models.

It is natural to say that (M) is locally indirectly identifiable from (M^a) if the binding function $b(\theta)$ is locally injective, and to introduce the indirect information matrix of (M) based on (M^a) as the asymptotic variance–covariance matrix (under M) of the vector obtained by the orthogonal projection of the components of:

$$\frac{1}{\sqrt{T}} \sum_{t=1}^{T} \frac{\partial \log f(y_t/x_t; \theta)}{\partial \theta}$$

on the space spanned by the components of:

$$\frac{1}{\sqrt{T}} \sum_{t=1}^{T} \left\{ \frac{\partial \log f^a(y_t/x_t; b(\theta))}{\partial \beta} - E_\theta \left[\frac{\partial \log f^a(y_t/x_t; b(\theta))}{\partial \beta} \Big/ \underline{z_t} \right] \right\}.$$

Note that the unconditional expectation

$$E_\theta \left[\frac{\partial \log f^a(y_t/x_t; b(\theta))}{\partial \beta} \right]$$

is equal to zero because of the definition of $b(\theta)$, but that, in general, the conditional expectation

$$E_\theta \left[\frac{\partial \log f^a(y_t/x_t; b(\theta))}{\partial \beta} \Big/ \underline{z_t} \right]$$

is different from zero.

It is clear that, under (M), the indirect information matrix, denoted by $II(\theta)$, is smaller, in the usual sense, than $I(\theta)$. Moreover, $II(\theta)$ has the following properties.

Proposition 4.7 | (i) The **indirect information matrix** $II(\theta)$ is equal to:

$$\frac{\partial b'}{\partial \theta}(\theta) J(\theta) \bar{I}^{-1}(\theta) J(\theta) \frac{\partial b}{\partial \theta'}(\theta),$$

where:

$$
\begin{aligned}
J(\theta) &= p \lim_{T} -\frac{1}{T} \sum_{t=1}^{T} \frac{\partial^2 \log f^a(y_t/x_t; b(\theta))}{\partial \beta \, \partial \beta'} \\
&= -E_\theta \left[\frac{\partial^2 \log f^a(y_t/x_t; b(\theta))}{\partial \beta \, \partial \beta'} \right], \\
\bar{I}(\theta) &= \lim_{T} V_\theta \left\{ \frac{1}{\sqrt{T}} \sum_{t=1}^{T} \left[\frac{\partial \log f^a(y_t/x_t; b(\theta))}{\partial \beta} \right. \right. \\
&\quad \left. \left. - E_\theta \left(\frac{\partial \log f^a(y_t/x_t; b(\theta))}{\partial \beta} \bigg/ \underline{z_t} \right) \right] \right\}.
\end{aligned}
$$

(ii) If the matrix $II(\theta)$ is invertible, (M) is locally indirectly identifiable from (M^a).

Proof. See Appendix 4B.

The first part of this property shows that, when the criterion of the indirect inference method is the log likelihood of an auxiliary model, the asymptotic variance–covariance matrix of the optimal indirect inference estimators is (see Proposition 4.4):

$$\left(1 + \frac{1}{S}\right) II^{-1}(\theta_0).$$

When S tends to infinity we obtain a kind of indirect Cramer–Rao bound, which is, as in the direct case, the inverse of the Indirect Information matrix.

The second part of Proposition 4.7 shows that the links between information and local identifiability are identical in the indirect and the direct cases.

Appendix 4A: Derivation of the Asymptotic Results

In this appendix we just sketch the proofs of the asymptotic properties of indirect inference estimators. The aim is to understand why these estimators are consistent, to get the form of their asymptotic variance–covariance matrices, and to give their asymptotic expansions in order to study their asymptotic equivalence. More precise proofs are given in Gouriéroux *et al.* (1993) and Smith (1993).

4A.1 Consistency of the estimators

To prove the consistency, we need several regularity conditions. The most important ones are:

(A1) The normalized function $\psi_T(y_T^s(\theta), \underline{z_T}; \beta)$ tends almost surely to a deterministic limit function $\psi_\infty(\theta, \beta)$ uniformly in (θ, β) when T goes to ∞.

(A2) This limit function has a unique maximum with respect to β: $b(\theta) = \arg\max_\beta \psi_\infty(\theta, \beta)$.

(A3) ψ_T and ψ_∞ are differentiable with respect to β, and $\frac{\partial \psi_\infty}{\partial \beta}(\theta, \beta) = \lim_T \frac{\partial \psi_T}{\partial \beta}(\underline{\bar{y}_T^s(\theta)}, \underline{z_T}; \beta)$.

(A4) The only solution of the asymptotic first order conditions is $b(\theta)$: $\frac{\partial \psi_\infty}{\partial \beta}(\theta, \beta) = 0 \Rightarrow \beta = b(\theta)$.

(A5) The equation $\beta = b(\theta)$ admits a unique solution in θ.

The proof of consistency is based on the study of the asymptotic optimization problem. Let us first consider the two intermediate estimators, $\hat{\beta}_T$ and $\hat{\beta}_{ST}(\theta)$. We have:

$$\hat{\beta}_T = \arg\max_\beta \psi_T(\underline{y_T}, \underline{z_T}; \beta) \to \arg\max_\beta \psi_\infty(\theta_0, \beta) = b(\theta_0),$$

$$\hat{\beta}_{ST}(\theta) = \arg\max_\beta \sum_{s=1}^{S} \psi_T(y_T^s(\theta), \underline{z_T}; \beta) \to \arg\max_\beta S\psi_\infty(\theta, \beta) = b(\theta).$$

Therefore $\hat{\beta}_T$ converges to $b(\theta_0)$, and $\hat{\beta}_{ST}(\cdot)$ converges to the binding function $b(\cdot)$. Then:

$$\hat{\theta}_{ST}(\Omega) = \arg\max_\theta \left[\hat{\beta}_T - \hat{\beta}_{ST}(\theta)\right]' \Omega \left[\hat{\beta}_T - \hat{\beta}_{ST}(\theta)\right]$$

$$\to \arg\min_\theta [b(\theta_0) - b(\theta)]' \Omega [b(\theta_0) - b(\theta)]$$

$$= \{\theta : b(\theta) = b(\theta_0)\} \text{ (as soon as } \Omega \text{ is positive definite)}$$

$$= \theta_0 \text{ (from (A5))}.$$

A similar argument based on the derivative $\frac{\partial \psi_\infty}{\partial \beta}$ gives the consistency of $\hat{\hat{\theta}}_{ST}(\Sigma)$.

4A.2 Asymptotic expansions

We need some additional regularity conditions, which essentially concern the second order differentiability of the functions ψ_T, ψ_∞ with respect to both parameters θ, β and the continuity of the derivatives. Applying the implicit function theorem will imply the first order differentiability of the binding function $b(\cdot)$. Moreover, we assume that:

(A6) $p\lim_{T\to\infty} -\dfrac{\partial^2\psi_T}{\partial\beta\,\partial\beta'}(\underline{y_T},\underline{z_T};b(\theta)) = -\dfrac{\partial^2\psi_\infty}{\partial\beta\,\partial\beta'}(\theta_0,b(\theta_0)) = J_0.$

(A7) $\sqrt{T}\dfrac{\partial\psi_T}{\partial\beta}(\underline{y_T},\underline{z_T};b(\theta_0)) \xrightarrow[T\to+\infty]{d} N(0,I_0^*).$

(A8) $\lim_{T\to\infty}\mathrm{cov}_0\left[\sqrt{T}\dfrac{\partial\psi_T}{\partial\beta}[\underline{y_T^{s_1}}(\theta_0),\underline{z_T};b(\theta_0)],\sqrt{T}\dfrac{\partial\psi_T}{\partial\beta}[\underline{y_T^{s_2}}(\theta_0),\underline{z_T};b(\theta_0)]\right]$
$= K_0$, for $s_1 \neq s_2$.

This implies:

$$K_0 = \lim_{T\to\infty} V_0\left[E_0\left(\sqrt{T}\dfrac{\partial\psi_T}{\partial\beta}(\underline{y_T},\underline{z_T};b(\theta))/\underline{z_T}\right)\right],$$

$$I_0^* - K_0 = \lim_{T\to\infty} V_0\left[\sqrt{T}\dfrac{\partial\psi_T}{\partial\beta}(\underline{y_T},\underline{z_T};b(\theta_0))\right.$$
$$\left. -E_0\left(\sqrt{T}\dfrac{\partial\psi_T}{\partial\beta}(\underline{y_T},\underline{z_T};b(\theta_0))/\underline{z_T}\right)\right]$$
$$= \bar{I}_0 \quad \text{(say)}.$$

Asymptotic expansions of $\hat{\beta}_T$ and $\hat{\beta}_{ST}(\theta_0)$

These are directly deduced from the first order conditions. For instance, we have:

$$\sqrt{T}\sum_{s=1}^S \dfrac{\partial\psi_T}{\partial\beta}(\underline{y_T^s}(\theta_0),\underline{z_T};\hat{\beta}_{ST}(\theta_0)) = 0,$$

or

$$\sqrt{T}\sum_{s=1}^S \dfrac{\partial\psi_T}{\partial\beta}(\underline{y_T^s}(\theta_0),\underline{z_T};b(\theta_0)) + \sum_{s=1}^S \dfrac{\partial^2\psi_T}{\partial\beta\,\partial\beta'}[\underline{y_T^s}(\theta_0),\underline{z_T};b(\theta_0)]$$
$$\times\sqrt{T}[\hat{\beta}_{ST}(\theta_0) - b(\theta_0)] = o_p(1),$$

$$\sqrt{T}[\hat{\beta}_{ST}(\theta_0) - b(\theta_0)] = \left[-\sum_{s=1}^S \dfrac{\partial^2\psi_T}{\partial\beta\,\partial\beta'}(\underline{y_T^s}(\theta_0),\underline{z_T};b(\theta_0))\right]^{-1}$$

$$\times \sqrt{T} \sum_{s=1}^{S} \frac{\partial \psi_T}{\partial \beta} \left(\underline{y_T^s}(\theta_0), \underline{z_T}; b(\theta_0) \right) + o_p(1)$$

$$= \frac{1}{S} \left[-\frac{\partial^2 \psi_\infty}{\partial \beta \, \partial \beta'} (\theta_0, b(\theta_0)) \right]^{-1}$$

$$\times \sqrt{T} \sum_{s=1}^{S} \frac{\partial \psi_T}{\partial \beta} \left(\underline{y_T^s}(\theta_0), \underline{z_T}; b(\theta_0) \right) + o_p(1),$$

$$\sqrt{T} [\hat{\beta}_{ST}(\theta_0) - b(\theta_0)] = \frac{J_0^{-1}}{S} \sqrt{T} \sum_{s=1}^{S} \frac{\partial \psi_T}{\partial \beta} \left(\underline{y_T^s}(\theta_0), \underline{z_T}; b(\theta_0) \right) + o_p(1).$$

$$(4A.1)$$

Note that, from (4A.1), it is clear that $\hat{\beta}_{ST}(\theta)$ is asymptotically equivalent to $\frac{1}{S} \sum_{s=1}^{S} \hat{\beta}_T^s(\theta_0)$ (with $\hat{\beta}_T^s(\theta_0) = \arg\max_\beta \psi_T[\underline{y_T^s}(\theta_0), \underline{z_T}; \beta]$), and to $\tilde{\beta}_{ST}(\theta_0) = \arg\max_\beta \psi_{ST}[\underline{y_{ST}^s}(\theta), \underline{z_{ST}}; \beta]$ (with $\underline{z_{kT+h}} = \underline{z_h}, k = 0, \ldots, S-1; h = 1, \ldots, T$), provided that we have an additive decomposition:

$$\frac{\partial \psi_T}{\partial \beta} (\underline{y_T}, \underline{z_T}; \beta) = \frac{1}{T} \sum_{t=1}^{T} \frac{\partial \psi_1}{\partial \beta} (\underline{y_t}, \underline{z_t}; \beta).$$

with a fixed number of variables in $\underline{y_t}$ and $\underline{z_t}$.

Similarly, we have:

$$\sqrt{T} [\hat{\beta}_T - b(\theta_0)] = J_0^{-1} \sqrt{T} \frac{\partial \psi_T}{\partial \beta} (\underline{y_T}, \underline{z_T}; b(\theta_0)) + o_p(1). \qquad (4A.2)$$

Asymptotic expansion of $\hat{\theta}_{ST}(\Omega)$

The first order condition for $\hat{\theta}_{ST}(\Omega)$ is:

$$\frac{\partial \hat{\beta}_{ST}'}{\partial \theta} [\hat{\theta}_{ST}(\Omega)] \Omega [\hat{\beta}_T - \hat{\beta}_{ST}(\hat{\theta}_{ST}(\Omega))] = 0.$$

An expansion around the limit value θ_0 gives:

$$\frac{\partial \hat{\beta}_{ST}'}{\partial \theta} (\theta_0) \Omega \sqrt{T} [\hat{\beta}_T - \hat{\beta}_{ST}(\theta_0)]$$

$$- \frac{\partial \hat{\beta}_{ST}'}{\partial \theta} (\theta_0) \Omega \frac{\partial \hat{\beta}_{ST}}{\partial \theta} (\theta_0) \sqrt{T} (\hat{\theta}_{ST}(\Omega) - \theta_0) = o_p(1).$$

$$\sqrt{T} [\hat{\theta}_{ST}(\Omega) - \theta_0] = \left[\frac{\partial b'(\theta_0)}{\partial \theta} \Omega \frac{\partial b(\theta_0)}{\partial \theta'} \right]^{-1} \frac{\partial b'}{\partial \theta} (\theta_0) \Omega$$

$$\times \sqrt{T} [\hat{\beta}_T - \hat{\beta}_{ST}(\theta_0)] + o_p(1).$$

$$(4A.3)$$

Asymptotic expansion of $\hat{\hat{\theta}}_{ST}(\Sigma)$

The first order condition is:

$$\left\{ \sum_{s=1}^{S} \frac{\partial^2 \psi_T}{\partial \theta \, \partial \beta'} [\underline{y}_T^s(\hat{\hat{\theta}}_{ST}), \underline{z_T}, \hat{\beta}_T] \right\} \Sigma \left\{ \sum_{s=1}^{S} \frac{\partial \psi_T}{\partial \beta} [\underline{y}_T^s(\hat{\hat{\theta}}_{ST}), \underline{z_T}, \hat{\beta}_T] \right\} = 0.$$

An expansion around the values θ_0, $b(\theta_0)$ of the parameters provides:

$$\left\{ \sum_{s=1}^{S} \frac{\partial^2 \psi_T}{\partial \theta \, \partial \beta'} [\underline{y}_T^s(\theta_0), \underline{z_T}, b(\theta_0)] \right\} \Sigma \left\{ \sqrt{T} \sum_{s=1}^{S} \frac{\partial \psi_T}{\partial \beta} [\underline{\bar{y}}_T^s(\theta_0), \underline{z_T}, b(\theta_0)] \right.$$

$$+ S \frac{\partial^2 \psi_\infty}{\partial \beta \, \partial \beta'} [\theta_0, b(\theta_0)] \sqrt{T} [\hat{\beta}_T - b(\theta_0)]$$

$$+ S \frac{\partial^2 \psi_\infty}{\partial \beta \, \partial \theta'} [\theta_0, b(\theta_0)] \sqrt{T} [\hat{\hat{\theta}}_{ST}(\Sigma) - \theta_0] \bigg\} = o_p(1),$$

or, using (4A.1)

$$\frac{\partial^2 \psi_\infty}{\partial \theta \, \partial \beta'} [\theta_0, b(\theta_0)] \Sigma \left\{ J_0 \sqrt{T} [\hat{\beta}_{ST}(\theta_0) - \hat{\beta}_T] \right.$$

$$+ \frac{\partial^2 \psi_\infty}{\partial \beta \, \partial \theta'} (\theta_0, b(\theta_0)) \sqrt{T} (\hat{\hat{\theta}}_{ST}(\Sigma) - \theta_0) \bigg\} = o_p(1).$$

Finally, we get:

$$\sqrt{T} (\hat{\hat{\theta}}_{ST}(\Sigma) - \theta_0) = \left\{ \frac{\partial^2 \psi_\infty}{\partial \theta \, \partial \beta'} [\theta_0, b(\theta_0)] \Sigma \frac{\partial^2 \psi_\infty}{\partial \beta \, \partial \theta'} [\theta_0, b(\theta_0)] \right\}^{-1}$$

$$\times \frac{\partial^2 \psi_\infty}{\partial \theta \, \partial \beta'} [\theta_0, b(\theta_0)] \Sigma J_0 \sqrt{T} [\hat{\beta}_T - \hat{\beta}_{ST}(\theta_0)] + o_p(1).$$

$$(4A.4)$$

Asymptotic equivalence of the estimators

We know that:

$$\frac{\partial b}{\partial \theta'} (\theta_0) = J_0^{-1} \frac{\partial^2 \psi_\infty}{\partial \beta \, \partial \theta'} [\theta_0, b(\theta_0)].$$

Therefore the asymptotic expansion of $\hat{\hat{\theta}}_{ST}(\Sigma)$ given in (4A.4) may also be written:

$$\sqrt{T} (\hat{\hat{\theta}}_{ST}(\Sigma) - \theta_0)$$

$$= \left[\frac{\partial b'}{\partial \theta} (\theta_0) J_0 \Sigma J_0 \frac{\partial b}{\partial \theta'} (\theta_0) \right]^{-1} \frac{\partial b'}{\partial \theta} (\theta_0) J_0 \Sigma J_0 \sqrt{T} [\hat{\beta}_T - \hat{\beta}_{ST}(\theta_0)] + o_p(1).$$

A comparison with expansion (4A.3) directly gives Proposition 4.3:

$$\sqrt{T} [\hat{\hat{\theta}}_{ST}(\Sigma) - \hat{\theta}_{ST}(J_0 \Sigma J_0)] = o_p(1).$$

Asymptotic distribution of the estimators

From (4A.1), (4A.2), we get:

$$\sqrt{T}[\hat{\beta}_T - \hat{\beta}_{ST}(\theta_0)] = J_0^{-1}\sqrt{T}\left[\frac{\partial \psi_T}{\partial \beta}(\underline{y_T}, \underline{z_T}; b(\theta_0))\right.$$

$$\left. -\frac{1}{S}\sum_{s=1}^{S}\frac{\partial \psi_T}{\partial \beta}(\underline{y_T^s}(\theta_0), \underline{z_T}; b(\theta_0))\right].$$

Therefore using (A7), (A8), we obtain:

$$\sqrt{T}[\hat{\beta}_T - \hat{\beta}_{ST}(\theta_0)] \xrightarrow[T \to +\infty]{d} N\left[0, J_0^{-1}\left[\left(1 + \frac{1}{S}\right)I_0^* - 2K_0 + \frac{S(S-1)}{S^2}K_0\right]J_0^{-1}\right]$$

$$= N\left[0, \left(1 + \frac{1}{S}\right)J_0^{-1}(I_0^* - K_0)J_0^{-1}\right]$$

$$= N\left[0, \left(1 + \frac{1}{S}\right)J_0^{-1}\bar{I}_0 J_0^{-1}\right]$$

$$= N\left[0, \left(1 + \frac{1}{S}\right)\Omega^{*-1}\right].$$

And finally, using (4A.3):

$$\sqrt{T}[\hat{\theta}_{ST}(\Omega) - \theta_0] \xrightarrow[T \to +\infty]{d} N[0, W(S, \Omega)],$$

where $W(S, \Omega)$ is given in Proposition 4.2.

The optimality of the matrix $\Omega = \Omega^*$ is a consequence of the Gauss–Markov theorem.

Appendix 4B: Indirect Information and Identification: Proofs

4B.1 Computation of $II(\theta)$

Let us consider the asymptotic variance–covariance matrix, under (M), of:

$$\left\{\frac{1}{\sqrt{T}}\sum_{t=1}^{T}\frac{\partial \log f_t(\theta)}{\partial \theta'}, \frac{1}{\sqrt{T}}\sum_{t=1}^{T}\left[\frac{\partial \log f_t^a[b(\theta)]}{\partial \beta'} - E_\theta\left(\frac{\partial \log f_t^a[b(\theta)]}{\partial \beta'}\Big/ \underline{z_t}\right)\right]\right\}'$$

(with $f_t(\theta) = f(y_t/x_t; \theta)$, $f_t^a(\beta) = f^a(y_t/x_t; \beta)$). This matrix is denoted by:

$$\begin{pmatrix} I(\theta) & I^P(\theta) \\ I^N(\theta) & \bar{I}(\theta) \end{pmatrix},$$

with:

$$I(\theta) = V_\theta \left(\frac{\partial \log f_t(\theta)}{\partial \theta} \right),$$

$$I^P(\theta) = [I^N(\theta)]'$$

$$= \sum_{k=0}^{\infty} \mathrm{cov}_\theta \left(\frac{\partial \log f_t(\theta)}{\partial \theta}, \frac{\partial \log f_{t+k}^a[b(\theta)]}{\partial \beta} \right),$$

(since, for $k < 0$,

$$\mathrm{cov}_\theta \left(\frac{\partial \log f_t(\theta)}{\partial \theta}, \frac{\partial \log f_{t+k}^a[b(\theta)]}{\partial \beta} \right)$$

$$= E_\theta \left[\frac{\partial \log f_t(\theta)}{\partial \theta} \frac{\partial \log f_{t+k}^a[b(\theta)]}{\partial \beta'} \right]$$

$$= E_\theta \left[E_\theta \left(\frac{\partial \log f_t(\theta)}{\partial \theta} \Big/ \underline{y_{t-1}}, \underline{z_t} \right) \frac{\partial \log f_{t+k}^a[b(\theta)]}{\partial \beta'} \right]$$

$$= 0)$$

and:

$$\bar{I}(\theta) = \sum_{k=-\infty}^{\infty} \mathrm{cov}_\theta \left[\left(\frac{\partial \log f_t^a[b(\theta)]}{\partial \beta} - E_\theta \left(\frac{\partial \log f_t^a[b(\theta)]}{\partial \beta} \Big/ \underline{z_t} \right) \right), \right.$$

$$\left. \left(\frac{\partial \log f_{t+k}^a[b(\theta)]}{\partial \beta} - E_\theta \left(\frac{\partial \log f_{t+k}^a[b(\theta)]}{\partial \beta} \Big/ \underline{z_t} \right) \right) \right],$$

$$= I^*(\theta) - K(\theta),$$

with:

$$I^*(\theta) = V_{as} \left(\frac{1}{\sqrt{T}} \sum_{t=1}^{T} \frac{\partial \log f_t^a[b(\theta)]}{\partial \beta} \right)$$

$$= \sum_{k=-\infty}^{\infty} \mathrm{cov}_\theta \left(\frac{\partial \log f_t^a[b(\theta)]}{\partial \beta}, \frac{\partial \log f_{t+k}^a[b(\theta)]}{\partial \beta} \right),$$

$$K(\theta) = V_{as} \left[\frac{1}{\sqrt{T}} \sum_{t=1}^{T} E_\theta \left(\frac{\partial \log f_t^a[b(\theta)]}{\partial \beta} \Big/ \underline{z_t} \right) \right]$$

$$= \sum_{k=-\infty}^{\infty} \mathrm{cov}_\theta \left[E_\theta \left(\frac{\partial \log f_t^a[b(\theta)]}{\partial \beta} \Big/ \underline{z_t} \right), E_\theta \left(\frac{\partial \log f_{t+k}^a[b(\theta)]}{\partial \beta} \Big/ \underline{z_{t+k}} \right) \right].$$

Therefore, the asymptotic variance–covariance matrix of the projection of the components of $\frac{1}{\sqrt{T}} \sum_{t=1}^{T} \log f_t(\theta)/\partial \theta$ on the space spanned by the components of

$$\frac{1}{\sqrt{T}} \sum_{t=1}^{T} \left[\frac{\partial \log f_t^a[b(\theta)]}{\partial \beta} - E \left(\frac{\partial \log f_t^a[b(\theta)]}{\partial \beta} \Big/ \underline{z_t} \right) \right]$$

is:

$$II(\theta) = I^P(\theta)\bar{I}^{-1}(\theta)I^N(\theta).$$

4B.2 Another expression of $I^P(\theta)$

From the definition of $b(\theta)$, we have:

$$E_\theta \frac{\partial \log f_t^a[b(\theta)]}{\partial \beta} = 0, \quad \forall \theta,$$

or:

$$E_z \left[\int \frac{\partial \log f_t^a[b(\theta)]}{\partial \beta} \left(\prod_{k=0}^{t-1} f_{t-k}(\theta) \right) f_0(\theta) \left(\prod_{k=0}^{t-1} dy_{t-k} \right) d\underline{y_0} \right] = 0, \quad \forall \theta,$$

where $f_0(\theta)$ is the conditional p.d.f. of $\underline{y_0}$ given the exogenous variables. Differentiating with respect to θ, we get:

$$E_\theta \left[\frac{\partial^2 \log f_t^a[b(\theta)]}{\partial \beta \, \partial \beta'} \right] \frac{\partial b(\theta)}{\partial \theta'} + \sum_{k=0}^{\infty} E_\theta \left[\frac{\partial \log f_{t+k}^a[b(\theta)]}{\partial \beta} \frac{\partial \log f_t(\theta)}{\partial \theta'} \right]$$

$$+ \lim_{t \to \infty} E_\theta \left[\frac{\partial \log f_t^a[b(\theta)]}{\partial \beta} \frac{\partial \log f_0(\theta)}{\partial \theta'} \right] = 0.$$

The last limit is zero under the usual mixing assumption, and therefore:

$$\frac{\partial b(\theta)}{\partial \theta'} = J^{-1}(\theta)[I^P(\theta)]',$$

and

$$I^P(\theta) = \frac{\partial b'(\theta)}{\partial \theta} J(\theta).$$

Finally, we get:

$$II(\theta) = \frac{\partial b'(\theta)}{\partial \theta} J(\theta)\bar{I}^{-1}(\theta)J(\theta)\frac{\partial b(\theta)}{\partial \theta'}.$$

If $II(\theta)$ is invertible, $\frac{\partial b(\theta)}{\partial \theta'}$ is of full column rank and the second part of Proposition 4.7 follows from the implicit function theorem.

5

Applications to Limited Dependent Variable Models

5.1 MSM and SML Applied to Qualitative Models

5.1.1 Discrete choice model

The problem of discrete choices made by the agents is at the origin of the method of simulated moments (McFadden 1989). In this subsection we first recall the form of the model (see Section 1.3.1), the expression of the log likelihood function, and the first order conditions. The model is defined from the underlying utility levels:

$$\begin{cases} U_{ij} = z_{ij}b_j + v_{ij}, & j = 1, \ldots, J, i = 1, \ldots, n, \\ \Leftrightarrow U_i = z_i b + v_i, & v_i \sim N(0, \Omega), \end{cases} \tag{5.1}$$

and from the endogenous dichotomous variables summarizing the choices:

$$y_{ij} = \mathbb{1}_{(j \text{ is retained})} = \mathbb{1}_{(U_{ij} > U_{ie}, \forall \ell \neq j)}. \tag{5.2}$$

The conditional discrete distributions of the endogenous variables are characterized by the probabilities

$$\begin{aligned} P_\theta[y_{ij} = 1/z_i] &= P_\theta[U_{ij} > U_{ie}, \forall \ell \neq j] \\ &= p_j(z_i; \theta) \quad \text{(say)}. \end{aligned} \tag{5.3}$$

The previous relationship can be seen as a moment condition, since it is equivalent to:

$$\begin{aligned} E_\theta[y_{ij}/z_i] &= p_j(z_i; \theta), \qquad j = 1, \ldots, J, \\ \Leftrightarrow E_\theta[y_i/z_i] &= p(z_i; \theta). \end{aligned} \tag{5.4}$$

With the notations of Chapter 2, we have $K(y_i, z_i) = y_i, k(z_i, \theta) = p(z_i; \theta)$. The log likelihood function is given by:

$$\begin{aligned} \log \ell(y/z; \theta) &= \sum_{i=1}^{n} \left[\sum_{j=1}^{J} y_{ij} \log p_j(z_i; \theta) \right] \\ &= \sum_{j=1}^{J} \sum_{i \in I_j} \log p_j(z_i; \theta), \end{aligned} \tag{5.5}$$

where I_j, $j = 1, \ldots, J$, is the subset of individuals for which $y_{ij} = 1$.
Finally, the likelihood equations are of the form:

$$\sum_{i=1}^{n} \sum_{j=1}^{J} \frac{y_{ij}}{p_j(z_i; \theta)} \frac{\partial p_j}{\partial \theta}(z_i; \theta) = 0,$$

or, since:

$$\sum_{j=1}^{J} \frac{\partial p_j}{\partial \theta}(z_i; \theta) = \frac{\partial}{\partial \theta}\left[\sum_{j=1}^{J} p_j(z_i; \theta)\right] = \frac{\partial}{\partial \theta}(1) = 0,$$

$$\sum_{i=1}^{n} \sum_{j=1}^{J} \frac{1}{p_j(z_i; \theta)} \frac{\partial p_j}{\partial \theta}(z_i; \theta) \left[y_{ij} - p_j(z_i; \theta)\right] = 0. \qquad (5.6)$$

It is an empirical orthogonality condition, where the instruments are asymptotically

$$Z_{ij}(z) = \frac{1}{p_j(z_i; \theta_0)} \frac{\partial p_j}{\partial \theta}(z_i; \theta_0).$$

This choice of instruments in the GMM allows us to reach efficiency. However, it has to be noted that such instruments depend on the unknown true value θ_0; therefore they have to be approximated by

$$\tilde{Z}_{ij}(z) = \frac{1}{p_j(z_i; \tilde{\theta})} \frac{\partial p_j}{\partial \theta}(z_i; \tilde{\theta}),$$

where $\tilde{\theta}$ is a consistent estimator of θ_0, and this replacement has no effect on the asymptotic distribution of the estimator.

5.1.2   Simulated methods

Let us introduce an unbiased simulator $\tilde{p}_j(z_i, u; \theta)$ of $p_j(z_i; \theta)$, and let us denote by $\bar{p}_j^S(z_i, u_{ij}^S; \theta) = \frac{1}{S} \sum_{s=1}^{S} \tilde{p}_j(z_i, u_{ij}^s; \theta)$ the average simulator, where u_{ij}^S is a notation for $(u_{ij}^s, s = 1, \ldots, S)$.

MSM

As seen in Chapter 2, we first have to select a set of instruments $Z_{ij}(z_i)$; then the MSM estimator is the solution of an optimization problem:

$$\min_{\theta} \left\{\sum_{i=1}^{n} \sum_{j=1}^{J} Z_{ij}(z_i) \left[y_{ij} - \bar{p}_j^S(z_i, u_{ij}^S; \theta)\right]\right\}'$$

$$\times \Omega \left\{\sum_{i=1}^{n} \sum_{j=1}^{J} Z_{ij}(z_i) \left[y_{ij} - \bar{p}_j^S(z_i, u_{ij}^S; \theta)\right]\right\}.$$

SML

The SML estimator is the solution of:

$$\hat{\theta}_{Sn} = \arg\max_{\theta} \sum_{i=1}^{n} \sum_{j=1}^{J} y_{ij} \log \bar{p}_j^S(z_i, u_{ij}^S; \theta)$$

$$= \arg\max_{\theta} \sum_{i=1}^{n} \sum_{i \in I_j} \log \bar{p}_j^S(z_i, u_{ij}^S; \theta),$$

and satisfies the first order conditions:

$$\sum_{i=1}^{n} \sum_{j=1}^{J} \frac{1}{\bar{p}_j^S(z_i, u_{ij}^S; \hat{\theta}_{Sn})} \frac{\partial}{\partial \theta} \bar{p}_j^S(z_i, u_{ij}^S; \hat{\theta}_{Sn}) \left[y_{ij} - \bar{p}_j^S(z_i, u_{ij}^S; \hat{\theta}_{Sn}) \right] = 0. \quad (5.7)$$

This orthogonality condition is not an empirical moment orthogonality condition. Indeed, even asymptotically,

$$Z_{ij}(\theta_0) = \frac{1}{\bar{p}_j^S(z_i, u_{ij}^S; \theta_0)} \frac{\partial \bar{p}_j^S(z_i, u_{ij}^S; \theta_0)}{\partial \theta}$$

is not an instrument, since it depends on the simulated values u_{ij}^S, which introduce a correlation between $Z_{ij}(\theta_0)$ and $y_{ij} - \bar{p}_j^S(z_i, u_{ij}^S; \theta_0)$.

Simulated instruments

It has been proposed to apply the MSM with instruments close to the Z appearing in the likelihood equations. To destroy the correlation previously discussed between Z and $y - \bar{p}^S$, the idea is to consider:

$$Z_{ij}^*(\theta) = \frac{1}{\bar{p}_j^S(z_i, v_{ij}^S; \theta)} \frac{\partial \bar{p}_j^S}{\partial \theta}(z_i, v_{ij}^S; \theta),$$

where :

$$\bar{p}_j^S(z_i, v_{ij}^S; \theta) = \frac{1}{S^*} \sum_{s=1}^{S^*} \tilde{p}_j(z_i, v_{ij}^s; \theta).$$

The v_{ij}^s are drawn independently of the u_{ij}^s and in the same distribution. Then we can look for the estimator $\tilde{\theta}_{Sn}$ solution of:

$$\sum_{i=1}^{n} \sum_{j=1}^{J} Z_{ij}^*(\tilde{\theta}_{Sn}) \left[y_{ij} - \bar{p}_j^S(z_i, u_{ij}^S; \tilde{\theta}_{Sn}) \right] = 0,$$

where $\tilde{\theta}_{Sn}$ is a consistent estimator of θ, when $n \to \infty$, and S is fixed. With such a choice, and with S^* and S sufficiently large, we may be close to the asymptotic efficiency.

5.1.3   Different simulators

We now have to discuss different possible unbiased simulators of the probabilities $p_j(z_i; \theta)$. A good simulator has to be smooth, and has to imply a good precision of the estimator, and short computer time. Some of these simulators have already been presented in previous chapters. Some others are specific to this qualitative framework.

The frequency simulator

The latent equations can be written:

$$U_i = z_i b + A u_i, \text{ where } AA' = \Omega, \qquad u_i \sim N[0, Id].$$

The frequency simulator initially proposed by McFadden (1989) and Pakes and Pollard (1989) consists in drawing the errors u_i^s, and then considering

$$\tilde{p}_j(z_i, u^s; \theta) = \mathbb{1}_{(z_{ij}b + A_j u_i^s > z_{il}b + A_l u_i^s, \forall l \neq j)}, \tag{5.8}$$

where A_j is the jth row of A.

These simulators have several drawbacks.

(i) If we use a moderate number of replications, the average simulator has a significant probability of taking the value zero. It is a problem for the SML method, where we have to compute the logarithm of this quantity.

(ii) Moreover, the frequency simulator is nondifferentiable (and even discontinuous) with respect to θ. This lack of smoothness does not allow the use of first order conditions, and introduces both numerical and theoretical difficulties (see Pakes and Pollard 1989).

(iii) Finally, this simulator is not very efficient for approximating the probability $p_j(z_i; \theta)$, especially when the number J is large. In such cases some probabilities p_j are small, and a rather large number of replications are needed to approximate them reasonably.

The importance sampling simulator based on latent variables

This simulator has already been introduced in examples 2.1 and 2.2. We introduce the vector v_j whose components are $v_{j\ell} = U_{ij} - U_{i\ell}$, $\ell = 1, \ldots, j-1, j+1, \ldots, J$, and whose distribution is known, up to the parameters. If $f_j(v_j/z_i; \theta)$ denotes the conditional p.d.f., we have:

$$p_j(z_i; \theta) = \int f_j(v_j/z_i; \theta) \mathbb{1}_{(v_{j\ell} > 0, \ell \neq j)} \, dv_j$$

$$= \int \frac{f_j(v_j/z_i; \theta)}{\varphi(v_j/z_i)} \mathbb{1}_{(v_{j\ell} > 0, \ell \neq j)} \varphi(v_j/z_i) \, dv_j$$

where φ is a known distribution with support $(\mathbb{R}^+)^{J-1}$. The simulator is:

$$\tilde{p}_j(z_i, v; \theta) = \frac{f_j(v/z_i; \theta)}{\varphi(v/z_i)}, \quad \text{where } v \sim \varphi(v/z_i).$$

If f_j is smooth with respect to θ, the same is true for $\tilde{p}_j$.

Note that, contrary to the frequency simulator, different simulations are used for the different alternatives j proposed to a same individual. Such a computation of approximated probabilities, alternative by alternative, will also appear in the other simulators and increases the precision of these simulators when the importance sampling functions are well chosen. Note, however, that, when different simulations are used for the different alternatives, the sum of these simulators over j is not equal to 1.

The Stern simulator

In qualitative models, including discrete choice models but also sequential choices, the main problem is to approximate the individual selection probabilities for given values of the parameter. These selection probabilities are of the form:

$$P[a_j \leq v_j \leq b_j, \quad j = 1, \ldots, m], \tag{5.9}$$

where $v = (v_1, \ldots, v_m)' \sim N(0, \Sigma)$. The values a_j, b_j and the variance–covariance matrix Σ are known as soon as we know the values of the explanatory variables and the values of the parameters. Therefore they depend on i and θ.

To build an unbiased simulator of the probability of the rectangle $D = \prod_{j=1}^m [a_j, b_j]$ for the normal distribution $N(0, \Sigma)$, Stern (1992) proposed to decompose the variance–covariance matrix Σ. Let us introduce the smallest eigenvalue λ of the matrix Σ; we have $\Sigma - \lambda I d_m \gg 0$, and therefore we can write:

$$\Sigma = \lambda I d_m + CC', \tag{5.10}$$

where C is an $(m \times m)$ matrix whose rank is $m - 1$ (or less if the multiplicity order of λ is strictly larger than 1). We deduce that the initial normal distribution $N(0, \Sigma)$ is also the distribution of:

$$v^* = Cu + \lambda w, \tag{5.11}$$

where u and w are independent, $u \sim N[0, I d_m]$, $w \sim N[0, I d_m]$.

Let us now consider the selection probability:

$$\begin{aligned} P[D] &= P\left[a_j \leq v_j^* \leq b_j, \quad j = 1, \ldots, m\right] \\ &= P\left[a_j \leq c_j u + \lambda w_j \leq b_j, \quad j = 1, \ldots, m\right], \\ &\quad \text{where } c_j \text{ is the } j\text{th row of } C, \end{aligned}$$

$$= E P \left[\frac{a_j - c_j u}{\lambda} \leq w_j \leq \frac{b_j - c_j u}{\lambda}, \quad j = 1, \ldots, m/u \right]$$

$$= E \left\{ \prod_{j=1}^{m} P \left[\frac{a_j - c_j u}{\lambda} \leq w_j \leq \frac{b_j - c_j u}{\lambda} / u \right] \right\}$$

$$= E \left\{ \prod_{j=1}^{m} \left[\Phi \left(\frac{b_j - c_j u}{\lambda} \right) - \Phi \left(\frac{a_j - c_j u}{\lambda} \right) \right] \right\}.$$

Therefore:

$$\tilde{p}(u) = \prod_{j=1}^{m} \left[\Phi \left(\frac{b_j - c_j u}{\lambda} \right) - \Phi \left(\frac{a_j - c_j u}{\lambda} \right) \right], \qquad (5.12)$$

where $u \sim N(0, Id_m)$ is an unbiased simulator of $P(D)$. This simulator is based on the general idea of conditioning introduced in previous chapters.

The GHK simulator

This simulator was first introduced by Geweke (1989) and has been used in various papers (Borsch-Supan and Hajivassiliou 1993, Hajivassiliou *et al.* 1996, Keane 1993, Hajivassiliou 1993*a, b, c*). It is sometimes called the **GHK (Geweke–Hajivassiliou–Keane) simulator**. The idea is to directly approximate the probability of a rectangle.

To simplify the presentation, we first consider the bidimensional case. We have to estimate the probability of a rectangular domain $P[v \in D] = P(v \in [a_1, b_1] \times [a_2, b_2])$, where $v \sim N(0, \Sigma)$.

We first transform the random term v to get a random vector with a standard normal distribution. The transformation may be chosen as a lower triangular matrix:

$$v = Au, \text{ where } A = \begin{bmatrix} a_{11} & 0 \\ a_{21} & a_{22} \end{bmatrix}, \quad u \sim N(0, Id_2), \quad a_{11} > 0, a_{22} > 0.$$
$$(5.13)$$

In terms of u_1, u_2 the selection probability is:

$$\begin{aligned} P[v \in D] &= P[a_1 < v_1 < b_1, \quad a_2 < v_2 < b_2] \\ &= P[a_1 < a_{11} u_1 < b_1, \quad a_2 < a_{21} u_1 + a_{22} u_2 < b_2] \\ &= P \left[\frac{a_1}{a_{11}} < u_1 < \frac{b_1}{a_{11}}, \quad \frac{a_2}{a_{22}} < \frac{a_{21}}{a_{22}} u_1 + u_2 < \frac{b_2}{a_{22}} \right] \\ &= P[\alpha_1 < u_1 < \beta_1, \quad \alpha_2 < u_2 + \gamma u_1 < \beta_2] \quad \text{(say)} \\ &= P[u \in D^*]. \end{aligned}$$

In the u-space the domain D^* has the form shown in Figure 5.1.

Now let us consider a drawing u_1^* in the standard normal distribution restricted (or conditional) to $[\alpha_1, \beta_1]$, and a drawing u_2^* in the standard normal restricted

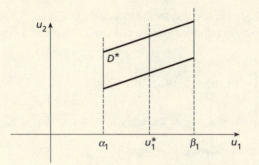

FIGURE 5.1: Domain D^*.

to $[\alpha_2 - \gamma u_1^*, \beta_2 - \gamma u_1^*]$. It is easily seen that the distribution of (u_1^*, u_2^*) is not the bivariate standard normal distribution restricted to D^*. However, an unbiased simulator of $P[v \in D]$ is:

$$\tilde{p}(u_1^*) = [\Phi(\beta_1) - \Phi(\alpha_1)][\Phi(\beta_2 - \gamma u_1^*) - \Phi(\alpha_2 - \gamma u_1^*)]. \qquad (5.14)$$

Indeed, we have:

$$
\begin{aligned}
E\tilde{p}(u_1^*) &= \int_{[\alpha_1,\beta_1]} \tilde{p}(u_1^*) \frac{\varphi(u_1^*)}{\Phi(\beta_1) - \Phi(\alpha_1)} \, du_1^* \\
&= \int_{[\alpha_1,\beta_1]} [\Phi(\beta_2 - \gamma u_1^*) - \Phi(\alpha_2 - \gamma u_1^*)]\varphi(u_1^*) \, du_1^* \\
&= P[(u_1, u_2) \in D^*].
\end{aligned}
$$

Note that u_2^* has not been used, but it has been introduced in order to prepare the general case.

Finally, it is easy to check that a drawing u_1^* in the standard normal distribution restricted to $[\alpha_1, \beta_1]$ is deduced from a drawing $\tilde{u}_1$ in the uniform distribution $U_{(0,1)}$ on $(0, 1)$ by the formula:

$$u_1^* = \Phi^{-1}\{[\Phi(\beta_1) - \Phi(\alpha_1)]\tilde{u}_1 + \Phi(\alpha_1)\}, \qquad (5.15)$$

since

$$
\begin{aligned}
P[u_1^* < x] &= P[\Phi(u_1^*) < \Phi(x)] \\
&= P\left[[\Phi(\beta_1) - \Phi(\alpha_1)]\tilde{u}_1 < \Phi(x) - \Phi(\alpha_1)\right] \\
&= [\Phi(x) - \Phi(\alpha_1)][\Phi(\beta_1) - \Phi(\alpha_1)]^{-1}.
\end{aligned}
$$

General case. Let us now consider the extension to a general dimension m. After the lower triangular transformation, the domain D^* has the following form:

$$\begin{cases} \alpha_1 \leq u_1 \leq \beta_1, \\ \alpha_2 \leq u_2 + \gamma_{21}u_1 \leq \beta_2, \\ \dots \\ \alpha_m \leq u_m + \gamma_{m,m-1}u_{m-1} + \cdots + \gamma_{m,1}u_1 \leq \beta_m. \end{cases}$$

Let us introduce the following drawings:

u_1^* in $N(0, 1)$ conditional to $[\alpha_1, \beta_1]$

u_2^* in $N(0, 1)$ conditional to $[\alpha_2 - \gamma_{21}u_1^*, \beta_2 - \gamma_{21}u_1^*]$

$\vdots$

u_{m-1}^* in $N(0, 1)$ conditional to $[\alpha_{m-1} - \gamma_{m-1,m-2}u_{m-2}^* - \cdots - \gamma_{m-1,1}u_1^*,$
$\qquad\qquad\qquad\qquad \beta_{m-1} - \gamma_{m-1,m-2}u_{m-2}^* - \cdots - \gamma_{m-1,1}u_1^*].$

An unbiased simulator of $P[u \in D^*] = P(v \in D)$ is:

$$\tilde{p}(u_1^*, \ldots, u_{m-1}^*) = [\Phi(\beta_1) - \Phi(\alpha_1)] \prod_{i=2}^{m} \{\Phi[\beta_i - \gamma_{i,i-1}u_{i-1}^* - \cdots - \gamma_{i,1}u_1^*]$$
$$-\Phi[\alpha_i - \gamma_{i,i-1}u_{i-1}^* - \cdots - \gamma_{i,1}u_1^*]\}. \tag{5.16}$$

5.2 Qualitative Models and Indirect Inference based on Multivariate Logistic Models

The indirect inference approach may be based on an approximation of the initial multivariate probit model for which the selection probabilities (or, equivalently, the log likelihood function) have a simple analytical expression. In this section we discuss an approximation based on multivariate logistic models (Gouriéroux *et al.* 1993, Gouriéroux and Jouneau 1994).

5.2.1 Approximations of a multivariate normal distribution in a neighbourhood of the no correlation hypothesis

Let us consider a random vector $Y = (Y_1, \ldots, Y_p)'$ with a Gaussian distribution $N(m, \Sigma)$. We introduce the correlation matrix R, whose entries are the correlation coefficients ρ_{ij}. The cumulative distribution function of Y is:

$$G(y_1, \ldots, y_p) = P[Y_1 < y_1, \ldots, Y_p < y_p]$$

$$= P\left(\frac{Y_1 - m_1}{\sigma_1} < \frac{y_1 - m_1}{\sigma_1}, \ldots, \frac{Y_p - m_p}{\sigma_p} < \frac{y_p - m_p}{\sigma_p}\right)$$

$$= \int_{-\infty}^{\frac{y_1 - m_1}{\sigma_1}} \cdots \int_{-\infty}^{\frac{y_p - m_p}{\sigma_1}} \frac{1}{(2\pi)^{p/2}} \frac{1}{\sqrt{\det R}} \exp\left(-\frac{1}{2} u' R^{-1} u\right) du.$$

Let us consider a neighbourhood of the no correlation hypothesis. Since R is close to the identity matrix, we have the expansion:

$$\frac{1}{(2\pi)^{p/2}} \frac{1}{\sqrt{\det R}} \exp\left(-\frac{1}{2} u' R^{-1} u\right) \simeq \frac{1}{(2\pi)^{p/2}} \exp\left[-\frac{1}{2} u'(Id + R - Id)^{-1} u\right]$$

$$\simeq \frac{1}{(2\pi)^{p/2}} \exp\left[-\frac{1}{2}[u'u - u'(R - Id)u]\right]$$

$$\simeq \frac{1}{(2\pi)^{p/2}} \left[1 + \frac{1}{2} u'(R - Id)u\right]$$

$$\times \exp\left(-\frac{1}{2} u'u\right)$$

$$= \prod_{i=1}^{p} \varphi(u_i)\left(1 + \sum_{k<\ell} \rho_{k\ell} u_k u_e\right).$$

Therefore a first order expansion of the c.d.f. is:

$$G(y_1, \ldots, y_p) \simeq \prod_{i=1}^{p} \Phi\left(\frac{y_i - m_i}{\sigma_i}\right)\left\{1 + \sum_{k<\ell} \rho_{k\ell} \frac{\varphi\left(\frac{y_k - m_k}{\sigma_k}\right)}{\Phi\left(\frac{y_k - m_k}{\sigma_k}\right)} \frac{\varphi\left(\frac{y_l - m_l}{\sigma_l}\right)}{\Phi\left(\frac{y_l - m_l}{\sigma_l}\right)}\right\}$$

$$= \tilde{G}(y_1, \ldots, y_p) \quad \text{(say).} \tag{5.17}$$

In the neighbourhood of the no correlation hypothesis, this function is also equivalent to:

$$G(y_1, \ldots, y_p) \simeq \prod_{i=1}^{p} \Phi\left[\frac{y_i - m_i}{\sigma_i} + \sum_{j<i} \rho_{ij} \frac{\varphi\left(\frac{y_j - m_j}{\sigma_j}\right)}{\Phi\left(\frac{y_j - m_j}{\sigma_j}\right)}\right]$$

$$= \tilde{\tilde{G}}(y_1, \ldots, y_p) \quad \text{(say).} \tag{5.18}$$

This is a local correction for the correlation effects by the introduction of Mill's ratios.

Finally, if we consider that the unidimensional normal distribution is well approximated by a logistic distribution,

$$\Phi(y) \simeq F\left(\frac{\pi y}{\sqrt{3}}\right), \quad \varphi(y) \simeq \frac{\pi}{\sqrt{3}} F\left(\frac{\pi y}{\sqrt{3}}\right)\left[1 - F\left(\frac{\pi y}{\sqrt{3}}\right)\right],$$

where $F(y) = [1 + \exp(-y)]^{-1}$, we get two other approximations:

$$G(y_1, \ldots, y_p) \simeq \prod_{i=1}^{p} F\left(\frac{\pi}{\sqrt{3}} \frac{y_i - m_i}{\sigma_i}\right)$$

$$\times \left[1 + \sum_{k<\ell} \frac{\pi^2 \rho_{kl}}{3} S\left(\frac{\pi}{\sqrt{3}} \frac{y_k - m_k}{\sigma_k}\right) S\left(\frac{\pi}{\sqrt{3}} \frac{y_l - m_l}{\sigma_l}\right)\right]$$

$$= \tilde{F}(y_1, \ldots, y_p) \qquad \text{(say)}, \tag{5.19}$$

and

$$G(y_1, \ldots, y_p) \simeq \prod_{i=1}^{p} F\left[\frac{\pi}{\sqrt{3}} \frac{y_i - m_i}{\sigma_i} + \sum_{j<i} \frac{\pi^2}{3} \rho_{ij} S\left(\frac{\pi}{\sqrt{3}} \frac{y_j - m_j}{\sigma_j}\right)\right]$$

$$= \tilde{\tilde{F}}(y_1, \ldots, y_p) \qquad \text{(say)}, \tag{5.20}$$

where $S(y) = 1 - F(y)$ is the survival function associated with the logistic distribution.

5.2.2   The use of the approximations when correlation is present

Let us consider the log likelihood function associated with a discrete choice model. It is given by:

$$L_n = \sum_{i=1}^{n} \sum_{j=1}^{J} y_{ij} \log P_\theta(U_{ij} > U_{i\ell}, \forall \ell \neq j)$$

$$= \sum_{i=1}^{n} \sum_{j=1}^{J} y_{ij} \log P_\theta(v_{ij\ell} < 0, \forall \ell \neq j),$$

where $\{v_{ij\ell} = U_{ie} - U_{ij}, l = 1, \ldots, j-1, j+1, \ldots, J\}$ has a multivariate normal distribution whose c.d.f. is $G(\cdot; m_{ij}(\theta), \Sigma_{ij}(\theta))$, and $m_{ij}(\theta)$ and $\Sigma_{ij}(\theta)$ denote the mean and the covariance matrix.

Therefore $L_n = \sum_{i=1}^{n} \sum_{j=1}^{J} y_{ij} \log G(0; m_{ij}(\theta), \Sigma_{ij}(\theta))$. This log likelihood function is untractable because of the multiple integrals appearing in G. However, it may be replaced by approximations such as:

$$\tilde{L}_n = \sum_{i=1}^{n} \sum_{j=1}^{J} y_{ij} \log \tilde{G}(0; m_{ij}(\beta), \Sigma_{ij}(\beta)),$$

or

$$\tilde{L}_n = \sum_{i=1}^{n} \sum_{j=1}^{J} y_{ij} \log \tilde{\tilde{G}}(0; m_{ij}(\beta), \Sigma_{ij}(\beta)),$$

or   (5.21)

$$\tilde{L}_n = \sum_{i=1}^{n} \sum_{j=1}^{J} y_{ij} \log \bar{F}(0; m_{ij}(\beta), \Sigma_{ij}(\beta)),$$

or

$$\tilde{L}_n = \sum_{i=1}^{n} \sum_{j=1}^{J} y_{ij} \log \tilde{\bar{F}}(0; m_{ij}(\beta), \Sigma_{ij}(\beta)),$$

which all lead to simple analytical forms of $\tilde{L}_n$.

These approximations can be used as the basis of the indirect inference approach. An indirect inference estimator of θ is derived by minimizing a quantity of the kind:

$$[\hat{\beta}_n - \hat{\beta}_{Sn}(\theta)]'\Omega[\hat{\beta}_n - \hat{\beta}_{Sn}(\theta)],$$

where

$$\hat{\beta}_n = \arg\max_{\beta} \tilde{L}_n(y; \beta),$$

$$\hat{\beta}_{Sn}(\theta) = \arg\max_{\beta} \sum_{s=1}^{S} \tilde{L}_n(y^s(\theta), \beta),$$

and $y^s(\theta)$ is a set of n simulated vectors $\tilde{y}_i(\theta)$ drawn from the discrete choice models.

Such an approach is consistent and has a good precision when the correlations are small (since $\tilde{L}_n$ is a good approximation of L), but also for much larger correlations. (See Appendix 5A for some Monte Carlo studies.)

5.3 Simulators for Limited Dependent Variable Models based on Gaussian Latent Variables

5.3.1 Constrained and conditional moments of a multivariate Gaussian distribution

Section 5.1 has described several simulators for probabilities of the form:

$$P\{a_j \leq v_j \leq b_j, \quad j = 1, \ldots, m\} = P[v \in D],$$

where $D = \prod_{j=1}^{m}[a_j, b_j]$ and $v = (v_1, \ldots, v_m)' \sim N(0, \Sigma)$.

It is also useful to introduce simulators of some more general moments constrained by $v \in D$. These moments may be of the form:

$$E[h(v)\mathbb{1}_D(v)] \qquad \text{(constrained moment)},$$

or:

$$E[h(v)/v \in D] = \frac{E[h(v)\mathbb{1}_D(v)]}{E[\mathbb{1}_D(v)]} \qquad \text{(conditional moment)},$$

where h is a given integrable function. For instance, conditional computations naturally appear in limited dependent variable models with truncation effects, when the variable is observed only if a given constraint $v \in D$ is satisfied. But conditional moments are also important if we perform a direct analysis of first order conditions in more classical frameworks such as discrete choice models, in particular if we apply simulated scores (see example 2.3). To illustrate this point, let us consider a Gaussian variable $\tilde{v} \sim N[\mu, \Sigma]$, and the probability:

$$P[\bar{a}_j \leq \tilde{v}_j \leq \bar{b}_j, \quad j = 1, \ldots, m] = P[a_j \leq v_j \leq b_j, \quad j = 1, \ldots, m],$$

where μ and Σ are unknown, whereas the $\bar{a}_j, \bar{b}_j$ are known, and where $v = \tilde{v} - \mu$, $a = \bar{a} - \mu, b = \bar{b} - \mu$.

The previous probability is a function of the parameters μ, Σ:

$$p[\mu, \Sigma] = \int \mathbb{1}_{\bar{D}}(\tilde{v}) \frac{1}{(2\pi)^{m/2}\sqrt{\det \Sigma}} \exp\left[-\frac{1}{2}(\tilde{v} - \mu)'\Sigma^{-1}(\tilde{v} - \mu)\right] d\tilde{v},$$

where $\bar{D} = \prod_{j=1}^{m}[\bar{a}_j, \bar{b}_j]$. When we consider the first order conditions associated with a maximum likelihood approach, we have to compute the derivatives:

$$\frac{\partial \log p}{\partial \mu}(\mu, \Sigma) \quad \text{and} \quad \frac{\partial \log p}{\partial \Sigma}(\mu, \Sigma).$$

Some direct computations give:

$$\begin{aligned}
\frac{\partial \log p}{\partial \mu}(\mu, \Sigma) &= \frac{1}{p(\mu, \Sigma)} \frac{\partial p}{\partial \mu}(\mu, \Sigma) \\
&= \frac{\Sigma^{-1} E[\mathbb{1}_{\bar{D}}(\tilde{v})(\tilde{v} - \mu)]}{E[\mathbb{1}_{\bar{D}}(\tilde{v})]} \\
&= \Sigma^{-1} E[v/v \in D],
\end{aligned}$$

and similarly:

$$\frac{\partial \log p}{\partial \Sigma}(\mu, \Sigma) = \frac{1}{2}\Sigma^{-1}[E(vv'/v \in D) - \Sigma]\Sigma^{-1}.$$

5.3.2 Simulators for constrained moments

A particular case of constrained moment $E[h(v)\mathbb{1}_D(v)]$ is the probability $P[v \in D]$, which corresponds to $h = 1$. It explains why the simulators described in this subsection are direct extensions of the ones presented in Section 5.1.3, and we will keep the same notations.

The Stern simulator

The Gaussian vector v may be decomposed in:

$$v = Cu + \lambda w,$$

where u and w are independent, $u \sim N(0, Id_m)$, $w \sim N(0, Id_m)$, and λ is a scalar, in practice the smallest eigenvalue of Σ. We have:

$$E[h(v)\mathbb{1}_D(v)] = E E[h(v)\mathbb{1}_D(v)/u].$$

Therefore $E[h(v)\mathbb{1}_D(v)/u^s]$, where u^s is drawn in the standard normal distribution $N(0, Id_m)$, is an unbiased simulator of the constrained moment. Now we have to check if the conditional expectation $E[h(v)\mathbb{1}_D(v)/u]$ has a simple analytical form. This expectation is equal to:

$$
\begin{aligned}
E[h(v)\mathbb{1}_D(v)/u] &= E[h[Cu + \lambda w]\mathbb{1}_D(Cu + \lambda w)/u] \\
&= \int h[Cu + \lambda w]\mathbb{1}_D(Cu + \lambda w) \prod_{j=1}^{m} (\varphi(w_j)\, dw_j) \\
&= \int h[Cu + \lambda w] \prod_{j=1}^{m} \mathbb{1}_{\left[\frac{a_j - C_j u}{\lambda}, \frac{b_j - C_j u}{\lambda}\right]}(w_j) \prod_{j=1}^{m} \varphi(w_j) \prod_{j=1}^{m} dw_j.
\end{aligned}
$$

Such an integral may be easily computed for some specific functions h, in particular when $h(v) = \prod_{j=1}^{m} v_j^{r_j}$. This class of h functions is interesting since we have seen that it naturally appears with $r_j = 0, 1, 2$, when we look at the score vectors. For such products of power functions, the previous multiple integral is a product of one-dimensional integrals, which are easily derived as soon as we know how to compute an expression of the form:

$$\Psi(t, \mu, r) = \int_{-\infty}^{t} (w - \mu)^r \varphi(w)\, dw, \qquad \text{for } r \in \mathbb{N}. \tag{5.22}$$

It is a simple exercise to establish the following recursion formula:

$$
\begin{aligned}
\Psi(t, \mu, 0) &= \Phi(t), \\
\Psi(t, \mu, r) &= (r - 1)\Psi(t, \mu, r - 2) - \mu\Psi(t, \mu, r - 1) \\
&\quad - (t - \mu)^{r-1}\varphi(t), \qquad \text{for } r \geq 1
\end{aligned} \tag{5.23}
$$

(with the convention $0 \cdot \Psi(t, \mu, -1) = 0$).

The GHK simulator

Let us recall that we first apply a triangular transformation A such that:

$$v = Au, \quad \text{where } u \sim N[0, Id_m].$$

Then we make explicit the constraints on u implied by $v \in D$:

$$\begin{cases} \alpha_1 \leq u_1 \leq \beta_1 \\ \alpha_2 \leq u_2 + \gamma_{2,1} u_1 \leq \beta_2 \\ \cdots \\ \alpha_m \leq u_m + \gamma_{m,m-1} u_{m-1} + \cdots + \gamma_{m,1} u_1 \leq \beta_m. \end{cases}$$

This set of constraints will be denoted:

$$u \in D^*.$$

Next, we introduce the following drawings:

u_1^* in $N(0,1)$ conditionally to $[\alpha_1, \beta_1]$,

u_2^* in $N(0,1)$ conditionally to $[\alpha_2 - \gamma_2 u_1^*, \beta_2 - \gamma_2 u_1^*]$

$\vdots$

u_m^* in $N(0,1)$ conditionally to $[\alpha_m - \gamma_{m,m-1} u_{m-1}^* - \cdots - \gamma_{m,1} u_1^*,$

$$\beta_m - \gamma_{m,m-1}, u_{m-1}^* - \cdots - \gamma_{m,1} u_1^*].$$

The distribution of $u^* = (u_1^*, \ldots, u_m^*)'$ is the **recursive truncated normal distribution** with p.d.f.:

$$g(u) = \mathbb{1}_{D^*}(u)$$

$$\times \prod_{j=1}^{m} \frac{\varphi(u_j)}{\Phi[\beta_j - \gamma_{j,j-1} u_{j-1} - \cdots - \gamma_{j,1} u_1] - \Phi[\alpha_j - \gamma_{j,j-1} u_{j-1} - \cdots - \gamma_{j1} u_1]}$$

$$= \mathbb{1}_{D^*}(u) \frac{\prod_{j=1}^{m} \varphi(u_j)}{\tilde{p}(u_1, \ldots, u_{m-1})}, \tag{5.24}$$

where $\tilde{p}$ has already been defined in (5.16) and where by convention the denominator is $\Phi(\beta_1) - \Phi(\alpha_1)$ for $j = 1$.

Proposition 5.1 | An unbiased simulator of $E[h(v) \mathbb{1}_D(v)]$ is $h[Au^*] \tilde{p}(u_1^*, \ldots, u_{m-1}^*)$, where u^* follows the recursive truncated normal distribution defined in (5.24).

Proof. We have:

$$E[h(Au^*) \tilde{p}(u_1^*, \ldots, u_{m-1}^*)]$$

$$= \int h(Au^*) \tilde{p}(u_1^*, \ldots, u_{m-1}^*) \mathbb{1}_{D^*}(u^*) \frac{\prod_{j=1}^{m} \varphi(u_j^*)}{\tilde{p}(u_1^*, \ldots, u_{m-1}^*)} \prod_{j=1}^{m} du_j^*$$

$$= \int h(Au^*) \mathbb{1}_{D^*}(u^*) \prod_{j=1}^{m} \varphi(u_j^*) \prod_{j=1}^{m} du_j^*$$

$$= E(h(Au) \mathbb{1}_{D^*}(u)), \text{ where } u \sim N(0, Id_m)$$

$$= E(h(v) \mathbb{1}_D(v)).$$

QED

The result is similar to the one derived in Section 5.1.2. Just note that it is now necessary to draw the last component u_m^* as soon as it appears in the function $h(Au^*)$.

5.3.3 Simulators for conditional moments

The question clearly is: How can the conditional distribution of v be drawn in given $v \in D$? We propose several answers to this question.

Acceptance–rejection methods

A crude acceptance–rejection method consists in drawing simulated values v^s, $s = 1, \ldots$, in the distribution of v until one of these values satisfies the constraint $v^s \in D$. This first value compatible with the domain is the first simulated value in the distribution conditional on $\{v \in D\}$. A drawback of such a practice is the large number of underlying drawings that may be necessary in order to get one effective simulated value in the conditional distribution, when $P(v \in D)$ is small.

The **accelerated acceptance–rejection method** will avoid this problem. It is based on the following lemma:

Lemma 5.1 | Let f and g be two p.d.f.s on $\mathbb{R}^m$ such that:
(i) the support of g is the domain D;
(ii) $\sup_{v \in D} \dfrac{f(v)}{g(v)} \leq \alpha < +\infty$.

Let us consider some independent drawings (v^s, x^s), $s = 1, \ldots$, of v^s in the distribution g and of x^s in the uniform distribution on $[0, 1]$.

Let us define the first drawing s_1 such that $f(v^s) \geq x^s \alpha g(v^s)$.

Then the distribution of $\tilde{v}^1 = v^{s_1}$ is:

$$ f(v) \mathbb{1}_D(v) \left[\int_D f(v) \, dv \right]^{-1}, $$

i.e. the distribution f conditional on $v \in D$.

Proof. We have:

$$
\begin{aligned}
P[v < \tilde{v}^1 < v + dv] &= P[v < v^1 < v + dv/v^1 \text{ is accepted }] \\
&= P[v < v^1 < v + dv/f(v^1) \geq x^1 \alpha g(v^1)] \\
&= \frac{P[v < v^1 < v + dv, \, f(v^1) \geq x^1 \alpha g(v^1)]}{P[f(v^1) \geq x^1 \alpha g(v^1)]} \\
&= \frac{g(v) \, dv f(v) [\alpha g(v)]^{-1}}{\int_D \frac{f(v)}{\alpha g(v)} g(v) \, dv} \mathbb{1}_D(v) \\
&= \frac{\mathbb{1}_D(v) f(v)}{\int_D f(v) \, dv} dv.
\end{aligned}
$$

QED

In this accelerated procedure the proportion of efficient drawings, i.e. the ones that satisfy the constraint, is on average:

$$
P[f(v^1) \geq x^1 \alpha g(v^1)] = \frac{\int_D f(v) \, dv}{\alpha}.
$$

Therefore from this point of view the accelerated approach is preferable to the crude one as soon as $\alpha < 1$. To get a good performance, we have to choose the auxiliary p.d.f. g such that $\bar{\alpha} = \sup_D \frac{f(v)}{g(v)}$ is as small as possible. Anyway we have:

$$
f(v) \leq \bar{\alpha} g(v), \qquad \text{if } v \in D,
$$

and by integration:

$$
\int_D f(v) \, dv \leq \bar{\alpha} \int_D g(v) \, dv = \bar{\alpha}.
$$

This gives $\int_D f(v) \, dv$ as the lower bound for $\bar{\alpha}$.

Example 5.1   Application to conditioning of the normal distribution

The previous lemma can be applied to the case of multivariate normal distributions, i.e. to simulations in the distribution of v conditional on $v \in D$, where $v \sim N[0, \Sigma]$. After some change of variable $v = Au, u \sim N[0, Id_m]$, it is equivalent to simulate in the distribution of u given $u \in D^*$, where D^* is defined in Section 5.3.2. In such a case we have:

$$
f(u) = \prod_{j=1}^m \varphi(u_j),
$$

and we may choose as auxiliary p.d.f. with support D^* the recursive truncated normal distribution (see (5.24)):

$$
g(u) = \mathbb{1}_{D^*}(u) \frac{\prod_{j=1}^m \varphi(u_j)}{\tilde{p}(u_1, \ldots, u_{m-1})}.
$$

We get:

$$\frac{f(u)}{g(u)} = \tilde{p}(u_1, \ldots, u_{m-1})$$

$$= \prod_{j=1}^{m} [\Phi(\beta_j - \gamma_{j,j-1} u_{j-1} - \cdots - \gamma_{j,1} u_1)$$

$$- \Phi(\alpha_j - \gamma_{j,j-1} u_{j-1} - \cdots - \gamma_{j,1} u_1)]$$

$$\leq \prod_{j=1}^{m} \sup_{x} [\Phi(\beta_j - x) - \Phi(\alpha_j - x)]$$

$$= \prod_{j=1}^{m} [2\Phi(\beta_j - \alpha_j) - 1].$$

The corresponding accelerated acceptance–rejection method consists in drawing some underlying simulated values—u^s in the recursive truncated normal distribution, x^s in the uniform distribution on $[0, 1]$—until the first index s_1 for which:

$$x^{s_1} \leq \frac{\tilde{p}(u_1^{s_1}, \ldots, u_{m-1}^{s_1})}{\prod_{j=1}^{m} [2\Phi(\beta_j - \alpha_j) - 1]}.$$

Then we compute $v^{s_1} = A u^{s_1}$, which follows the normal distribution $N(0, \Sigma)$ conditioned by $v \in D$.

The Gibbs sampling simulator

The basis of the Gibbs sampling is the characterization of a multivariate distribution by the set of all univariate conditional distributions.

Lemma 5.2 | Let $x = (x_1, \ldots, x_m)'$ be a random vector with a strictly positive density function $f(x)$ with respect to a product of measures $\otimes_{j=1}^{m} d\mu_j(x_j)$. Then the multivariate distribution is completely characterized by the knowledge of the conditional distributions $f_j(x_j/x_{-j})$, $j = 1, \ldots, m$, where x_{-j} stands for $(x_1, \ldots, x_{j-1}, x_{j+1}, \ldots, x_m)$, i.e. the set of all the variables except the one with index j.

Proof. We give it for the bidimensional case. Let us introduce the marginal distributions $f_1(x_1)$, $f_2(x_2)$ of x_1 and x_2. From the Bayes formula, we have:

$$f_1(x_1) = f_2(x_2) \frac{f_1(x_1/x_2)}{f_2(x_2/x_1)}.$$

Integrating with respect to $d\mu_1(x_1)$, we get:

$$f_2(x_2) = \left[\int \frac{f_1(x_1/x_2)}{f_2(x_2/x_1)} \, d\mu_1(x_1) \right]^{-1}.$$

Therefore the marginal distributions (and also the joint distribution) are known as soon as we know the two conditional distributions.

QED

Remark 5.1

The condition of strict positivity of the multivariate p.d.f. is necessary for the characterization, as shown by the following counterexample. The distributions $P_\alpha = \alpha U_{(0,\frac{1}{2})}^{\otimes 2} + (1 - \alpha) U_{(\frac{1}{2},1)}^{\otimes 2}$, where $\alpha \in [0, 1]$, have the same conditional distributions. These conditional distributions are either $U_{(0,\frac{1}{2})}$ or $U_{(\frac{1}{2},1)}$ and are independent of the scalar α.

Proposition 5.2 | Let $f_j(x_j/x_{-j})$ be the conditional p.d.f. associated with a multivariate p.d.f. $f(x)$. We recursively define a Markov process of order 1, $x^\tau = (x_1^\tau, \dots, x_m^\tau)$, in the following way:

(i) x^0 is given;

(ii) the distribution of x_1^τ given $x^{\tau-1}$ is: $f_1(x_1^\tau / x_2^{\tau-1}, \dots, x_m^{\tau-1}) = f_1(x_1^\tau / x_{-1}^{\tau-1})$; the distribution of x_2^τ given $x_1^\tau, x^{\tau-1}$ is: $f_2(x_2^\tau / x_1^\tau, x_3^{\tau-1}, \dots, x_m^{\tau-1})$;

$\vdots$

the distribution of x_m^τ given $x_1^\tau, \dots, x_{m-1}^\tau, x^{\tau-1}$ is: $f_m(x_m^\tau / x_1^\tau, \dots, x_{m-1}^\tau) = f_m(x_m^\tau / x_{-m}^\tau)$.

Then the stationary distribution of the Markov process is f.

Proof. We will check the property for the bidimensional case. Let us assume that the distribution of $x^{\tau-1}$ is $f(x_1^{\tau-1}, x_2^{\tau-1})$; we have to prove that the distribution of x^τ is also f. The marginal distribution of x_1^τ is:

$$\int \int f_1(x_1^\tau / x_2^{\tau-1}) f(x_1^{\tau-1}, x_2^{\tau-1}) \, dx_1^{\tau-1} \, dx_2^{\tau-1}$$

$$= \int f_1(x_1^\tau / x_2^{\tau-1}) f_2(x_2^{\tau-1}) \, dx_2^{\tau-1}$$

$$= f_1(x_1^\tau),$$

(where $f_1(x_1)$ and $f_2(x_2)$ are the marginal p.d.f.s of $f(x_1, x_2)$).

Since the conditional distribution of x_2^τ given x_1^τ is $f_2(x_2^\tau / x_1^\tau)$, the result follows.

QED

From the previous property we can approximately simulate a drawing in f in the following way (called the Gibbs sampler):

(i) First we choose some initial value x^0.

(ii) Then we successively draw in the conditional distributions following the procedure of Proposition (5.2), to derive a simulated path of the Markov process $x^{\tau,s}$, $\tau = 0, \ldots, T$.

It is possible to prove that there exists a number ρ, $0 < \rho < 1$, such that, for any function h,

$$\left| Eh(x^{T,s}) - \int h(x) f(x) \, dx \right| < K_h \rho^T, \tag{5.25}$$

where K_h is a constant depending on h.

Therefore, for T sufficiently large, $x^{T,s}$ may be considered a good approximation of a drawing in f. Note that the x^τs, $\tau > T$, can also be considered as drawn from f, but that they are not independent.

Example 5.2 Application to the conditioning of a normal distribution

Let us apply the previous approach to a drawing of a value $\tilde{v}$ from the normal distribution $N[0, \Sigma]$ conditioned by $\tilde{v} \in D = \prod_{j=1}^m [a_j, b_j]$. The multivariate distribution is:

$$f_D(\tilde{v}) = \mathbb{1}_D(\tilde{v}) \frac{1}{P[v \in D]} \frac{1}{(2\pi)^{m/2}\sqrt{\det \Sigma}} \exp\left(-\frac{1}{2}\tilde{v}'\Sigma^{-1}\tilde{v}\right),$$

where $v \sim N[0, \Sigma]$.

The p.d.f. is difficult to use directly since $P[v \in D]$ has an intractable form. What about the different univariate conditional distributions? The conditional p.d.f.s are such that:

$$\begin{aligned}
f_j(w_j/\tilde{v}_{-j}) \, dw_j &\simeq P[w_j < \tilde{v}_j < w_j + dw_j/\tilde{v}_{-j}] \\
&= P[w_j < v_j < w_j + dw_j/v_{-j} = \tilde{v}_{-j}, v \in D] \\
&= P[w_j < v_j < w_j + dw_j/v_{-j} = \tilde{v}_{-j}, a_j < v_j < b_j],
\end{aligned}$$

since the components $\tilde{v}_k$, $k \neq j$, already satisfy the constraints. Therefore we see that the density function $f_j(w_j/\tilde{v}_{-j})$ is the p.d.f. of the conditional distribution of v_j given $v_{-j} = \tilde{v}_{-j}$, reconditioned by $v_j \in [a_j, b_j]$. The conditional distribution of v_j given $v_{-j} = \tilde{v}_{-j}$ is the normal distribution:

$$N[0, \sigma_{c,j}^2],$$

where

$$\begin{aligned}
\sigma_{c,j}^2 &= \Sigma_{jj} - \Sigma_{j,-j}(\Sigma_{-j,-j})^{-1}\Sigma_{-j,j}, \\
\Sigma_{jj} &= V(v_j), \quad \Sigma_{j,-j} = \text{cov}(v_j, v_{-j}), \quad \Sigma_{-j,-j} = V(v_{-j}).
\end{aligned}$$

The conditional p.d.f. $f_j(\tilde{v}_j/\tilde{v}_{-j})$ is directly deduced, and has an analytical form:

$$f_j(\tilde{v}_j/\tilde{v}_{-j}) = \mathbb{1}_{(a_j,b_j)}(\tilde{v}_j) \frac{1}{\Phi\left(\dfrac{b_j}{\sigma_{c,j}}\right) - \Phi\left(\dfrac{a_j}{\sigma_{c,j}}\right)} \frac{1}{\sigma_{c,j}\sqrt{2\pi}} \exp\left(-\frac{1}{2}\frac{\tilde{v}_j^2}{\sigma_{c,j}^2}\right).$$

Therefore the successive conditional drawings of the Gibbs sampling will be easily performed.

5.4 Empirical Studies

In this section we briefly describe empirical studies that have appeared in the literature. Essentially, we consider models that could not have been estimated without simulation techniques, because of the presence of high dimensional integrals.

5.4.1 Labour supply and wage equation

Following the seminal approach by Heckman (1981), the labour force participation is based on the comparison of the maximum wage offered and the reservation wage. More precisely, let us consider a panel data set on n individuals, $i = 1, \ldots, n$, each observed at periods $t = 1, \ldots, T$. We write the latent model as:

$$\begin{cases} \log w_{it} = m_{it} + u_{it}, \\ y_{it}^* = \log w_{it} - \log w_{it}^* = \mu_{it} + v_{it}, \end{cases} \tag{5.26}$$

where w_{it}, w_{it}^* are the offered and reservation wages respectively, m_{it}, μ_{it} are the conditional means, and u_{it}, v_{it} some error terms. These latent variables are used to define the sequence of individual decisions: the worker i is unemployed at $t \iff y_{it}^* < 0$.

Let an indicator dummy variable be defined as $d_{it} = 0$ iff $y_{it}^* < 0$, and $d_{it} = 1$ otherwise. Then the employment–unemployment history of the individual is characterized by the vector of indicators $d_{i1}, \ldots, d_{iT}$.

For studying some questions such as the persistence of aggregate unemployment or its evolution over the business cycle, it is necessary to specify carefully all the dynamic aspects of the latent model. It is known that for duration models several dependences have to be considered:

- the state dependence, i.e. the effect of the current state occupied by an individual;

- the duration dependence, i.e. the effect of the length of the current spell of unemployment; a spurious duration dependence may also be due to unobserved individual heterogeneity;

- the history dependence, e.g. the effect of the cumulated length of unemployment spells before the current spell (lagged duration dependence), or the effect of the number of past spells (occurrence dependence);

- the habit persistence, i.e. effect of lagged values of w_{it}, w_{it}^*, ...

In summary, the dynamic aspects may be captured either by introducing some lagged endogenous variables among the explanatory variables, or by considering some particular structures of the error terms, such as a decomposition in an unobserved individual effect (the omitted heterogeneity), or an additional time individual term with an autoregressive structure—for instance,

$$\begin{cases} u_{it} = \alpha_i + \tilde{u}_{it}, \\ \tilde{u}_{i,t} = \rho\tilde{u}_{i,t-1} + \varepsilon_{i,t}, \end{cases} \qquad \begin{cases} v_{it} = \beta_i + \tilde{v}_{i,t}, \\ \tilde{v}_{i,t} = r\tilde{v}_{i,t-1} + \eta_{it}, \end{cases} \tag{5.27}$$

where α_i, β_i, $\varepsilon_{i,t}$, $\eta_{i,t}$ are independent Gaussian variables, with zero mean and variances σ_α^2, σ_β^2, σ_ε^2, σ_η^2, respectively.

The estimation of the parameters may be based on different kinds of observation. In practice, these observations may correspond either to the states d_{it}, $i = 1, \ldots, N$, $t = 1, \ldots, T$ (if it is a pure discrete time duration model—see Muhleisen 1993), or to observations of the states d_{it} and of the wage w_{it} when the worker is employed, $d_{it} = 1$ (see e.g. Bloemen and Kapteyn 1990, Keane 1993, Magnac, Robin and Visser 1995). In such a nonlinear framework, even the estimations of the coefficients of the static explanatory variables may be very sensitive to misspecifications of the dynamics.

To examine this point, we reproduce in Table 5.1 some results obtained in Muhleisen (1993). The parameters are estimated by optimizing a simulated log likelihood function. Since this likelihood is a function of some probabilities associated with the multivariate normal distribution, the GHK simulator has been used. Because the performance of the GHK estimator depends on the accuracy of the computations, owing to its recursive structure, a pseudo-random number generator with 20-digit precision has been used (Kennedy and Gentle 1980).

5.4.2 Test of the rational expectation hypothesis from business survey data[1]

The main assumption for rational expectations (RE) is that prediction errors are uncorrelated with any variable in the information available at the previous date. If y_t^* is the variable to be predicted, and y_t^{*e} is the expectation of this variable held at date $t - 1$, the RE assumption implies for instance that the linear regression of y_t^* on y_t^{*e}, y_{t-1}^*, y_{t-1}^{*e},

$$y_t^* = a_0 + a_1 y_t^{*e} + a_2 y_{t-1}^* + a_3 y_{t-1}^{*e} + u_t, \tag{5.28}$$

---

[1]See Nerlove and Schuermann (1992).

TABLE 5.1: The participation equation[a].

Variable	AR(1) error	AR(1) error + random effect
Constant	2.74 (4.5)	2.72 (4.4)
Age (130)	1.23 (1.3)	1.93 (1.3)
Age^2/1000	−0.55 (1.4)	−0.55 (1.4)
Nationality (1 = foreign)	−0.013 (0.14)	−0.023 (0.24)
Disability (1 = yes)	−0.22 (2.12)	−0.22 (2.13)
No. of children (age 0–6)	0.04 (0.51)	0.04 (0.5)
(age 7–10)	−0.12 (1.6)	−0.11 (1.6)
(age 11–15)	−0.14 (1.8)	−0.13 (1.8)
Partnership (1 = yes)	0.06 (0.6)	0.07 (0.6)
State (1 = north/west)	−0.24 (2.7)	−0.24 (2.6)
Region (1 = rural)	−0.06 (0.6)	−0.06 (0.7)
Years of schooling/10	0.15 (0.8)	0.16 (0.8)
Job status (1 = blue collar)	−0.23 (2.4)	−0.23 (2.3)
Union membership	0.09 (1.2)	0.09 (1.1)
$d_{i,t-1}$	−2.35 (15.2)	−2.44 (13.5)
$d_{i,t-2}$	−0.015 (0.13)	0.05 (0.38)
$d_{i,t-3}$	−0.25 (2.5)	−0.23 (2.30)
$d_{i,t-4}$	−0.49 (4.0)	−0.47 (3.8)
$\prod_{j=1}^{4} d_{i,t-j}$	−0.05 (0.3)	−0.05 (0.3)
Lagged unemployment	−0.07 (6.0)	−0.07 (5.8)
Male unemployment rate	−0.98 (3.4)	−0.98 (3.4)
σ_α^2		0.015 (0.40)
ρ	0.14 (1.9)	0.090 (0.99)

[a] The data are taken from six waves of the Socio-Economic Panel for West Germany for the years 1984–1989, and concern 12 000 individuals. The estimations are performed using only the history of the states, and two schemes are considered for the error term v_{it}: a pure autoregressive scheme $\beta_i = 0$, and the complete scheme also including the random effect β_i. The different explanatory variables, including some lagged endogenous ones, are included in a linear way in μ_{it}.

is such that $a_0 = a_2 = a_3 = 0$, $a_1 = 1$.

In practice, it is possible to have some time–individual data on expectations and realizations from business surveys. Unfortunately, these data are qualitative, with alternatives such as:

$$\nearrow \quad \longrightarrow \quad \searrow .$$

In a first approach we may consider that such data are deduced from the underlying quantitative variable by truncation. For instance, the qualitative variable associated with y_{it}^* is:

$$y_{it} = \begin{cases} 1\,(\searrow), & \text{if } y_{it}^* \leq z_{it}b - \alpha, \\ 2\,(\rightarrow), & \text{if } z_{it}b - \alpha < y_{it}^* < z_{it}b + \alpha, \\ 3\,(\nearrow), & \text{if } z_{it}b + \alpha < y_{it}^*, \end{cases} \tag{5.29}$$

where i is the individual index and t the date. Let us consider the simple case of two dates, $T - 1$ and T. We may specify the distribution of the latent variables $y_{i,T}^*, y_{i,T}^{*e}, y_{i,T-1}^*, y_{i,T-1}^{*e}$ as multivariate normal:

$$\begin{bmatrix} y_{i,T}^* \\ y_{i,T}^{*e} \\ y_{i,T-1}^* \\ y_{i,T-1}^{*e} \end{bmatrix} \sim N \left[\begin{pmatrix} z_{i,T}c \\ z_{i,T}d \\ z_{i,T-1}c \\ z_{i,T-1}d \end{pmatrix}, \begin{pmatrix} \sigma_{11} & \sigma_{12} & \sigma_{13} & \sigma_{14} \\ & \sigma_{22} & \sigma_{23} & \sigma_{24} \\ & & \sigma_{11} & \sigma_{12} \\ & & & \sigma_{22} \end{pmatrix} \right],$$

where $z_{i,T}$ are observable exogenous variables and where there is independence between individuals. The associated distribution of the qualitative observed variables $(y_{i,T}, y_{i,T}^e, y_{i,T-1}, y_{i,T-1}^e)$, $i = 1, \ldots, N$, will contain four-dimensional integrals and will depend on the parameter $\theta = (c', d', b', \alpha, \sigma_{ij})'$.

Nerlove and Schuermann (1992) have estimated such a multinomial probit model (without explanatory variables), and considered the test of the RE hypothesis. It requires a preliminary transformation of the constraints ($a_0 = a_2 = a_3 = 0$, $a_1 = 1$) into constraints on the components of θ. Such constraints include:

$$c = d, \quad \sigma_{12} = \sigma_{22}, \quad \ldots .$$

The sample consisted of 1007 manufacturing firms for the fourth quarter of 1986 ($T - 1$) and the first quarter of 1987 (T), and the estimation has been performed using the smooth recursive conditioning simulator (GHK). The number of replications was 20. The RE hypothesis has been rejected from the set of data.

Appendix 5A: Some Monte Carlo Studies

As seen in Chapter 4, the asymptotic and finite sample properties of indirect inference estimators are improved if the auxiliary model or criterion is well chosen, especially if the binding function is close to the identity function in the just identified case. Therefore it may be useful to evaluate the approximations of the bivariate

Gaussian c.d.f. proposed in Section 4.2. Let us denote by $\Phi_2(x, y; \rho)$ the c.d.f. of the normal distribution:

$$N\left[\begin{pmatrix} 0 \\ 0 \end{pmatrix}, \begin{pmatrix} 1 & \rho \\ \rho & 1 \end{pmatrix}\right],$$

and let us consider the approximated c.d.f. of the form:

$$G(x, y, r, m_x, m_y, \sigma_x, \sigma_y)$$
$$= \frac{1}{\sigma_x \sigma_y} \Phi\left(\frac{x - m_x}{\sigma_x}\right) \Phi\left(\frac{y - m_y}{\sigma_y}\right)$$
$$\times \left\{1 + r\left[1 - \Phi\left(\frac{x - m_x}{\sigma_x}\right)\right]\left[1 - \Phi\left(\frac{y - m_y}{\sigma_y}\right)\right]\right\}.$$

Then we may look at the solution of the minimization problem

$$\min_{r, m_x, m_y, \sigma_x, \sigma_y} \bar{K}(m_x, m_y, \sigma_x, \sigma_y, r, \rho),$$

where:

$$\bar{K}(m_x, m_y, \sigma_x, \sigma_y, r, \rho)$$
$$= \int\int_{\mathcal{R}^2} \varphi(x, y; \rho) K(x, y, m_x, m_y, \sigma_x, \sigma_y, r, \rho) \, dx \, dy,$$
$$K(x, y, m_x, m_y, \sigma_x, \sigma_y, r, \rho)$$
$$= \Phi_2(x, y; \rho) \log \frac{\Phi_2(x, y; \rho)}{G(x, y, r, m_x, m_y, \sigma_x, \sigma_y)}$$
$$+ [1 - \Phi_2(x, y, \rho)] \log \frac{1 - \Phi_2(x, y, \rho)}{1 - G(x, y, r, m_x, m_y, \sigma_x, \sigma_y)}.$$

The criterion $\bar{K}$ is a Kullback–Leibler information criterion measuring a discrepancy between the two distributions Φ_2 and G, where Φ_2 corresponds to the initial model, and the observations are qualitative and dichotomous. The solution of the minimization problem gives the values of the binding function for the values of the parameters 0, 0 (for the means), 1, 1 (for the variances), and ρ for the correlation. It is easily checked that the two components of the binding function associated with the means are equal, $m_x(\rho) = m_y(\rho)$, and that the same is true for the components associated with the variances $\sigma_x(\rho) = \sigma_y(\rho)$. Figures 5A.1–5A.3 describe the three functions $m_x(\rho)$, $\sigma_x(\rho)$, and $r(\rho)$. It is directly seen that the approximation has nice properties in the domain $\rho \in [0, \frac{1}{3}]$ since for these values of ρ we have:

$$m_x(\rho) \simeq 0, \qquad \sigma_x(\rho) \simeq 1, \qquad r(\rho) \simeq \rho.$$

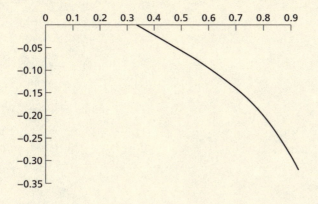

FIGURE 5A.1: The component of the binding function $m_x(\cdot)$.

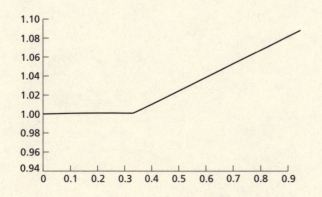

FIGURE 5A.2: The component of the binding function $\sigma_x(\cdot)$.

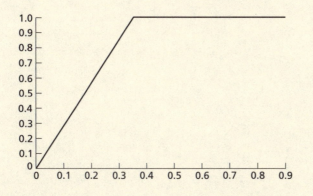

FIGURE 5A.3: The component of the binding function $r(\cdot)$.

6

Applications to Financial Series

6.1 Estimation of Stochastic Differential Equations from Discrete Observations by Indirect Inference

6.1.1 The principle

Models without factors

Let us consider a continuous time process satisfying a stochastic differential equation:

$$dy_t = g(\theta, y_t)\, dt + h(\theta, y_t)\, dW_t, \tag{6.1}$$

where (W_t) is a standard Brownian motion. If the only available observations correspond to integer dates $1, 2, \ldots, T$, it is not possible in general to determine the analytical form of the density of the observations $\ell(y_1, \ldots, y_T; \theta)$. However, the path of the continuous time process (y_t) may be simulated with a good accuracy. The idea is to introduce the discrete time analogue (or Euler approximation) of (6.1) corresponding to a small time unit δ (such that $1/\delta$ is an integer). More precisely, we define the process $\left(y_t^{(\delta)}\right)$ such that:

$$y_t^{(\delta)} = y_{k\delta}^{(\delta)} \qquad \text{if} \quad k\delta \le t < (k+1)\delta, \tag{6.2}$$

where

$$y_{(k+1)\delta}^{(\delta)} = y_{k\delta}^{(\delta)} + \delta g\left(\theta, y_{k\delta}^{(\delta)}\right) + h\left(\theta, y_{k\delta}^{(\delta)}\right)\sqrt{\delta}\varepsilon_k^{(\delta)},$$

and $(\varepsilon_k^{(\delta)}, k$ varying$)$ is a Gaussian white noise with unit variance.

Then, for each parameter value θ, we can simulate $y_{k\delta}^{(\delta)s}(\theta)$, $k = 1, \ldots, [T/\delta]$, $s = 1, \ldots, S$, using (6.2), and deduce simulated values for the observation dates by just selecting the values corresponding to integer indexes:

$$y_t^s(\theta) = y_t^{(\delta)s}(\theta) \quad \text{(i.e. with } k = t/\delta). \tag{6.3}$$

It is known that $\left(y_t^{(\delta)}\right)$ tends in distribution to (y_t) when δ tends to zero at a sufficient rate (see e.g. Guard 1988). Therefore (6.3) will provide an accurate simulation of y as soon as δ is sufficiently small.

Instrumental models

Different instrumental models may be introduced to estimate the parameter θ of the diffusion equation. The most natural one is the discrete time version of (6.1) with the time unit $\delta = 1$:

$$y_t = y_{t-1} + g(\beta, y_{t-1}) + h(\beta, y_{t-1})\varepsilon_t \quad (M^a). \tag{6.4}$$

This is a nonlinear autoregressive model, with an explicit form of the log likelihood function:

$$L_T^a(\beta) = \sum_{t=1}^{T} \left\{ -\frac{1}{2} \log 2\pi - \frac{1}{2} \log h^2(\beta, y_{t-1}) - \frac{1}{2} \frac{[y_t - y_{t-1} - g(\beta, y_{t-1})]^2}{h^2(\beta, y_{t-1})} \right\}. \tag{6.5}$$

The pseudo-maximum likelihood estimator $\hat{\beta}_T = \arg_\beta \max L_T^a(\beta)$ is frequently used in financial applications to estimate θ_0, but it is inconsistent. The indirect inference approach based on L_T^a will correct the bias arising from the time discretization.

It is also possible to introduce some other kinds of auxiliary models, such as GARCH models, as suggested in Engle and Lee (1994).

Models with factors

A similar approach may be followed for more general models based on the evolution of underlying factors, y_t^* say. These models may be written:

$$\begin{cases} dy_t^* = g(\theta, y_t^*) \, dt + h(\theta, y_t^*) \, dW_t, \\ y_t = a(y_t^*), \end{cases} \tag{6.6}$$

where a is given. The different processes may be multivariate with corresponding sizes for the matricial functions.

Well-known examples of such models include stochastic volatility models. Such models contain a subsystem describing the evolution of asset prices S_t (say), and a second subsystem giving the evolution of some state variables with an effect on the price volatility:

$$\begin{cases} dS_t = \mu_\theta[S_t, \sigma_\theta(Z_t)] \, dt + \sigma_\theta(Z_t) \, dW_t^S, \\ dZ_t = g_\theta(Z_t) \, dt + \gamma_\theta(Z_t) \, dW_t^Z, \end{cases} \tag{6.7}$$

where $\binom{W_t^S}{W_t^Z}$ is a Brownian motion, with possible instantaneous correlation (see e.g. Scott 1987, Wiggins 1987, Hull and White 1987, for pricing problems in this framework). In practice, the only available observations are price values at discrete dates, and the factors driving the volatility are unobserved.

As above, it is possible to simulate $(y_1, \ldots, y_T) = (S_1, \ldots, S_T)$ by using a time discretization of system (6.7) with a small time unit δ. In this simulation step it is necessary jointly to simulate the observable and latent processes $\left[S_t^{(\delta)}, Z_t^{(\delta)} \right]$.

The discretized version of (6.7) with time unit $\delta = 1$ may be chosen as auxiliary model (M^a). It is given by:

$$\begin{cases} S_t = S_{t-1} + \mu_\theta[S_{t-1}, \sigma_\theta(Z_{t-1})] + \sigma_\theta(Z_{t-1})\varepsilon_t^S, \\ Z_t = Z_{t-1} + g_\theta(Z_{t-1}) + \gamma_\theta(Z_{t-1})\varepsilon_t^Z, \\ \text{where } \begin{pmatrix} \varepsilon_t^S \\ \varepsilon_t^Z \end{pmatrix} \text{ is a Gaussian white noise with variance–covariance matrix } \Omega. \end{cases}$$

$$(6.8)$$

The auxiliary parameter is $\beta = [\theta', \text{vech}\, \Omega']'$. System (6.8) defines a nonlinear state space modelling for which the likelihood function has an untractable form. However the parameters β may be estimated by some Kalman filter type methods (see Section 6.3.2). These methods would give inconsistent estimators of β even if (6.8) were valid; however, first, (6.8) is an approximated model; second, we are interested in consistent estimators of θ not of β; and third, indirect inference will correct for the inconsistency.

Some other examples of factor models are time deformed processes (see e.g. Clark 1973, and Ghysels *et al.* 1994a). In such models we introduce two underlying processes: (i) a price process, expressed in intrinsic time (market time) and following a stochastic differential equation:

$$dS_t^* = \mu(S_t^*)\, dt + \sigma(S_t^*)\, dW_t^*,$$

and (ii) the changing time process Z, which gives the relation between calendar time and market time. This increasing process may also be assumed to follow a stochastic differential equation:

$$dZ_t = a(Z_t)\, dt + b(Z_t)\, dC_t,$$

where the two processes (W_t^*) and (C_t) are independent Brownian and gamma processes, respectively.

The observations are the prices at some discrete dates in calendar time, S_t, $t = 1, \ldots, T$, where $S_t = S_{Z_t}^*$.

In the following subsections we describe several applications of this kind which have recently appeared in the literature.

6.1.2   Comparison between indirect inference and full maximum likelihood methods

Such comparisons are possible only for specific models for which the distribution of discretized observations is tractable. Two Monte Carlo studies are presented below and correspond to the geometric Brownian motion and the Ornstein–Uhlenbeck models (see Gouriéroux *et al.* 1993, and Broze *et al.* 1995a).

Geometric Brownian motion with drift

This well-known model has been widely used in finance and is the basis of the derivation of the Black–Scholes formula for option pricing. The price y_t of the underlying asset is assumed to satisfy the stochastic differential equation:

$$\frac{dy_t}{y_t} = \mu\,dt + \sigma\,dW_t, \tag{6.9}$$

where W_t is a standard Brownian motion and μ and σ are the drift and volatility parameters respectively. By applying Ito's formula, we get the equivalent form:

$$d(\log y_t) = \left(\mu - \frac{\sigma^2}{2}\right)dt + \sigma\,dW_t. \tag{6.10}$$

We deduce from (6.10) the exact discretized version of (6.9), which corresponds to a random walk with drift in the log price:

$$\log y_t = \log y_{t-1} + \left(\mu - \frac{\sigma^2}{2}\right) + \sigma\varepsilon_t, \quad (\varepsilon_t) \sim \text{IIN}(0, 1), \tag{6.11}$$

and to a lognormal distribution for the price. Therefore the parameters μ, σ may be estimated by the full maximum likelihood method, i.e. by:

$$(\hat{\mu}_1, \hat{\sigma}_1^2)' = \arg\max_{\mu,\sigma^2}\left[-\frac{T}{2}\log 2\pi - \frac{T}{2}\log\sigma^2 \right.$$
$$\left. -\frac{1}{2\sigma^2}\sum_{t=1}^{T}\left(\log y_t - \log y_{t-1} - \mu + \frac{\sigma^2}{2}\right)^2\right].$$

We may also introduce the direct Euler approximation of (6.9):

$$\begin{aligned} y_t &= y_{t-1} + \mu^* y_{t-1} + \sigma^* y_{t-1}\varepsilon_t^* \\ &= (1 + \mu^*)y_{t-1} + \sigma^* y_{t-1}\varepsilon_t^*, \quad (\varepsilon_t^*) \sim \text{IIN}(0, 1), \end{aligned} \tag{6.12}$$

which gives an autoregressive form for (y_t) with some conditional heteroscedasticity. A naive estimator is derived by taking the (pseudo-)maximum likelihood estimator corresponding to (6.12):

$$(\hat{\mu}_2, \hat{\sigma}_2^2)' = \arg\max_{\mu,\sigma^2}\left[-\frac{T}{2}\log 2\pi \right.$$
$$\left. -\frac{1}{2}\sum_{t=1}^{T}\log(\sigma^2 y_{t-1}^2) - \frac{1}{2}\sum_{t=1}^{T}\frac{(y_t - (1 + \mu)y_{t-1})^2}{\sigma^2 y_{t-1}^2}\right].$$

This estimator is equal to the empirical moments:

$$\hat{\mu}_2 = \frac{1}{T} \sum_{t=1}^{T} \frac{y_t}{y_{t-1}} - 1, \qquad \hat{\sigma}_2^2 = \frac{1}{T} \sum_{t=1}^{T} \left(\frac{y_t}{y_{t-1}} - \frac{1}{T} \sum_{t=1}^{T} \frac{y_t}{y_{t-1}} \right)^2.$$

It is inconsistent, since the discretization (6.12) is not the right one. The asymptotic bias is easily derived. For $\hat{\mu}_2$, we have:

$$E\hat{\mu}_2 = E\left(\frac{y_t}{y_{t-1}}\right) - 1 = E \exp\left(\log \frac{y_t}{y_{t-1}}\right) - 1$$

$$= E\left[\exp\left(\mu - \frac{\sigma^2}{2} + \sigma \varepsilon_t\right)\right] - 1$$

$$= \exp\left(\mu - \frac{\sigma^2}{2}\right) E(\exp \sigma \varepsilon_t) - 1$$

$$= \exp \mu - 1. \qquad \text{(from 6.11)}$$

The bias, i.e. $E\hat{\mu}_2 - \mu = (\exp \mu) - (1 + \mu)$, is always positive. Finally, we can correct for this bias by applying indirect inference on the basis of the auxiliary model (6.12). We get a third estimator, $(\hat{\mu}_3, \hat{\sigma}_3^2)$.

To compare the properties of these three methods—maximum likelihood, naive, and indirect inference—we reproduce in figures 6.1 and 6.2 the results of a Monte Carlo study (with 200 replications). The true values of the parameters are $\mu = 0.2$, $\sigma = 0.5$, and the number of observations is $T = 150$. Indirect inference is applied with $S = 1$ simulation and with $\delta = 1/10$.

The positive bias of the naive estimator, and the complete correction by indirect inference, are clearly seen in the two figures. The indirect inference estimator is even less biased in finite samples than the ML estimator for the volatility parameter (see Section 4.4). Of course, the distribution of the indirect inference estimator is less concentrated than the distribution of the ML estimator, a consequence of the asymptotic efficiency of the latter. But we have to remind ourselves that the indirect inference method has been performed with only one replication and that the concentration might have been improved by increasing the number S. Table 6.1 summarizes the statistical properties of the three estimators.

Estimation of an Ornstein–Uhlenbeck process

An Ornstein–Uhlenbeck process is a solution of the differential equation:

$$dy_t = k(a - y_t)\, dt + \sigma\, dW_t. \qquad (6.13)$$

It is a three parameter model, with a mean reverting effect: if y_t is at some date far from a, it tends to go back to this value in the following periods (if k is positive). k is a return to the mean parameter, σ the volatility, and a a 'long-run

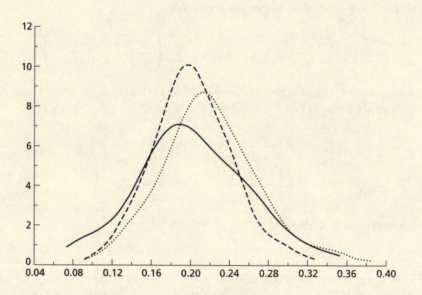

FIGURE 6.1: Geometric Brownian motion, estimation of μ: ——— indirect estimator, – – – ML estimator, $\cdots\cdots$ naive estimator.

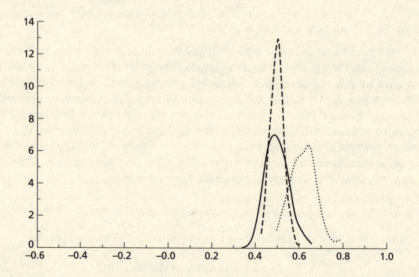

FIGURE 6.2: Geometric Brownian motion, estimation of σ: ——— indirect estimator, – – – ML estimator, $\cdots\cdots$ naive estimator.

TABLE 6.1: First and second order moments.

Estimator		Mean	Bias	Standard deviation	Root mean square error
ML	μ	0.201	0.001	0.040	0.040
	σ	0.503	0.003	0.030	0.030
Indirect	μ	0.201	0.001	0.057	0.057
	σ	0.499	−0.001	0.087	0.087
Naive	μ	0.220	0.020	0.049	0.053
	σ	0.624	0.124	0.061	0.138

equilibrium' around which the path (y_t) is varying. Such a model also admits an exact discretization, which is:

$$y_t = a(1 - \exp(-k)) + (\exp(-k))y_{t-1} + \sigma \left(\frac{1 - \exp(-2k)}{2k} \right)^{1/2} \varepsilon_t, \quad (6.14)$$

where $(\varepsilon_t) \sim \mathrm{IIN}(0, 1)$. It corresponds to a linear autoregressive formulation of order 1. It provides some other interpretations of parameters: for instance, the value of k is directly linked with the serial autocorrelation, while a is the mean of the process.

As in the previous subsection, we are going to compare three estimation methods: the ML estimator based on (6.14), the PML (or naive) estimator based on the crude discretization

$$y_t = y_{t-1} + k^*(a^* - y_{t-1}) + \sigma^*\varepsilon_t^*, \quad (\varepsilon_t^*) \sim \mathrm{IIN}(0, 1),$$

and the indirect inference estimator, also based on (6.15). In this simple example it is easy to look for asymptotic properties of the naive estimator since (6.14) and (6.15) have the same structure. The limits for the naive estimators are:

$$a^* = a, \qquad k^* = 1 - \exp(-k) < k, \qquad \sigma^* = \sigma \left(\frac{1 - \exp(-2k)}{2k} \right)^{1/2} < \sigma.$$

Therefore the bias correction by indirect inference is essentially useful for the two parameters k, σ; in fact, it turns out that the ML and the naive estmators of a and a^* are identical. Figures 6.3 and 6.4 give the distributions of the three estimators, where the Monte Carlo study has been performed with $k = 0.8, a = 0.1, \sigma = 0.06$, $T = 250, S = 1$, and a simulation time unit of $1/10$.

6.1.3 Specification of the volatility

The previous two examples are very specific since the associated continuous time models have exact discretizations, which is not the case in more general frameworks. However, we have seen that indirect inference is a good way to correct the

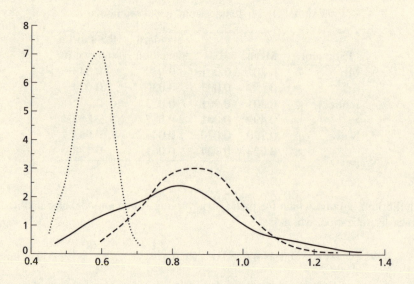

FIGURE 6.3: The Ornstein–Uhlenbeck process, estimation of k: ——— indirect estimator, – – – ML estimator, · · · · · · naive estimator.

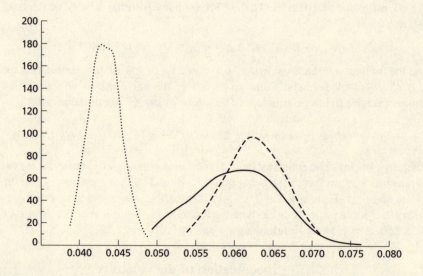

FIGURE 6.4: The Ornstein–Uhlenbeck process, estimation of σ: ——— indirect estimator, – – – ML estimator, · · · · · · naive estimator.

TABLE 6.2: First and second order moments of the estimators.

Estimator		Mean	Bias	Standard deviation	Root mean square error
ML	k	0.859	0.059	0.122	0.135
	a	0.100	0.000	0.005	0.005
	σ	0.063	0.003	0.004	0.005
Indirect	k	0.811	0.011	0.170	0.170
	a	0.100	0.000	0.007	0.007
	σ	0.060	0.000	0.005	0.005
Naive	k	0.574	−0.226	0.051	0.232
	a	0.100	0.000	0.005	0.005
	σ	0.043	−0.017	0.002	0.017

asymptotic biases on volatility parameters. In this section we consider other models with stochastic volatilities and with infeasible maximum likelihood estimators. (See also Monfardini 1996 for applications of indirect inference on discrete time stochastic volatility models.)

The Brennan–Schwartz model for the short-term interest rate[1]

Among the models proposed in Chan *et al.* (1992), where the short-term interest rate is assumed to satisfy:

$$dr_t = (\alpha + \beta r_t)\, dt + \sigma_0 r_t^{\gamma}\, dW_t,$$

the Brennan–Schwartz model (1979) corresponds to the constraint $\gamma = 1$.

Broze *et al.* (1993) have estimated such models from rates of return on US Treasury bills with one month to maturity. The short-term interest rate is identified with the one-month rate. The data cover the period January 1972–November 1991, and contain 239 observations. The evolution of this rate in first difference clearly shows the presence of conditional heteroscedasticity.

A generalized version of (6.16) in which the volatility term has been replaced by

$$\sigma_t = \sigma_0(r_t^{\gamma} + \sigma_1), \tag{6.15}$$

has first been estimated from the (misspecified) discretized version, taking into account the stationarity condition $0 \leq \gamma \leq 1$. The results are given in Table 6.3.

If these estimators were consistent for the parameters of the underlying continuous time model (which is not the case, since they have been derived from the

---

[1] See Broze *et al.* (1993); see also DeWinne (1994).

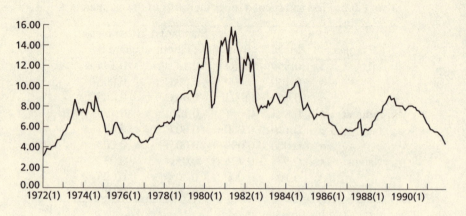

FIGURE 6.5: The US Treasury bill interest rate.

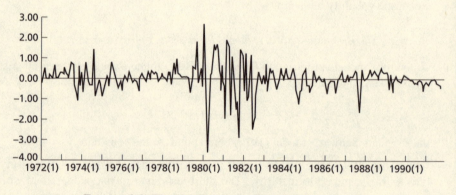

FIGURE 6.6: The US Treasury bill in difference.

TABLE 6.3: Estimations from the discretized version.

Parameter	α	$\beta + 1$	σ_0	σ_1	γ
Estimation	0.23	0.97	0.094	-1.73	1

TABLE 6.4: Estimation by indirect inference.

Parameter	α	$\beta + 1$	σ_0	σ_1	γ
Estimation	0.03	0.98	0.102	-0.08	1

discretized version), we would have concluded that the Chan *et al.* model is mis-specified. Indeed, the estimation of γ reaches the limit point between stationarity and nonstationarity, and the constant term σ_1 in the variance is significantly different from zero.

However, such a conclusion may be valid only after a bias correction of the previous estimators. This correction has been performed by indirect inference based on a discretized version with a time unit of $1/10$ (see Table 6.4).

The γ estimator still reaches the limit point, which confirms the misspecification. In fact, it means that the unconstrained estimator of γ, i.e. without imposing the inequality constraint $\gamma \leq 1$, would have taken a value strictly larger than one. The estimators of parameters β, σ_0 are not strongly modified. On the contrary, the estimations of α and σ_1 are much more sensitive to the discretization of the model. Given the previous Monte Carlo results, this is not surprising for the volatility parameter σ_1. Concerning the α parameter, the effect is probably a consequence of the constraint on γ. The unconstrained estimator of γ (a volatility parameter) is strongly modified by discretization of the model. Imposing the constraint $\gamma = 1$ transfers this modification to another parameter measuring the nonstationarity phenomenon; α is such a parameter.

The informational content of option prices

Pastorello *et al.* (1994) were interested in comparing the informational content of option prices and stock prices for the parameters associated with the dynamics of the volatility. For this purpose, they first introduced a stochastic volatility model of the form:

$$\begin{cases} \dfrac{dS_t}{S_t} = \mu \, dt + \sigma_t \, dW_t^S, \\ d\log\sigma_t = k(a - \log\sigma_t) \, dt + \sigma \, dW_t^\sigma, \end{cases} \qquad (6.16)$$

where S_t, σ_t denote the stock price and the volatility respectively, and where (W_t^S), (W_t^σ) are two independent standard Brownian motions. Therefore the log volatility satisfies an Orstein–Uhlenbeck model, and, conditional on the volatility process, the stock prices have a lognormal formulation with a time varying volatility.

The option prices are deduced from the arbitrage free conditions. Let us consider a European call option on the asset S, maturing at time T, with strike K. It delivers at date T the terminal value $\max(0, S_T - K)$. By arbitrage free arguments, its price at date t is a discounted expected value of this terminal cash flow, where the expectation is taken with respect to a pricing (risk-neutral) probability Q, and conditionally to the information available at t:

$$P_t(T, K) = \exp[-r(T - t)]E_t^Q \max(0, S_T - K)]. \tag{6.17}$$

In the previous expression the instantaneous interest rate r is assumed to be fixed and deterministic. Even if we assume that the option price only depends on the two underlying factors (S_t, σ_t), we are in a framework of incomplete markets, and the valuation probability Q is not defined in a unique way. However, for the particular dynamics (6.16), it is possible to exhibit all the admissible probabilities Q (see Hull and White 1987); moreover, if we assume that there is no risk premium associated with the risk on volatility (the volatility of the volatility), we get a unique pricing formula:

$$P_t(T, K) = S_t \left[E_t \Phi \left(\frac{x_t}{u_{t,T}} + \frac{u_{t,T}}{2} \right) - \exp(-x_t) E_t \Phi \left(\frac{x_t}{u_{t,T}} - \frac{u_{t,T}}{2} \right) \right], \tag{6.18}$$

where the expectations are taken with respect to the historical probability (the one associated with (6.16)), where:

$$x_t = \log \frac{S_t}{K \exp[-r(T - t)]}, \qquad u_{t,T} = \left[\int_t^T \sigma_u^2 \, du \right]^{\frac{1}{2}}, \tag{6.19}$$

and Φ is the c.d.f. of the standard normal distribution.

The formula (6.18) is an extension of the Black–Scholes formula (see Black and Scholes 1973), which corresponds to the limit case of a constant deterministic volatility $\bar{\sigma}$. In such a case the formula reduces to:

$$P_t^{BS}(T, K, \bar{\sigma}) = S_t \left[\Phi \left(\frac{x_t}{\bar{\sigma}\sqrt{T - t}} + \frac{\bar{\sigma}\sqrt{T - t}}{2} \right) \right.$$
$$\left. - \exp(-x_t) \Phi \left(\frac{x_t}{\bar{\sigma}\sqrt{T - t}} - \frac{\bar{\sigma}\sqrt{T - t}}{2} \right) \right].$$

In Pastorello *et al.* (1993), the observations are stock prices $S_t, t = 1, \ldots, T$, and prices of at-the-money options, i.e. options such that $x_t = 0$, corresponding to a sequence of maturities $\tau = T - t$. The observations are denoted by:

$$y_t^* = (S_t, P_t), \qquad t = 1, \ldots, T,$$

where:

$$P_t = P_t[t + \tau, S_t \exp r(T - t)]$$
$$= S_t \left[2E_t \Phi \left(\frac{u_{t,t+\tau}}{2} \right) - 1 \right]. \tag{6.20}$$

Only one maturity τ is introduced date by date in order to avoid deterministic relationships between observations. Indeed, such relationships will exist as soon as we introduce two options or more date by date, since the dynamic model (6.16) only depends on just two underlying factors.

In practice, option prices are often normalized by the Black–Scholes formula in order to correct partially for the maturity and strike effects. This normalized price, called implicit volatility and denoted by σ_t^I, is defined as the solution of:

$$P_t^{BS}(T, K, \sigma_t^I) = P_t,$$

and for at-the-money options it is given by:

$$\sigma_t^I = \frac{2}{\sqrt{\tau}} \Phi^{-1} \left[E_t \Phi \left(\frac{u_{t,t+\tau}}{2} \right) \right]$$

$$= \frac{2}{\sqrt{\tau}} \Phi^{-1} \left\{ E_t \Phi \left[\frac{1}{2} \left(\int_t^{t+\tau} \sigma_u^2 \, du \right)^{1/2} \right] \right\}. \tag{6.21}$$

It is of course equivalent to considering the observations $y_t^*, t = 1, \ldots, T$, or the observations $y_t = (S_t, \sigma_t^I), t = 1, \ldots, T$.

Three estimation methods of the parameters a, k, σ have been considered by Pastorello *et al.*

(i) In the first one, they use the observations $S_t, t = 1, \ldots, T$, only on the stock prices. Then the parameters μ, a, k, σ are estimated by indirect inference using as auxiliary model the discretized version of system (6.18) with a time unit of $1/10$.

(ii) In the second one, they use the data only on option prices, i.e. the observed values of the implicit volatility, and they apply the Ornstein–Uhlenbeck model directly to these volatilities. Since this dynamic admits an exact discretized version, it is equivalent to estimating the AR(1) formulation:

$$\log \sigma_t^I = a(1 - \exp(-k)) + (\exp(-k)) \log \sigma_{t-1}^I + \sigma \left(\frac{1 - \exp(-2k)}{2k} \right)^{1/2} \varepsilon_t. \tag{6.22}$$

This idea of directly replacing the unobserved volatility by the implicit volatility derived from the option price is not correct. Since the underlying volatility is stochastic, we know from (6.21) that σ_t^I does not coincide with σ_t, and does not follow the Ornstein–Uhlenbeck dynamics.

(iii) The third estimation method is also based only on the data on option prices. It uses the auxiliary model (6.22), and then is corrected by indirect inference.

These three methods have been applied to a set of artificially generated data on $(S_t, P_t), t = 1, \ldots, T$. The values of the parameters retained for the data generating process have been fixed to reasonable levels:

TABLE 6.5: Summary statistics of estimators of k.

	Indirect inference based on (S_t)	Indirect inference based on (σ_t^I)	Uncorrected method based on (σ_t^I)
Mean	0.173	0.117	0.142
Standard error	0.131	0.030	0.026

TABLE 6.6: Summary statistics of estimators of a.

	Indirect inference based on (S_t)	Indirect inference based on (σ_t^I)	Uncorrected method based on (σ_t^I)
Mean	−6.46	−6.42	−6.70
Standard error	0.11	0.04	0.02

$\mu = 4.6\%$ per year, which is the average nominal return on Treasury bills for the period 1948–83.

$k = 0.116$, $a = -6.422$, $\sigma = 0.192$, which correspond to the estimates reported in Melino and Turnbull (1990).

The Monte Carlo experiments have been performed with a sample size $T = 720$, corresponding to daily returns. Some summary statistics are given in Tables 6.5–6.7.

Since the parameter σ measuring the magnitude of the random character of the volatility is rather high, the implicit volatilities σ_t^I are bad proxies of the underlying volatilities, and the application of the uncorrected method based on the observations (σ_t^I) leads to strongly biased estimators.

The other important remark concerns the relative precision of the estimators based on the stock prices (S_t) and the option prices (σ_t^I). It clearly appears that the option prices are much more informative, especially for the parameters k and σ, which measure the time correlation and the random character of the volatility. Of course,

TABLE 6.7: Summary statistics of estimators of σ.

	Indirect inference based on (S_t)	Indirect inference based on (σ_t^I)	Uncorrected method based on (σ_t^I)
Mean	0.245	0.195	0.065
Standard error	0.134	0.039	0.003

better results may have been obtained by a joint use of the two kinds of observation, but the improvement of the precision would not be very important compared with the one based uniquely on the information summarized in the implicit volatility; moreover, all the methods using stock price data are sensitive to misspecification errors concerning the dynamics of (S_t). Indeed, we have to recall that the pricing formulas that are derived from the arbitrage free conditions do not depend on the form of the instantaneous expected return $\mu(t, S_t, \sigma_t)$ such that:

$$\frac{dS_t}{S_t} = \mu(t, S_t, \sigma_t) \, dt + \sigma_t \, dW_t^S.$$

6.2   Estimation of Stochastic Differential Equations from Moment Conditions

The parameters of stochastic differential equations may also be estimated by methods of moments. In this section we present both exact and simulated methods of moments.

6.2.1   Moment conditions deduced from the infinitesimal operator[2]

Infinitesimal operators

Let us consider a strictly stationary continuous time vector Markov process (y_t). We may introduce the family of operators (G_t), defined on square integrable functions by:

$$G_t \varphi(y) = E[\varphi(y_t)/y_0 = y]. \tag{6.23}$$

Definition 6.1 | The **infinitesimal operator** of the Markov process is the derivative at $t = 0$ of the operator G_t; it is denoted by A and given by $A = \lim_{t \to 0} \frac{1}{t}(G_t - Id)$.

Since the limit $\lim_{t \to 0} \frac{1}{t}(G_t \varphi - \varphi)$ does not necessarily exist for all square integrable functions, the infinitesimal operator is in fact defined on a subset of the set of square integrable functions. This subset is called the domain of the infinitesimal operator and is denoted by D.

---

[2]See Hansen and Scheinkman (1995), and Conley *et al.* (1994).

Proposition 6.1 | If the Markov process (y_t) satisfies the stochastic differential equation

$$dy_t = \mu(y_t)\,dt + \sigma(y_t)\,dW_t,$$

where (W_t) is a multivariate standard Brownian motion, the infinitesimal operator is given by:

$$A\varphi(y) = \frac{d\varphi(y)}{dy'}\mu(y) + \frac{1}{2}\mathrm{Tr}\left[\sigma(y)\sigma'(y)\frac{d^2\varphi(y)}{dy\,dy'}\right].$$

Proof. See Appendix 6A.

A similar approach for defining another infinitesimal operator may also be followed for the reverse time process. More precisely, we may introduce the sequence of operators (G_t^*) defined by:

$$G_t^*\varphi(y) = E[\varphi(y_0)/y_t = y], \tag{6.24}$$

and their derivative at zero:

$$A^* = \lim_{t \to 0}\frac{1}{t}(G_t^* - Id). \tag{6.25}$$

We denote by D^* the domain of A^*.

Proposition 6.2 | G_t^* (resp. A^*) is the adjoint operator of G_t (resp. A) for the scalar product associated with the marginal distribution of y_t.

Proof. Indeed, we have

$$\begin{aligned}
E[\varphi(y_t)\tilde{\varphi}(y_0)] &= E[E(\varphi(y_t)/y_0)\tilde{\varphi}(y_0)]\\
&= E[G_t\varphi(y_0)\tilde{\varphi}(y_0)]\\
&= \langle G_t\varphi, \tilde{\varphi}\rangle.
\end{aligned}$$

Similarly, we have:

$$\begin{aligned}
E[\varphi(y_t)\tilde{\varphi}(y_0)] &= E[\varphi(y_t)E[\tilde{\varphi}(y_0)/y_t]]\\
&= E[\varphi(y_t)G_t^*\tilde{\varphi}(y_t)]\\
&= \langle \varphi, G_t^*\tilde{\varphi}\rangle.
\end{aligned}$$

We deduce the result from the definition of an adjoint operator:

$$\langle G_t\varphi, \tilde{\varphi}\rangle = \langle \varphi, G_t^*\tilde{\varphi}\rangle.$$

QED

Note that the scalar product is the one associated with the marginal probability distribution of y_t, which is time independent because of the stationarity assumption. The determination of the operator A^* sometimes requires the computation of the stationary distribution of the process. However, for most stationary univariate diffusions the two operators are equal: $A^* = A$ (see Hansen and Scheinkman 1995).

Moment conditions

Proposition 6.3 | (i) We have:

$$E A\varphi(y_t) = 0, \quad \forall \varphi \in D.$$

(ii) We have:

$$E[A\varphi(y_{t+1})\tilde{\varphi}(y_t) - \varphi(y_{t+1})A^*\tilde{\varphi}(y_t)] = 0,$$
$$\forall \varphi \in D, \quad \forall \tilde{\varphi} \in D^*.$$

Proof: (i) We have:

$$E[G_t\varphi(y_0)] = E E[\varphi(y_t)/y_0]$$
$$= E\varphi(y_t)$$
$$= E\varphi(y_0).$$

Therefore $E\left[\frac{1}{t}(G_t - Id)\varphi(y_0)\right] = 0$, and by taking the limit, $E A\varphi(y_0) = 0$.

(ii) Since A and G_1 commute, we have:

$$E[A\varphi(y_{t+1})\tilde{\varphi}(y_t)] = E[E(A\varphi(y_{t+1})/y_t)\tilde{\varphi}(y_t)]$$
$$= E[G_1 A\varphi(y_t)\tilde{\varphi}(y_t)]$$
$$= \langle G_1 A\varphi, \tilde{\varphi}\rangle$$
$$= \langle A G_1\varphi, \tilde{\varphi}\rangle$$
$$= \langle \varphi, G_1^* A^*\tilde{\varphi}\rangle$$
$$= E[\varphi(y_{t+1})G_1^* A^*\tilde{\varphi}(y_{t+1})]$$
$$= E[\varphi(y_{t+1})E(A^*\tilde{\varphi}(y_t)/y_{t+1}]$$
$$= E[\varphi(y_{t+1})A^*\tilde{\varphi}(y_t)].$$

QED

We must add that the second set of moment conditions can be extended to functions without multiplicative forms. If $\varphi(y_t, y_{t+1})$ is such a function of the two arguments, we get, for univariate diffusion equations,

$$
E\left[\mu(y_{t+1})\frac{\partial\varphi}{\partial y_{t+1}}(y_t, y_{t+1}) + \frac{1}{2}\sigma^2(y_{t+1})\frac{\partial^2\varphi}{\partial y_{t+1}^2}(y_t, y_{t+1})\right]
$$
$$
= E\left[\mu(y_t)\frac{\partial\varphi}{\partial y_t}(y_t, y_{t+1}) + \frac{1}{2}\sigma^2(y_{t+1})\frac{\partial^2\varphi}{\partial y_{t+1}^2}(y_t, y_{t+1})\right].
$$

These moment conditions may be used directly as the basis of exact moment methods in some simple cases. For instance let us consider the Chan *et al.* (1992) model introduced in Section 6.1. It corresponds to the stochastic differential equation:

$$
dr_t = (\alpha + \beta r_t)\,dt + \sigma_0 r_t^\gamma\,dW_t.
$$

We have, for a function φ possibly depending on the parameter,

$$
A\varphi_\theta(r_t) = (\alpha + \beta r_t)\frac{d\varphi_\theta}{dr}(r_t) + \frac{1}{2}\sigma_0^2 r_t^{2\gamma}\frac{d^2\varphi_\theta}{dr^2}(r_t), \tag{6.26}
$$

and the moment condition $E A\varphi_\theta(r_t) = 0$ is:

$$
E\left[(\alpha + \beta r_t)\frac{d\varphi_\theta}{dr}(r_t) + \frac{1}{2}\sigma_0^2 r_t^{2\gamma}\frac{d^2\varphi_\theta}{dr^2}(r_t)\right] = 0. \tag{6.27}
$$

In practice, we may introduce several functions φ and the associated moment conditions. For instance, we may introduce exponential functions $\varphi_j(r) = \exp(-a_j r)$, $j = 1, \ldots, p$, and the moment conditions will be:

$$
E\left[\exp(-a_j r_t)\left(\alpha + \beta r_t - \frac{a_j}{2}\sigma_0^2 r_t^{2\gamma}\right)\right] = 0. \tag{6.28}
$$

Properties of the method

Up to now, practical implementations of the previous ideas have been performed only for some specific modellings (see Conley *et al.* 1994). Therefore, we will essentially discuss some general properties of the associated method of moments. As usual, there is the problem of a suitable choice of the moment conditions, i.e of the functions φ, since the precisions of the estimators will depend on this choice. In particular, it would be interesting to know the loss of information resulting from the use of the conditions $E A\varphi(y_t) = 0$, which are essentially marginal conditions and only take the local dynamic into account through the infinitesimal operator A.

We see from the Chan *et al.* (1992) example (see (6.27)), that the moment conditions derived from the infinitesimal operators may be not sufficient to identify the parameters of interest. If γ is clearly identifiable, the other parameters α, β, σ_0^2 will be determined up to a multiplicative factor.

In fact, the main drawback of the Hansen–Scheinkman (1994) approach seems to be its difficulty of implementation for unobservable factor models. We shall illustrate this point using the stochastic volatility model considered in Pastorello *et al.* (1994). (Another illustration for a time deformed process is given in Ghysels *et al.* (1994*a*).) The model is defined by:

$$\begin{cases} dS_t = \mu S_t \, dt + \sigma_t S_t \, dW_t^S, \\ d \log \sigma_t = k(a - \log \sigma_t) \, dt + \sigma \, dW_t^\sigma, \end{cases}$$

or by introducing the bivariate process $y_t = \binom{S_t}{\log \sigma_t}$:

$$dy_t = \left[\begin{array}{c} \mu y_{1t} \\ k(a - y_{2t}) \end{array} \right] dt + \left[\begin{array}{cc} y_{1t} \exp y_{2t} & 0 \\ 0 & \sigma \end{array} \right] dW_t.$$

Therefore, considering φ functions independent of the parameter, we have:

$$A\varphi(y_t) = \mu y_{1t} \frac{\partial \varphi(y_t)}{\partial y_1} + k(a - y_{2t}) \frac{\partial \varphi}{\partial y_2}(y_t)$$

$$+ \frac{1}{2} \left[y_{1t}^2 \exp(2y_{2t}) \frac{\partial^2 \varphi}{\partial y_1^2}(y_t) + \sigma^2 \frac{\partial^2 \varphi}{\partial y_2^2}(y_t) \right].$$

Let us now assume that the only available data are the stock prices $S_t = y_{1t}$. In such a case, the only moment conditions that can be used as a basis for GMM are the ones for which $A\varphi(y_t)$ depends only on the first coordinate y_{1t}, and this for all the admissible values of the parameters. This constraint is equivalent to:

$$y_1 \frac{\partial \varphi}{\partial y_1}(y), \quad \frac{\partial \varphi}{\partial y_2}(y), \quad y_2 \frac{\partial \varphi}{\partial y_2}(y), \quad y_1^2 \exp(2y_2) \frac{\partial^2 \varphi(y)}{\partial y_1^2}, \quad \frac{\partial^2 \varphi(y)}{\partial y_2^2},$$

simultaneously independent of y_2, and it is satisfied only by the affine functions of $y_1 : \varphi(y) = a + by_1$. Therefore the approach provides uninteresting moment conditions in the case of parameter independent φ functions.

6.2.2   Method of simulated moments

We have seen that exact methods of moments were difficult to implement, especially in the case of unobservable factors. An alternative method is the method of simulated moments. Since the analytical forms of the conditional distribution of y_t given $\underline{y_{t-1}}$ are in general not simulable, the MSM has to be applied to static cross moments (see Chapter 2). Such an approach has been followed by Duffie and Singleton (1993). As before, the use of static moments only is likely to introduce a loss of precision, especially for the parameters summarizing the nonlinear features of the dynamics. It seems at least useful to take into account the third and fourth order moments Ey_t^3, Ey_t^4 in the case of stochastic volatility models, since we know that the existence of a stochastic volatility increases the tails of the marginal distribution, and in particular the kurtosis (see e.g. Engle 1982), together with cross order moments such as $E(y_t^2 y_{t-k}^2)$ to capture the conditional heteroscedasticity and $E(|y_t||y_{t-k}|)$ to capture the leverage effect (see Andersen and Sorensen 1993).

6.3   Factor Models

6.3.1   Discrete time factor models

The modelling of financial time series may also be performed through discrete time processes. In such a case the absence of analytical forms for the conditional p.d.f. is not due to problems of time aggregation, but generally comes from the unobservability of some latent processes (the factors) that drive the dynamics. After some preliminary transformations, this kind of model may be written as an (M^*) model (see (1.21)) of the form:

$$\begin{cases} y_t = r_1(y_{t-1}, y_t^*, \varepsilon_{1t}; \theta), \\ y_t^* = r_2(y_{t-1}, y_{t-1}^*, \varepsilon_{2t}; \theta), \end{cases} \tag{6.29}$$

where the functions $r_1(y_{t-1}, y_t^*, \cdot; \theta)$ and $r_2(y_{t-1}, y_{t-1}^*, \cdot; \theta)$ define a one to one relationship between $(\varepsilon_{1t}, \varepsilon_{2t})$ and (y_t, y_t^*), and where (ε_{1t}), (ε_{2t}) are independent white noises with known distributions. The $y_t, t = 1, \ldots, T$, variables are observable, but the factors $y_t^*, t = 1, \ldots, T$, are unobservable.

As mentioned in Section 1.3.4, conditional p.d.f.s are easily derived from system (6.3). These are the conditional p.d.f. of y_t given y_{t-1}, y_t^*, denoted by $f(y_t/y_{t-1}, y_t^*; \theta)$, and the conditional p.d.f. of y_t^* given y_{t-1}, y_{t-1}^*, denoted by $f^*(y_t^*/y_{t-1}, y_{t-1}^*; \theta)$. We then deduce the p.d.f. of $y_T = (y_1, \ldots, y_T)$, $y_T^* = (y_1^*, \ldots, y_T^*)$ given the information y_0, y_0^*:

$$f_0(y_T, y_T^*; \theta) = \prod_{t=1}^{T} f(y_t/y_{t-1}, y_t^*; \theta) f^*(y_t^*/y_{t-1}, y_{t-1}^*; \theta). \tag{6.30}$$

If the process (y_t, y_t^*) is strongly stationary and T is large, the effect of the initial conditions y_0, y_0^* becomes negligible when studying the asymptotic properties of the estimators. Therefore we will not discuss this problem of initial values. The likelihood function (conditional to y_0, y_0^*) has the form of a multivariate integral:

$$f_0(y_T; \theta) = \int \prod_{t=1}^{T} \left[f(y_t/y_{t-1}, y_t^*; \theta) f^*(y_t^*/y_{t-1}, y_{t-1}^*; \theta) \, d\mu(y_t^*) \right], \tag{6.31}$$

where $\mu(y_t^*)$ denotes the dominating measure.

Example 6.1   Factor ARCH models

Multivariate ARCH models naturally contain a large number of parameters, and it is necessary to introduce constraints in order to make this number smaller. A natural approach, compatible with the needs of financial theory and with some features of financial series which often have common evolutions in the volatilities, leads to the introduction of unobserved factors (Diebold and Nerlove 1989, Engle *et al.* 1990, King *et al.* 1990, and Gouriéroux *et al.* 1991).

Let us consider for instance the model with one exogenous factor of the Diebold–Nerlove type:

$$y_t = \lambda y_t^* + \varepsilon_t, \tag{6.32}$$

where (y_t) is the observable n-dimensional process, (ε_t) is a Gaussian white noise with an unknown variance–covariance matrix Ω, (y_t^*) is the unidimensional factor independent of (ε_t), and λ is the n-dimensional sensitivity vector of the components of y_t to the common factor y_t^*. We assume that the factor follows an ARCH(1) formulation (Engle 1982):

$$y_t^* \sim N(0, \alpha_0 + \alpha_1 y_{t-1}^{*2}), \tag{6.33}$$

conditional on y_{t-1}, y_{t-1}^* (with, for instance, the identification constraints $\alpha_0 > 0$, $\alpha_1 > 0$, $\alpha_0 + \alpha_1 = 1$).

In this example, we have:

$$\begin{cases} f(y_t/\underline{y_{t-1}}, y_t^* : \theta) = \dfrac{1}{(2\pi)^{n/2}} \dfrac{1}{\sqrt{[b]\det \Omega}} \exp\left[-\dfrac{1}{2}(y_t - \lambda y_t^*)'\Omega^{-1}(y_t - \lambda y_t^*)\right], \\[2em] f^*(y_t^*/\underline{y_{t-1}}, y_{t-1}^* : \theta) = \dfrac{1}{(2\pi)^{1/2}} \dfrac{1}{\sqrt{[b]\alpha_0 + \alpha_1 y_{t-1}^{*2}}} \exp\left[-\dfrac{1}{2}\dfrac{y_t^{*2}}{\alpha_0 + \alpha_1 y_{t-1}^{*2}}\right]. \end{cases}$$

6.3.2   State space form and Kitagawa's filtering algorithm[3]

The dynamic model (6.29) appears as a nonlinear state space system, where the first subsystem is the measurement equation and the second is the transition equation. In a linear state space system it is well known that the Kalman filter is an algorithm allowing for the exact computation of the conditional p.d.f. of y_t given $\underline{y_{t-1}}$ (and the initial conditions). In this subsection we will discuss the possibility of such an exact algorithm for nonlinear models, and show that, except for some specific cases, the exact computation of the likelihood function is not possible. Then it will be necessary to use either numerical or simulated methods.

---

[3] See Kitagawa (1987).

Kitagawa's algorithm explains how to compute recursively the conditional p.d.f. $f(y^{*t-1}_{t-p}/\underline{y_{t-1}})$, in the particular case of model (6.29):

$$y_t = r_1(\underline{y_{t-1}}, y^{*t}_{t-p}, \varepsilon_{1t}; \theta) \qquad (6.34)$$

$$y^*_t = r_2(\underline{y_{t-1}}, y^{*t-1}_{t-p}, \varepsilon_{2t}; \theta), \qquad (6.35)$$

with the notation $y^{*t}_{t-k} = (y^{*'}_t, y^{*'}_{t-1}, \dots, y^{*'}_{t-k})'$.

It requires several steps.

Step 1: Time updating

Let us assume that the p.d.f. $f(y^{*t-1}_{t-p}/\underline{y_{t-1}})$ is given. Then we deduce the conditional p.d.f.

$$f(y^{*t}_{t-p}/\underline{y_{t-1}}) = f(y^*_t/\underline{y_{t-1}}, y^{*t-1}_{t-p})f(y^{*t-1}_{t-p}/\underline{y_{t-1}}),$$

where the first term of the RHS in directly deduced from (6.35).

Step 2: One step prediction

We deduce

$$f(y_t, y^{*t}_{t-p}/\underline{y_{t-1}}) = f(y_t/\underline{y_{t-1}}, y^{*t}_{t-p})f(y^{*t}_{t-p}/\underline{y_{t-1}})$$

where the first term of the RHS is known from (6.34) and the second is given by Step 1.

Then, integrating out y^{*t}_{t-p}, we get:

$$f(y_t/\underline{y_{t-1}}) = \int f(y_t, y^{*t}_{t-p}/\underline{y_{t-1}}) \, d\mu^{\otimes p+1}\left(y^{*t}_{t-p}\right),$$

which is the general term of the likelihood function.

Step 3: Measure updating

From Step 2, we get

$$f(y^{*t}_{t-p}/\underline{y_t}) = \frac{f(y_t, y^{*t}_{t-p}/\underline{y_{t-1}})}{f(y_t/\underline{y_{t-1}})}.$$

And, integrating out y_{t-p}, we obtain $f(y^{*t}_{t-p+1}/\underline{y_t})$, which is the input of the next iteration.

In summary, Kitagawa's algorithm provides a recursive computation of the multiple integral defining the likelihood function.

Such an algorithm is not so simple to implement, since it requires the computation of integrals. These computations can be done explicitly in the case of linear Gaussian state space models, where Kitagawa's algorithm coincides with the Kalman filter, and when the factor y_t^* is discrete with a finite number of possible values—$b_1, \ldots, b_J$, say. In such a case the integrals reduce to finite sums (see Hamilton 1989). In the general case, and if p is small, these integrals could be approximated by numerical methods (see Kitagawa 1987) or by simulation methods.

6.3.3 An auxiliary model for applying indirect inference on factor ARCH models[4]

Since exact computation of the likelihood function can be performed when the factor takes only a finite number of values, a natural idea is to apply indirect inference to an approximated version of the ARCH model in which the factor has been state discretized. Let us consider the factor ARCH model introduced in (6.32) and (6.33) and a partition of the range of y_t^* in J given classes (a_j, a_{j+1}), $j = 0, \ldots, J - 1$, where $a_0 = -\infty$, $a_J = +\infty$. The state discretized factor is defined by:

$$\tilde{y}_t = b_j, \qquad \text{if } y_t^* \in (a_j, a_{j+1}),$$

where b_j are given real numbers, such as the centres of the classes, except for the two extreme ones.

The dynamics of the discretized factor may be defined in accordance with the dynamics of the initial one by:

$$
\begin{aligned}
P[\tilde{y}_t = b_j / \tilde{y}_{t-1} = b_l] &= P[y_t^* \in (a_j, a_{j+1}) / y_{t-1}^* \in (a_l, a_{l+1})] \\
&\simeq P[y_t^* \in (a_j, a_{j+1}) / y_{t-1}^* = b_l] \\
&= \Phi\left[\frac{a_{j+1}}{(\alpha_0 + \alpha_1 b_l^2)^{1/2}}\right] - \Phi\left[\frac{a_j}{(\alpha_0 + \alpha_1 b_l^2)^{1/2}}\right] \\
&= P_{jl}(\alpha_0, \alpha_1) \qquad \text{(say)}.
\end{aligned}
$$

Then the initial factor ARCH model is replaced by the proxy model:

$$y_t = \lambda \tilde{y}_t + \varepsilon_t,$$

where (ε_t), $(\tilde{y}_t)$ are independent, $(\varepsilon_t) \sim \text{IIN}(0, \Omega)$, and $(\tilde{y}_t)$ is a qualitative Markov process with transition probabilities $P_{jl}(\alpha_0, \alpha_1)$. This auxiliary model can be estimated by the maximum likelihood method, using Kitagawa's algorithm. Then the correction for the state discretization of the factors is performed by indirect inference.

---

[4] See Gouriéroux et al. (1993) and Gouriéroux (1992).

TABLE 6.8: Estimations of the SVM.

Parameter	Static model 1	Static model 2	Model 3	Model 4
b_0	−0.15 (0.04)	−0.28 (0.05)	−0.002 (0.002)	−0.007 (0.008)
b_1	0	0.18 (0.005)	0	0.06 (0.01)
b_2	0	0	0.96 (0.01)	0.96 (0.02)
ρ	0	0	0	0.09 (0.02)
η	0.76 (0.05)	0.71 (0.05)	0.16 (0.03)	0.16 (0.03)
log likelihood	−2937	−2928	−2898	−2890

[a]Standard errors are in parentheses. *Source*: Danielsson (1993).

6.3.4   SML applied to a stochastic volatility model[5]

Stochastic volatility models (SVM) may also be directly defined in discrete time. Danielsson (1993) considered such a model with the structure:

$$\begin{cases} y_t = \sigma_t u_t, \\ u_t = \rho u_{t-1} + \varepsilon_t, \\ \sigma_t^2 = \exp[b_0 + b_1|y_{t-1}| + b_2 \log \sigma_{t-1}^2 + \eta v_t], \end{cases} \tag{6.36}$$

where (ε_t), (v_t) are independent Gaussian white noises with zero mean and unit variance. Therefore there is a stochastic volatility which is predetermined, and generally not observable. This lack of observability implies a likelihood function with the form of a T-variate integral:

$$L_T(\theta) = \int \cdots \int \prod_{t=1}^{T} \left\{ \frac{1}{\sigma_t \sqrt{2\pi}} \exp - \frac{\left(y_t - \frac{\sigma_t \rho}{\sigma_{t-1}} y_{t-1} \right)^2}{2\sigma_t^2} \right.$$

$$\left. \times \frac{\sqrt{2}}{\sigma_t \eta \sqrt{\pi}} \exp - \frac{1}{2\eta^2} \left[\log \sigma_t^2 - b_0 - b_1|y_{t-1}| - b_2 \log \sigma_{t-1}^2 \right] d\sigma_t \right\}.$$

The expression of the likelihood function is simplified only in the static case: $\rho = b_2 = 0$.

The previous model has been estimated by the SML method using eight years of daily observations of Standard and Poor's 500 index for the years 1980–7 [$T = 2022$], and an accelerated Gaussian importance sampler. Several estimation results are given in Table 6.8 depending on the parameters of the model which are a priori constrained to zero. In particular, the first two columns of the table correspond to static cases.

---

[5]Danielsson (1994).

As expected, the coefficient b_2 giving the specific dynamic of the volatility is highly significant. Moreover, the coefficient b_1 is also significant, which means that the volatility does not admit an autonomous evolution.

Appendix 6A: Form of the Infinitesimal Operator

Proof. We shall just sketch the proof. We have:

$$A\varphi(y) = \lim_{dt \to 0} E\left[\frac{1}{dt}[\varphi(y_{t+dt}) - \varphi(y_t)]/y_t = y\right],$$

by using the stationarity assumption. A second order expansion around the value $y_t = y$ provides:

$$A\varphi(y) = \lim_{dt \to 0} E\left[\frac{1}{dt}\frac{d\varphi}{dy'}(y)\,dy_t/y_t = y\right]$$

$$+ \lim_{dt \to 0} E\left[\frac{1}{2\,dt}\,dy_t'\,\frac{d^2\varphi}{dy\,dy'}(y)\,dy_t/y_t = y\right]$$

$$= \lim_{dt \to 0} E\left[\frac{d\varphi}{dy'}(y)\mu(y) + \frac{d\varphi}{dy'}(y)\sigma(y)\frac{dW_t}{dt}\Big/y_t = y\right]$$

$$+ \lim_{dt \to 0} E\left[\frac{1}{2\,dt}(\mu(y)\,dt + \sigma(y)dW_t)'\frac{d^2\varphi(y)}{dy\,dy'}(\mu(y)\,dt\right.$$

$$\left. + \sigma(y)\,dW_t)/y_t = y\right]$$

$$= \frac{d\varphi}{dy'}(y)\mu(y) + \lim_{dt \to 0}\frac{1}{2\,dt}E\left[[\sigma(y)\,dW_t]'\frac{d^2\varphi(y)}{dy\,dy'}\sigma(y)\,dW_t/y_t = y\right],$$

since $E[dW_t/y_t = y] = 0$, and the other terms are negligible. Finally, we get:

$$A\varphi(y) = \frac{d\varphi}{dy'}(y)\mu(y) + \lim_{dt \to 0}\frac{1}{2\,dt}E\left\{\mathrm{Tr}\left([\sigma(y)\,dW_t]'\frac{d^2\varphi(y)}{dy\,dy'}\sigma(y)dW_t\right)\right\}$$

$$= \frac{d\varphi}{dy'}(y)\mu(y) + \lim_{dt \to 0}\frac{1}{2\,dt}E\mathrm{Tr}\left[\frac{d^2\varphi(y)}{dy\,dy'}\sigma(y)\,dW_t\,dW_t'\sigma'(y)\right]$$

$$= \frac{d\varphi}{dy'}(y)\mu(y) + \lim_{dt \to 0}\frac{1}{2\,dt}\mathrm{Tr}\left[\frac{d^2\varphi(y)}{dy\,dy'}\sigma(y)E(dW_t\,dW_t')\sigma'(y)\right]$$

$$= \frac{d\varphi}{dy'}(y)\mu(y) + \frac{1}{2}\mathrm{Tr}\left[\frac{d^2\varphi(y)}{dy\,dy'}\sigma(y)\sigma'(y)\right],$$

since $E[dW_t\,dW_t'] = dt\,Id$.

QED

7

Applications to Switching Regime Models

7.1 Endogenously Switching Regime Models

7.1.1 Static disequilibrium models

The canonical static disequilibrium model is defined as:

$$\begin{cases} y_{1t}^* = z_{1t}a_1 + \sigma_1\varepsilon_{1t} \\ y_{2t}^* = z_{2t}a_2 + \sigma_2\varepsilon_{2t} \\ y_t = \min(y_{1t}^*, y_{2t}^*) \qquad t = 1, \ldots, T, \end{cases} \tag{7.1}$$

where z_{1t}, z_{2t} are (row) vectors of observable exogenous variables, y_{1t}^* and y_{2t}^* are latent endogenous variables, y_t is observed, and $(\varepsilon_{1t}, \varepsilon_{2t})$ are independently $N(0, I_2)$ distributed. The parameter vector is $\theta = (a_1', a_2', \sigma_1, \sigma_2)'$.

In this simple canonical case the likelihood function is easily computed and is equal to:

$$\prod_{t=1}^{T} \left[\frac{1}{\sigma_1} \varphi\left(\frac{y_t - z_{1t}a_1}{\sigma_1} \right) \Phi\left(\frac{z_{2t}a_2 - y_t}{\sigma_2} \right) + \frac{1}{\sigma_2} \varphi\left(\frac{y_t - z_{2t}a_2}{\sigma_2} \right) \Phi\left(\frac{z_{1t}a_1 - y_t}{\sigma_1} \right) \right],$$

$$\tag{7.2}$$

where φ and Φ are the p.d.f. and the c.d.f. of $N(0, 1)$ respectively.

However, in multimarket disequilibrium models with nonlinear demand or supply functions, or in models with micro markets (see Laroque and Salanié 1989), the likelihood function becomes very complicated, and in some cases untractable. In order to solve this problem, Laroque and Salanié (1989) introduced various versions of the simulated pseudo-maximum likelihood (SPML) method. Moreover, in Laroque and Salanié (1994) an evaluation of these methods based on experiments is given. In these experiments the model retained is the previous canonical model in which (z_{1t}, z_{2t}) is a bivariate vector following

$$N\left[\begin{pmatrix} 5 \\ 5 \end{pmatrix}, \begin{pmatrix} 0 & 0 \\ 0 & 0.5 \end{pmatrix} \right]$$

independently for any t and where $a_1 = a_2 = \sigma_1 = \sigma_2 = 1$.

The estimation methods considered are the full information maximum likelihood method, three versions of the pseudo-maximum likelihood methods, called PML1,

PML2, and QGPML, and their simulated analogues, called SMPL1, SMPL2, and SPMLG. The three PML methods are obtained by maximizing the following pseudo-likelihood functions:

$$\text{PML1:} \quad \prod_{t=1}^{T} \varphi[y_t - m_1(z_t, \theta)]$$

$$\text{PML2:} \quad \prod_{t=1}^{T} \frac{1}{[v(z_t, \theta)]^{\frac{1}{2}}} \varphi\left[\frac{y_t - m_1(z_t, \theta)}{[v(z_t, \theta)]^{\frac{1}{2}}}\right]$$

$$\text{QGPML:} \quad \prod_{t=1}^{T} \varphi\left[\frac{y_t - m_1(z, \theta)}{[v(z_t, \hat{\theta}_{2T})]^{\frac{1}{2}}}\right],$$

where $\hat{\theta}_{2T}$ is a preliminary estimate of θ based on the PML2 method and where $m_1(z_t, \theta)$ and $v(z_t, \theta)$ are, respectively, the mean and the variance of y_t derived from the model and given by:

$$m_1(z, \theta) = z_1 a_1 \Phi\left(\frac{z_2 a_2 - z_1 a_1}{s}\right) + z_2 a_2 \Phi\left(\frac{z_1 a_1 - z_2 a_2}{s}\right) - s\varphi\left(\frac{z_1 a_1 - z_2 a_2}{s}\right),$$

with $s^2 = \sigma_1^2 + \sigma_2^2$ and:

$$v(z, \theta) = m_2(z, \theta) - m_1^2(z, \theta)$$

with:

$$m_2(z, \theta) = (z_1^2 a_1^2 + \sigma_1^2)\Phi\left(\frac{z_2 a_2 - z_1 a_1}{s}\right) + (z_2^2 a_2^2 + \sigma_2^2)\Phi\left(\frac{z_1 a_1 - z_2 a_2}{s}\right)$$
$$- s(z_1 a_1 + z_2 a_2)\varphi\left(\frac{z_1 a_1 - z_2 a_2}{s}\right).$$

In other words, these PML methods are based on normal pseudo-likelihood functions, although y_t is clearly not normal; note that in this case, the PML1 and the QGPML reduce, respectively, to the nonlinear and the quasi-generalized nonlinear least squares methods.

The simulated analogues of these methods are obtained by replacing $m_1(z_t, \theta)$ and $v(z_t, \theta)$ by approximations $m_1^S(z_t, \theta)$ and $v^S(z_t, \theta)$ based on simulations, namely:

$$m_1^S(z_t, \theta) = \frac{1}{S} \sum_{s=1}^{S} \min(z_{1t} a_1 + \sigma_1 \varepsilon_{1t}^s, z_{2t} a_2 + \sigma_2 \varepsilon_{2t}^s)$$

and:

$$v^S(z_t, \theta) = \frac{S}{S-1}\left[m_2^S(z_t, \theta) - (m_1^S(z_t, \theta))^2\right],$$

TABLE 7.1: Mean estimates on the retained samples (out of 200 samples); constrained estimator $\sigma_1 = \sigma_2 = \sigma$.

Coefficient (true value)	T	FIML	PML1	SPML1 $S=5$	$S=10$	$S=20$	PML2	SPML2 $S=5$	$S=10$	$S=20$
a_1	20	1.04	1.06	0.98	1.01	1.07	1.02	1.06	1.04	1.05
	50	1.03	1.07	0.95	0.96	1.00	1.02	1.09	1.09	1.05
(1.00)	80	1.03	1.09	0.95	0.97	0.98	1.02	1.10	1.07	1.05
a_2	20	1.04	1.26	1.00	1.03	1.04	1.03	1.08	1.07	1.04
	50	1.02	1.29	0.96	0.96	0.99	1.03	1.09	1.05	1.05
(1.00)	80	1.02	1.26	0.94	0.95	0.96	1.02	1.09	1.05	1.04
σ	20	0.88	1.84	0.64	0.79	1.01	0.88	1.23	1.02	0.94
	50	0.94	1.98	0.37	0.44	0.64	0.94	1.32	1.06	0.99
(1.00)	80	0.95	1.98	0.30	0.40	0.51	0.95	1.36	1.08	1.00

Coefficient (true value)	T	QGPML	SQGPML $S=5$	$S=10$	$S=20$
a_1	20	1.04	0.99	1.02	1.07
	50	1.06	0.96	0.98	0.98
(1.00)	80	1.08	0.96	0.98	0.99
a_2	20	1.27	1.01	1.02	1.06
	50	1.30	0.97	0.97	0.98
(1.00)	80	1.25	0.96	0.95	0.97
σ	20	1.74	0.72	0.76	1.07
	50	1.94	0.45	0.54	0.61
(1.00)	80	1.89	0.42	0.43	0.54

with:

$$m_2^S(z_t, \theta) = \frac{1}{S} \sum_{s=1}^{S} \left[\min(z_{1t}a_1 + \sigma_1\varepsilon_{1t}^s, z_{2t}a_2 + \sigma_2\varepsilon_{2t}^s) \right]^2,$$

where $(\varepsilon_{1t}^s, \varepsilon_{2t}^s)$, $s = 1, \ldots, S$ are drawn independently in $N(0, I_2)$.

It is readily seen from the expression for m_1 that σ_1 and σ_2 are not first order identifiable and that only $s = (\sigma_1^2 + \sigma_2^2)^{1/2}$ is first order identifiable; so, when implementing the first order PML methods PML1, QGPML, and their simulated analogues SMPL1 and SQGPML, the constraint $\sigma_1 = \sigma_2 = \sigma$ has been imposed.

The Monte Carlo study conducted by Laroque and Salanié (1994) shows many results on spurious maxima, on importance sampling, on the estimated asymptotic standard errors of the estimators, on their empirical standard deviations, and on their biases. The results on the biases in the constrained case ($\sigma_1 = \sigma_2 = \sigma$) are summarized in Table 7.1. As expected, the second order PML and SPML methods are better than the first order ones, especially for the estimation of a_2 and σ. However, the PML1 and QGPML methods are here dominated by their simulated analogues. The PML2 and SPML2 methods with $S = 10$ or 20 give very similar results, both of them being very close to those of the FIML method.

7.1.2   Dynamic disequilibrium models

SPML methods

Let us now consider the following dynamic disequilibrium model:

$$
\begin{cases}
y_{1t}^* = z_{1t}a_1 + y_{1,t-1}^* b_1 + y_{2,t-1}^* c_1 + \sigma_1 \varepsilon_{1t} \\
y_{2t}^* = z_{2t}a_2 + y_{1,t-1}^* b_2 + y_{2,t-1}^* c_2 + \sigma_2 \varepsilon_{2t} \\
y_t = \min(y_{1t}^*, y_{2t}^*) \\
t = 1, \dots, T,
\end{cases}
\tag{7.3}
$$

where z_{1t}, z_{2t} are (row) vectors of observable exogenous variables, y_{1t}^* and y_{2t}^* are latent endogenous variables, y_t is observed, and $(\varepsilon_{1t}, \varepsilon_{2t})$ are independently $N(0, I_2)$ distributed. (The cases of more than one lag or of autocorrelated disturbances are straightforward extensions.)

The likelihood function of such a model is intractable. In order to evaluate the complexity of this function, let us first introduce the notations:

$$
y_t^* = \max(y_{1t}^*, y_{2t}^*)
$$
$$
r_t = \mathbb{1}_{\{y_{1t}^* < y_{2t}^*\}},
$$

where r_t is the regime indicator.

There is a one to one relationship between (y_{1t}^*, y_{2t}^*) and (y_t, y_t^*, r_t), and the conditional p.d.f. of (y_t, y_t^*, r_t) given $\mathcal{I}_{t-1} = (y_{1,t-1}^*, y_{2,t-1}^*, \underline{z_t}) = (y_{t-1}, y_{t-1}^*, r_{t-1}, \underline{z_t})$ is

$$
f_t(y_t, y_t^*, r_t / \mathcal{I}_{t-1}; \theta) = \frac{\mathbb{1}_{\{y_t < y_t^*\}}}{\sigma_1 \sigma_2} \left[\varphi \left(\frac{y_t - m_{1t}^*(\theta)}{\sigma_1} \right) \varphi \left(\frac{y_t^* - m_{2t}^*(\theta)}{\sigma_2} \right) \mathbb{1}_{\{1\}}(r_t) \right.
$$
$$
\left. + \varphi \left(\frac{y_t - m_{2t}^*(\theta)}{\sigma_2} \right) \varphi \left(\frac{y_t^* - m_{1t}^*(\theta)}{\sigma_1} \right) \mathbb{1}_{\{0\}}(r_t) \right], \quad (7.4)
$$

where $m_{1t}^*(\theta)$ and $m_{2t}^*(\theta)$ are the conditional expectations of y_{1t}^* and y_{2t}^* given $\mathcal{I}_{t-1}$, i.e.

$$
m_{1t}^*(\theta) = z_{1t}a_1 + y_{1,t-1}^* b_1 + y_{2,t-1}^* c_1,
$$
$$
m_{2t}^*(\theta) = z_{2t}a_2 + y_{1,t-1}^* b_2 + y_{2,t-1}^* c_2,
$$

and θ is a notation for the parameter set $(a_1', a_2', b_1, b_2, c_1, c_2, \sigma_1, \sigma_2)'$. Note that the p.d.f. $f_t(y_t, y_t^*, r_t / \mathcal{I}_{t-1}; \theta)$ given in (7.4) is taken with respect to the measure $\lambda_2 \otimes (\delta_0 + \delta_1)$, where λ_2 is the Lebesgue measure on $\mathbb{R}^2$ and δ_0, δ_1 are the unit masses on 0 and 1.

We can deduce the p.d.f. of $y_{\underline{T}}$, $y_{\underline{T}}^*$, $r_{\underline{T}}$ (given some initial values):

$$
\prod_{t=1}^{T} f_t(y_t, y_t^*, r_t / \mathcal{I}_{t-1}; \theta).
\tag{7.5}
$$

Therefore the likelihood function, or the p.d.f., of y_T is:

$$\ell_T(\theta) = \sum_{r_T} \int \prod_{t=1}^{T} f_t(y_t, y_t^*, r_t/\mathcal{I}_{t-1}; \theta) \prod_{t=1}^{T} dy_t^*. \tag{7.6}$$

This likelihood function appears as a sum of 2^T T-dimensional integrals, and is, therefore, a priori intractable.

In this context, it is possible to use the simulated PML method based on static (or unconditional) moments. More precisely, let us define

$$Y_t = (y_t, y_{t-1}, \ldots, y_{t-k})', \qquad \text{for some } k,$$
$$M_t(\theta) = E_\theta(Y_t/z_t),$$
$$V_t(\theta) = V_\theta(Y_t/z_t).$$

The PML1 and PML2 methods, based on normal pseudo-likelihood functions and on static (or unconditional) moments, consist in minimizing, respectively,

$$\sum_{t=1}^{T} \|Y_t - M_t(\theta)\|^2$$

and

$$\sum_{t=1}^{T} \left[\log \det V_t(\theta) + (Y_t - M_t(\theta))' V_t^{-1}(\theta)(Y_t - M_t(\theta)) \right].$$

Since $M_t(\theta)$ and $V_t(\theta)$ do not have closed forms, we consider their simulated analogues in which $M_t(\theta)$ and $V_t(\theta)$ are replaced by approximations based on path simulations of the model, $Y_t^s(\theta)$ $s = 1, \ldots, S$:

$$M_t^S(\theta) = \frac{1}{S} \sum_{s=1}^{S} Y_t^s(\theta)$$

$$V_t^S(\theta) = \frac{1}{S-1} \sum_{s=1}^{S} \left[Y_t^s(\theta) - M_t^S(\theta) \right] \left[Y_t^s(\theta) - M_t^S(\theta) \right]'.$$

Laroque and Salanié (1993) proposed a Monte Carlo study based on

$$\begin{cases} y_{1t}^* = z_{1t}a_1 + by_{1,t-1}^* + \sigma_1\varepsilon_{1t} \\ y_{2t}^* = z_{2t}a_2 + \sigma_2\varepsilon_{2t} \\ y_t = \min(y_{1t}^*, y_{2t}^*), \end{cases} \tag{7.7}$$

where the z_{1t} are independently distributed in $N(2.5, 2.5^2)$, $z_{2t} = 5$, $(\varepsilon_{1t}, \varepsilon_{2t})$ follow independently $N(0, I_2)$, $a_1 = a_2 = \sigma_1 = \sigma_2 = 1$, $b = 0.5$, $T = 50$, $S = 10, 20, 50$, $k = 0$, and 200 replications have been performed.

The results obtained for the SPML2 estimates are reproduced in Table 7.2. As can be seen, the estimation biases are rather small in spite of the fact that k has been taken equal to 0, i.e. Y_t is simply y_t.

TABLE 7.2: Monte Carlo experiment in the dynamic disequilibrium model.

	True value	Mean estimate			Dispersion of estimate		
		$S = 10$	$S = 20$	$S = 50$	$S = 10$	$S = 20$	$S = 50$
a_1	1.00	1.02	1.04	1.07	0.22	0.24	0.31
b	0.50	0.50	0.50	0.49	0.06	0.06	0.05
a_2	1.00	1.01	1.00	0.99	0.08	0.06	0.05
σ_1	1.00	1.03	0.99	0.98	0.28	0.26	0.32
σ_2	1.00	1.04	1.00	0.96	0.25	0.23	0.20

SML methods

Lee (1995) has proposed two SML methods based on the following decompositions of $f_t(y_t, y_t^*, r_t/\mathcal{I}_{t-1}; \theta)$:

$$f_t(y_t, y_t^*, r_t/\mathcal{I}_{t-1}; \theta) = f_t(y_t^*/y_t, r_t, \mathcal{I}_{t-1}; \theta) f_t(y_t/r_t, \mathcal{I}_{t-1}; \theta) f_t(r_t/\mathcal{I}_{t-1}; \theta) \tag{7.8}$$

and

$$f_t(y_t, y_t^*, r_t/\mathcal{I}_{t-1}; \theta) = f_t(y_t^*/y_t, r_t, \mathcal{I}_{t-1}; \theta) f_t(r_t/y_t, \mathcal{I}_{t-1}; \theta) f_t(y_t/\mathcal{I}_{t-1}; \theta). \tag{7.9}$$

Using decomposition (7.8), the likelihood function (7.6) appears as the expectation of the function $\prod_{t=1}^T f_t(y_t/r_t, \mathcal{I}_{t-1}; \theta)$ with respect to the variables $y_1^*, \ldots, y_T^*$, $r_1, \ldots, r_T$, and using the probability distribution whose p.d.f. is:

$$\prod_{t=1}^T f_t(y_t^*/y_t, r_t, \mathcal{I}_{t-1}; \theta) f_t(r_t/\mathcal{I}_{t-1}; \theta).$$

Drawing independently S paths $(y_t^{*s}(\theta), r_t^s(\theta), t = 1, \ldots, T)$, $s = 1, \ldots, S$, in this distribution, we get an unbiased simulator of $\ell_T(\theta)$

$$\frac{1}{S} \sum_{s=1}^S \prod_{t=1}^T f_t(y_t/r_t^s(\theta), \mathcal{I}_{t-1}^s(\theta); \theta), \tag{7.10}$$

where $\mathcal{I}_{t-1}^s(\theta) = \{\underline{y_{t-1}}, y_{t-1}^{*s}(\theta), r_{t-1}^s(\theta), \underline{z_t}\}$.

Similarly, using decomposition (7.9) we get another unbiased simulator:

$$\frac{1}{S} \sum_{s=1}^S \prod_{t=1}^T f_t(y_t/\mathcal{I}_{t-1}^s(\theta); \theta),$$

where the S paths $(y_t^{*s}(\theta), r_t^s(\theta), t = 1, \ldots, T), s = 1, \ldots, S$, have been drawn independently in the distribution whose p.d.f. is:

$$\prod_{t=1}^{T} f_t(y_t^*/y_t, r_t, \mathcal{I}_{t-1}; \theta) f_t(r_t/y_t, \mathcal{I}_{t-1}; \theta).$$

The latter method gives better results than the former, and in this case the three required p.d.f.s are:

$$f_t(y_t/\mathcal{I}_{t-1}; \theta) = \frac{1}{\sigma_1} \varphi \left(\frac{y_t - m_{1t}^*(\theta)}{\sigma_1} \right) \Phi \left(\frac{m_{2t}^*(\theta) - y_t}{\sigma_2} \right)$$
$$+ \frac{1}{\sigma_2} \varphi \left(\frac{y_t - m_{2t}^*(\theta)}{\sigma_2} \right) \Phi \left(\frac{m_{1t}^*(\theta) - y_t}{\sigma_1} \right)$$

$$f_t(1/y_t, \mathcal{I}_{t-1}; \theta) = \frac{1}{\sigma_1} \varphi \left(\frac{y_t - m_{1t}^*(\theta)}{\sigma_1} \right) \Phi \left(\frac{m_{2t}^*(\theta) - y_t}{\sigma_2} \right) \bigg/ f_t(y_t/\mathcal{I}_{t-1}; \theta),$$

$$f_t(y_t^*/y_t, r_t, \mathcal{I}_{t-1}; \theta) = \mathbb{1}_{\{y_t^* > y_t\}} \left[\frac{1}{\sigma_2} \mathbb{1}_{\{1\}}(r_t) \varphi \left(\frac{y_t^* - m_{2t}^*(\theta)}{\sigma_2} \right) \bigg/ \Phi \left(\frac{m_{2t}^*(\theta) - y_t}{\sigma_2} \right) \right.$$
$$\left. + \frac{1}{\sigma_1} \mathbb{1}_{\{0\}}(r_t) \varphi \left(\frac{y_t^* - m_{1t}^*(\theta)}{\sigma_1} \right) \bigg/ \Phi \left(\frac{m_{1t}^*(\theta) - y_t}{\sigma_1} \right) \right].$$

The last two p.d.f.s show how to draw r_t and y_t^* at each date t: first r_t is drawn in the distribution on $\{0, 1\}$ defined by $f_t(1/y_t, \mathcal{I}_{t-1}; \theta)$, then y_t^* is drawn in the truncated normal distribution defined by $f_t(y_t^*/y_t, r_t, \mathcal{I}_{t-1}; \theta)$. (We have seen in Section 5.1.3 how to realize such a drawing efficiently.)

The results of a Monte Carlo study using this method are reported in Lee (1995) and seem encouraging; however, it seems difficult to extend this approach to more complicated models where the likelihood function is intractable even in the static case (for instance, multimarket models).

7.2 Exogenously Switching Regime Models

7.2.1 Markovian vs. non-Markovian models

We consider the case of a model with two regimes, denoted by $r_t = 1$ and $r_t = 0$. The generalization to the case of k regimes is straightforward. These regimes are driven by a Markov chain, defined by:

$$r_t = \mathbb{1}_{\{0\}}(r_{t-1}) \mathbb{1}_{[\pi_0, 1]}(u_t) + \mathbb{1}_{\{1\}}(r_{t-1}) \mathbb{1}_{[0, \pi_1]}(u_t), \tag{7.11}$$

where the u_t follow independently $\mathcal{U}_{[0,1]}$, the uniform distribution on $[0, 1]$; π_0 and π_1 are, respectively, the probabilities of staying in state 0 and state 1.

Let us now assume that the observed endogenous variable y_t is given by:

$$y_t = g(y_{t-p}^{t-1}, r_{t-p}^t, v_t; \theta), \tag{7.12}$$

where $\{v_t\}$ is a white noise independent of $\{u_t\}$, with a known distribution, where $y_{t-p}^{t-1} = (y_{t-1}, \ldots, y_{t-p})$, $r_{t-p}^t = (r_t, \ldots, r_{t-p})$, and g is a known function.

The conditional distribution of (y_t, r_t) given (y_{t-1}, r_{t-1}) depends only on $(y_{t-p}^{t-1}, r_{t-p}^{t-1})$, and the process (y_t, r_t) is jointly Markovian of order p. (Note that this would remain true if r_t were Markovian of order p and if the transition probabilities were functions of y_{t-p}^{t-1}.)

In this case Kitagawa's algorithm, described in Section 6.3.2, can be used to compute the likelihood function (by taking $y_t^* = r_t$). The integrals appearing in this algorithm are sums over the 2^{p+1} possible values of r_{t-p}^t, and the algorithm may be tractable if p is not too large. The algorithm thus obtained has been used by Hamilton in various contexts, in particular in a switching $AR(p)$ model (Hamilton 1989) in which (7.12) is specified as:

$$\Phi(L)(y_t - r_t) = \sigma v_t,$$

where $\Phi(L)$ is a polynomial of degree p in the lag operator L, with $\Phi(0) = 1$.

However, when (y_t, r_t) is not Markovian such an algorithm cannot be used, since the number of terms in the sums at date t would be 2^t, which makes these sums rapidly uncomputable.

So, we will extend the model defined by (7.11), (7.12), and in this more general framework we will define inference methods based on simulations.

7.2.2   A switching state space model and the partial Kalman filter[1]

Let us consider a switching state space model defined by:

$$y_t = \mu(r_{t-p}^t, y_{t-p}^{t-1}) + A(r_{t-p}^t, y_{t-p}^{t-1})y_t^* + B(r_{t-p}^t, y_{t-p}^{t-1})\varepsilon_t, \tag{7.13}$$

$$y_t^* = \nu(r_{t-p}^t, y_{t-p}^{t-1}) + C(r_{t-p}^t, y_{t-p}^{t-1})y_{t-1}^* + D(r_{t-p}^t, y_{t-p}^{t-1})\eta_t, \tag{7.14}$$

$$r_t = \mathbb{1}_{\{0\}}(r_{t-1})\mathbb{1}_{[\pi_0(y_{t-p}^{t-1}),1]}(u_t) + \mathbb{1}_{\{1\}}(r_{t-1})\mathbb{1}_{[0,\pi_1(y_{t-p}^{t-1})]}(u_t), \tag{7.15}$$

where $\{\varepsilon_t\}$, $\{\eta_t\}$ are independent standard Gaussian white noises, $\{u_t\}$ is a white noise, independent of $\{\varepsilon_t\}\{\eta_t\}$, whose marginal distribution is $\mathcal{U}_{[0,1]}$, the uniform distribution on $[0, 1]$ and y_0, z_0, r_0 are nonrandom.

The dimensions of y_t and y_t^* are denoted by n and k respectively. The regime indicator variable r_t is assumed to take two values 0 and 1, but an extension to any finite number of regimes is straightforward, y_t is observable, r_t is unobservable, and y_t^* is (at least partially) unobservable.

---

[1]This subsection refers to Billio and Monfort (1995).

Note that, from (7.15), y_t^* does not cause r_t in the Granger sense, but y_t may cause r_t and, therefore, r_t may be not strongly exogenous but only predetermined.

The framework defined by (7.13)–(7.15) contains many interesting models as particular cases: switching ARMA models (which may have a nontrivial moving average part), switching factor models, dynamic switching regressions, deformed time models, models with endogenously missing data, and so on (see Billio and Monfort 1995).

The partial Kalman filter, denoted by $\text{KF}(r_T)$, is defined as the Kalman filter mechanically applied to the linear state space model obtained from (7.13), (7.14) for any given sequence $\underline{r_T}$.

It can be shown that, if the assumption of noncausality from y_t^* to r_t (implied by (7.15)) holds, the conditional distributions $\mathcal{L}(y_t^*/\underline{y_{t-1}}, \underline{r_t})$, $\mathcal{L}(y_t^*/\underline{y_t}, \underline{r_t})$, and $\mathcal{L}(y_t/\underline{y_{t-1}}, \underline{r_t})$ are normal distributions whose expectations and variance–covariance matrices are the outputs of the partial Kalman filter:

$$\tilde{y}_{t/t-1}^*(\underline{r_t}), \qquad \tilde{\Sigma}_{t/t-1}(\underline{r_t})$$
$$\tilde{y}_{t/t}^*(\underline{r_t}), \qquad \tilde{\Sigma}_{t/t}(\underline{r_t})$$
$$\tilde{y}_{t/t-1}(\underline{r_t}), \qquad \tilde{M}_{t/t-1}(\underline{r_t}).$$

These outputs are very useful tools for the computation of the likelihood function of the model, or of the filters of y_t^* and r_t. (Similarly a partial Kalman smoother can be defined and used for the computation of the smoothers of y_t^* and r_t.) In particular, the p.d.f. $f(y_t/\underline{y_{t-1}}, \underline{r_t})$ of $N(\tilde{y}_{t/t-1}(\underline{r_t}), \tilde{M}_{t/t-1}(\underline{r_t}))$ will be useful for the computation of the likelihood function.

7.2.3   Computation of the likelihood function

The basic sequential sampling method

Let us define, for any $\underline{r_T}$, the partial likelihood function as:

$$\tilde{\ell}_T(\underline{r_T}) = \prod_{t=1}^{T} f(y_t/\underline{y_{t-1}}, \underline{r_t}), \tag{7.16}$$

and let us denote by P the probability distribution on $\{0, 1\}^T$ defined by:

$$\prod_{t=1}^{T} p(r_t/\underline{y_{t-1}}, \underline{r_{t-1}}),$$

where $p(i/\underline{y_{t-1}}, \underline{r_{t-1}}), i = 0, 1$, are the probabilities of the Bernoulli distributions:

$$\mathcal{B}\left[(1 - \pi_0(y_{t-p}^{t-1}))\mathbb{1}_{\{0\}}(r_{t-1}) + \pi_1(y_{t-p}^{t-1})\mathbb{1}_{\{1\}}(r_{t-1})\right].$$

The likelihood function ℓ_T can be written as:

$$\ell_T = \Sigma_{r_T} f(y_T, r_T)$$

$$= \Sigma_{r_T} \prod_{t=1}^{T} f(y_t/y_{t-1}, r_t) p(r_t/y_{t-1}, r_{t-1})$$

$$= E^P \tilde{\ell}_T(r_T). \tag{7.17}$$

In theory, this formula provides an unbiased simulator of ℓ_T and a way of approximating ℓ_T from S independent simulated paths $\{\tilde{r}_t^s\}$, $s = 1, \ldots, S$, drawn in P; this approximation is:

$$\frac{1}{S} \sum_{s=1}^{S} \prod_{t=1}^{T} f(y_t/y_{t-1}, \tilde{r}_t^s). \tag{7.18}$$

However this method provides very poor results and must be improved.

Sequentially optimal sampling (SOS) methods

Using arguments based on the sequential optimality of importance sampling methods, several improvements of the basic sequential sampling method have been proposed (in Billio and Monfort 1995).

(i) The first order sequentially optimal sampling (SOS(1)) method is based on the following unbiased simulator of ℓ_T:

$$f^*(y_1) \frac{1}{S} \sum_{s=1}^{S} \prod_{t=2}^{T} f^*(y_t/y_{t-1}, \tilde{r}_{t-1}^s), \tag{7.19}$$

where:

$$f^*(y_t/y_{t-1}, \tilde{r}_{t-1}) = \sum_{r=0}^{1} f(y_t/y_{t-1}, r, \tilde{r}_{t-1}) p(r/y_{t-1}, \tilde{r}_{t-1}),$$

$$f^*(y_1) = f^*(y_1/y_0, r_0), \tag{7.20}$$

and where the S paths $(\tilde{r}_t^s, r = 1, \ldots, T - 1)$, $s = 1, \ldots, S$, have been independently drawn in the distribution on $\{0, 1\}^{T-1}$ defined by:

$$\prod_{t=1}^{T-1} p^*(\tilde{r}_t/y_t, \tilde{r}_{t-1})$$

with

$$p^*(r_t/y_t, \tilde{r}_{t-1}) = \frac{f(y_t/y_{t-1}, r_t, \tilde{r}_{t-1}) p(r_t/y_{t-1}, \tilde{r}_{t-1})}{f^*(y_t/y_{t-1}, \tilde{r}_{t-1})}. \tag{7.21}$$

(ii) The second order sequentially optimal sampling (SOS(2)) method uses the unbiased simulator (assuming T even):

$$f^*(y_2, y_1) \frac{1}{S} \sum_{s=1}^{S} \prod_{k=2}^{T/2} f^*(y_{2k}, y_{2k-1}/\underline{y_{2k-2}}, \tilde{r}^s_{2k-2}), \qquad (7.22)$$

where

$$f^*(y_{t+1}, y_t/\underline{y_{t-1}}, \tilde{r}_{t-1})$$

$$= \sum_{r_{t+1}=0, r_t=0}^{1} [f(y_t/\underline{y_{t-1}}, r_t, \tilde{r}_{t-1}) f(y_{t+1}/\underline{y_t}, r_{t+1}, r_t, \tilde{r}_{t-1}) p(r_t/\underline{y_{t-1}}, \tilde{r}_{t-1})$$

$$\times p(r_{t+1}/\underline{y_t}, r_t, \tilde{r}_{t-1})], \qquad (7.23)$$

and where each of the S paths $(\tilde{r}^s_t, t = 1, \ldots, T-2)$, $s = 1, \ldots, S$, has been drawn by pairs using sequentially the probabilities

$$p^*(r_{t+1}, r_t/\underline{y_{t+1}}, \tilde{r}_{t-1}) = \left[f(y_t/\underline{y_{t-1}}, r_t, \tilde{r}_{t-1}) f(y_{t+1}/\underline{y_t}, r_{t+1}, r_t, \tilde{r}_{t-1}) \right.$$

$$\left. \times p(r_t/\underline{y_{t-1}}, \tilde{r}_{t-1}) p(r_{t+1}/\underline{y_t}, r_t, \tilde{r}_{t-1}) \right] / \left[f^*(y_{t+1}, y_t/\underline{y_{t-1}}, \tilde{r}_{t-1}) \right]. \quad (7.24)$$

(iii) A strong second order sequentially optimal sampling (SOS*(2)) has also been proposed and is based on the unbiased simulator:

$$f^*(y_1) f^{**}(y_2/y_1) \frac{1}{S} \sum_{s=1}^{S} \prod_{t=3}^{T} f^{**}(y_t/\underline{y_{t-1}}, \tilde{r}^s_{t-2}),$$

where

$$f^{**}(y_{t+1}/\underline{y_t}, \tilde{r}_{t-1}) = \sum_{r_t=0}^{1} f^*(y_{t+1}/\underline{y_t}, r_t, \tilde{r}^{t-1}) p^*(r_t/\underline{y_t}, \tilde{r}_{t-1})$$

$$= \left\{ \sum_{r_t=0, r_{t+1}=0}^{1} [f(y_{t+1}/\underline{y_t}, r_{t+1}, r_t, \tilde{r}_{t-1}) p(r_{t+1}/y^t, r_t, \tilde{r}_{t-1}) \right.$$

$$\left. \times f(y_t/\underline{y_{t-1}}, r_t, \tilde{r}_{t-1}) p(r_t/\underline{y_{t-1}}, \tilde{r}_{t-1})] \right\} / \left\{ \sum_{s_t=0}^{1} [f(y_t/\underline{y_{t-1}}, r_t, \tilde{r}_{t-1}) \right.$$

$$\left. \times p(r_t/\underline{y_{t-1}}, \tilde{r}_{t-1})] \right\}, \qquad (7.25)$$

and where the S paths $(\tilde{r}^s_t, t = 1, \ldots, T-2)$ have been sequentially drawn from:

$$p^{**}(r_t/\underline{y_{t+1}}, \tilde{r}_{t-1})$$

$$= f(y_t/\underline{y_{t-1}}, r_t, \tilde{r}_{t-1}) p(r_t/\underline{y_{t-1}}, \tilde{r}_{t-1}) \left\{ \sum_{r_{t+1}=0}^{1} [f(y_{t+1}/\underline{y_t}, r_{t+1}, r_t, \tilde{r}_{t-1}) \right.$$

$$\left. \times p(r_{t+1}/\underline{y_t}, r_t, \tilde{r}_{t-1})] \right\} / \left\{ \sum_{r_t=0, r_{t+1}=0}^{1} [f(y_{t+1}/\underline{y_t}, r_{t+1}, r_t, \tilde{r}_{t-1}) \right.$$

$$\left. \times p(r_{t+1}/\underline{y_t}, r_t, \tilde{r}_{t-1}) f(y_t/\underline{y_{t-1}}, r_t, \tilde{r}_{t-1}) p(r_t/\underline{y_{t-1}}, \tilde{r}_{t-1})] \right\}. \qquad (7.26)$$

TABLE 7.3: ($T = 100$).

Simulator	Simulated likelihood mean	Log simulated likelihood mean	Variance $\times 10^5$
BASIC	3.52×10^{-20}	1.4314	1.2×10^{-34}
SOS(1)	0.9902	1.0001	288
SOS(2)	1.0096	0.9999	199
SOS*(2)	1.0078	0.9999	12

This procedure could be generalized to an SOS*(p) method; but, clearly, the computational burden increases with p—in the limit case $p = T$ we would get the exact likelihood function.

Monte Carlo study

In order to evaluate the performances of the previous methods, we consider a simple case in which the likelihood function is computable by Hamilton's algorithm, namely the switching AR(1) model:

$$y_t = \mu_0 + (\mu_1 - \mu_0)r_t + \varphi[z_{t-1} - \mu_0 - (\mu_1 - \mu_0)r_{t-1}] + \sigma\varepsilon_t, \quad (7.27)$$

with:

$$\mu_0 = -0.72, \qquad \mu_1 = 0.94, \qquad \varphi = 0.32, \qquad \sigma = 0.5,$$

where r_t is a two state Markov chain defined by $\pi_0 = 0.89$ (probability of staying at 0) and $\pi_1 = 0.84$ (probability of staying at 1), and $\{\varepsilon_t\}$ is a standard Gaussian white noise independent of $\{r_t\}$.

We considered samples of various lengths T drawn from this process.

For each of the four previous methods (BASIC, SOS(1), SOS(2), SOS*(2)) we computed $S = 10\,000$ simulations of the value of the likelihood function at the true parameter. Each simulation was divided by the true value of the likelihood function, and Table 7.3 gives, for $T = 100$, the mean of these normalized simulations, the log of this mean divided by the log of the likelihood function, and the estimated variance of the mean of the normalized simulations.

From Table 7.3 it is clear that the basic method does not work at all, whereas the SOS(1), SOS(2), SOS*(2) give satisfactory results and the ordering of their respective performances is as expected.

Figure 7.1 shows the variability of the various simulators. Note that we have plotted the log simulators in order to be able to show them on the same graph (with the same scale).

Figure 7.2 shows the convergence rate of the log simulated mean for the various methods (except the basic method, which does not converge). From this figure it appears that the SOS*(2) method is the best: for this method, the mean is close to 1 as soon as S is larger than 50.

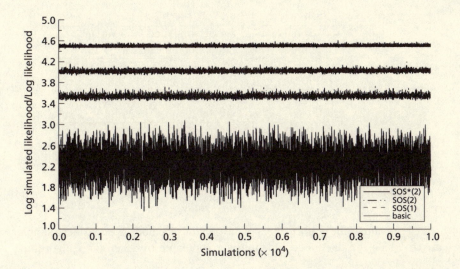

FIGURE 7.1: Log simulated likelihood/log likelihood, AR model, $T = 100$; $S = 10\,000$.

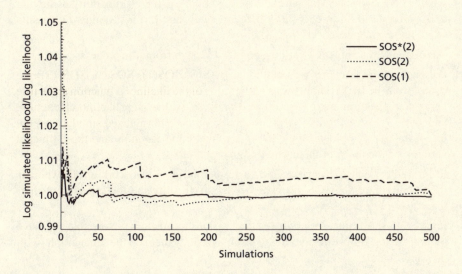

FIGURE 7.2: Convergence of the log simulated likelihood/log likelihood, AR model, $T = 100$; $S = 500$.

REFERENCES

AIT-SAHALIA, Y. (1996), 'Non Parametric Pricing of Interest Rate Derivative Securities', Econometrica, 64: 527–64.

AMARO de MATOS, J. (1994), 'MSM Estimators of American Option Pricing Models', INSEAD Discussion Paper, presented at AFFI Meeting, Tunis.

ANDERSEN, T., and B. SORENSEN (1993), 'GMM Estimation of a Stochastic Volatility Model: A Monte-Carlo Study', Discussion Paper, Northwestern University.

ANDERSON, B., and J. B. MOORE (1979), 'Optimal Filtering', Prentice-Hall, Englewood Cliffs, NJ.

ANDREWS, D. (1993), 'Exactly Median Unbiased Estimation of First Order Autoregressive/Unit Root Models', Econometrica, 61: 139–65.

BERRY, S., and A. PAKES (1990), 'The Performance of Alternative Simulation Estimators', Discussion Paper, Yale University.

BIANCHI, C., R. CESARI, and L. PANATTONI (1993), 'Alternative Estimators of a Diffusion Model of the Term Structure of Interest Rate: A Monte Carlo Comparison', Discussion Paper presented at ESEM, Uppsala.

BIERINGS, H., and K. SNEEK (1989), 'Pseudo-Maximum Likelihood Techniques in a Simple Rationing Model for the Dutch Labour Market', mimeo, University of Limburg and Free University of Amsterdam.

BILLIO, M., and A. MONFORT (1995), 'Switching State Space Models: Likelihood Function, Filtering and Smoothing', Discussion Paper no. 9557, CREST.

BLACK, F., and M. SCHOLES (1973), 'The Pricing of Options and Corporate Liabilities', Journal of Political Economy, 81: 637–59.

BLOEMEN, H., and A. KAPTEYN (1990), 'The Joint Estimation of a Non-Linear Labour Supply Function and a Wage Equation Using Simulated Response Probabilities', Discussion Paper, Tilburg University.

BOLDUC, D. (1992), 'Generalized Autoregressive Errors in the Multivariate Probit Model', Transportation Research B—Methodological, 26: 155–70.

—— (1994), 'Estimation of Multinomial Probit Models Using Maximum Simulated Likelihood with Analytical Derivatives and GHK Choice Probability Simulator', Discussion Paper, Laval University.

—— and M. KACI (1991), 'Estimation des modèles probit polytomiques: un survol des techniques', Discussion Paper 9127, Laval University.

BÖRCH-SUPAN, A., and V. HAJIVASSILIOU (1993), 'Smooth Unbiased Multivariate Probability Simulators for Maximum Likelihood Estimation of Limited Dependent Variable Models', Journal of Econometrics, 58: 347–68.

—— —— L. KOTLIKOFF, and J. MORRIS (1991), 'Health, Children, and Elderly Living Arrangements: a Multiperiod, Multinational Probit Model with Unobserved Heterogeneity and Autocorrelated Errors', in Topics in the Economics of Aging, D. Wise (ed.), University of Chicago Press.

BOSSAERTS, P. (1989), 'The Asymptotic Normality of Method of Simulated Moments Estimators of Option Pricing Models', Discussion Paper, Carnegie Mellon University.

—— and P. Hillion (1988), 'Method of Moment Tests of Contingent Claims Asset Pricing Models', Discussion Paper, Carnegie Mellon University.

BRENNAN, M., and E. SCHWARTZ (1979), 'A Continuous Time Approach to the Pricing of Bonds', Journal of Banking and Finance, 3: 135–53.

BROWN, B. (1990), 'Simulation Based Semi-Parametric Estimation and Prediction in Nonlinear Systems', Discussion Paper, Rice University.

—— and R. S. MARIANO (1984), 'Residual-Based Procedure for Prediction and Estimation in Nonlinear Simultaneous Systems', Econometrica, 52: 321–43.

BROZE, L., and C. GOURIÉROUX (1993), 'Covariance Estimators and Adjusted Pseudo-Maximum Likelihood Method', CORE Discussion Paper 9313.

—— O. SCAILLET, and J. M. ZAKOÏAN (1995), 'Testing for Continuous-Time Models of the Short Term Interest Rate', Journal of Empirical Finance, 2, 199–223.

—— —— and J M ZAKOÏAN (1995a), 'Quasi Indirect Inference for Diffusion Processes', CORE Discussion Paper 9505.

—— —— —— (1995*b*), 'Tests de Spécification fondés sur des simulations: le cas des diffusions', Discussion Paper, CORE.

BUTLER, J. S., and R. MOFFITT (1982), 'A Computationally Efficient Quadrature Procedure for One-Factor Multinomial Probit Model', Econometrica, 50: 761–4.

CANOVA, F. (1992), 'Statistical Inference by Calibration', Discussion Paper, Brown University.

CHAN, K., G. KAROLYI, F. LONGSTAFF, and A. SANDERS (1992), 'An Empirical Comparison of Alternative Models of the Short Term Interest Rate', Journal of Finance, 47: 1209–27.

CHESHER, A., and T. LANCASTER (1983), 'The Estimation of Models of Labour Market Behaviour', Review of Economic Studies, 50: 609–24.

CLARK, P. (1973), 'A Subordinated Stochastic Process Model with Finite Variance for Speculative Prices', Econometrica, 41: 135–55.

CLEMENT, E. (1994), 'Inférence statistique des processus de diffusion', Discussion Paper 9404, CREST.

COLEMAN, J. (1990), 'Solving the Stochastic Growth Model by Policy-Function Iteration', Journal of Business and Economic Statistics, 8: 27–30.

CONLEY, T., L. HANSEN, E. LUTTMER, and J. SCHEINKMAN (1994), 'Estimating Subordinated Diffusions from Discrete Data', Discussion Paper, University of Chicago.

COX, D. R. (1961), 'Test of Separate Families of Hypotheses', in Proceedings of the Fourth Berkeley Symposium on Mathematical Statistics and Probability, i, University of California Press, Berkeley, 105–23.

DACUNHA-CASTELLE, D., and D. FLORENS (1986), 'Estimation of the Coefficient of a Diffusion from Discrete Observation', Stochastics, 19: 263–84.

DANIELSSON, J. (1993), 'Multivariate Stochastic Volatility', Discussion Paper, University of Iceland.

—— (1994), 'Stochastic Volatility in Asset Prices: Estimation with Simulated Maximum Likelihood', Journal of Econometrics, 64: 375–400.

—— and J.-F. RICHARD (1993), 'Accelerated Gaussian Importance Sampler with Application to Dynamic Latent Variable Models', Journal of Applied Econometrics, 8: 153–73.

DELLAPORTAS, P., and A. SMITH (1993), 'Bayesian Inference for Generalized Linear and Proportional Hazards Models via Gibbs Sampling', Applied Statistics, 42: 443–59.

DEN HAAN, W., and A. MARCET (1994), 'Accuracy in Simulations', Review of Economic Studies, 61: 3–17.

DE WINNE, R. (1994), 'Processus de diffusion de taux d'intérét et correction du biais de discrétisation', mimeo, FUCAM.

DIEBOLD, F., and M. NERLOVE (1989), 'The Dynamic of Exchange Rate Volatility: a Multivariate Latent Factor ARCH Model', Journal of Applied Econometrics, 4: 1–22.

DUFFIE, D., and K. SINGLETON (1993), 'Simulated Moments Estimation of Markov Models of Asset Prices', Econometrica, 61: 929–52.

ENGLE, R. (1982), 'Autoregressive Conditional Heteroscedasticity with Estimates of the Variance of United Kingdom Inflations', Econometrica, 50: 987–1007.

—— and G. LEE (1994), 'Estimating Diffusion Models of Stochastic Volatility', Discussion Paper, University of California at San Diego.

—— V. NG, and M. ROTHSCHILD (1990), 'Asset Pricing with a Factor ARCH Covariance Structure: Empirical Estimates for Treasury Bills', Journal of Econometrics, 45: 213–37.

ERDEN, T., and M. KEANE (1992), 'A Dynamic Structural Model for Estimating Market Structure in Panel Data', Discussion Paper, University of Alberta.

FRACHOT, A., and C. GOURIÉROUX (1994), Titrisation et remboursements anticipés, Economica, Paris.

—— J. P. LESNE, and E. RENAULT (1995), 'Indirect Inference Estimation of Factor Models of the Yield Curve', Discussion Papers, Université d'Evry.

GALLANT, A. R. (1987), Nonlinear Statistical Models, John Wiley, New York.

—— and G. TAUCHEN (1996), 'Which Moments to Match?', Econometric Theory (forthcoming).

—— and H. WHITE (1988), A Unified Theory of Estimation and Inference for Nonlinear Dynamic Models, Basil Blackwell, Oxford.

—— D. HSIEH, and G. TAUCHEN (1994), 'Estimation of Stochastic Volatility Models with Diagnostics', Discussion Paper, Duke University.

GELFAND, A., and A. SMITH (1990), 'Sampling Based Approaches to Calculating Marginal Densities', Journal of the American Statistical Association, 85: 398–409.

—— S. HILLS, A. RACINE POON, and A. SMITH (1990), 'Illustration of Bayesian Inference in Normal Data Models using Gibbs Sampling', Journal of the American Statistical Association, 85: 972–85.

—— A. SMITH, and T. LEE (1992), 'Bayesian Analysis of Constrained Parameter and Truncated Data Problems', Journal of the American Statistical Association, 87: 523–32.

GENON-CATALOT, V. (1990), 'Maximum Contrast Estimation for Diffusion Processes from Discrete Observations', Statistics, 21: 99–116.

GEWEKE, J. (1989a), 'Efficient Simulation from the Multivariate Normal Distribution Subject to Linear Inequality Constraints and the Evolution of Constraint Probabilities', Discussion Paper, Duke University.

—— (1989b), 'Statistical Inference in Dynamic Behavioral Models using the Simulated Multinomial Likelihood Function', Discussion Paper, North Carolina University.

—— (1991), 'Efficient Simulation From the Multivariate Normal and Student t-Distributions Subject to Linear Constraints', Computing Science and Statistics, Proceedings of the Twenty Third Symposium on the Interface. Computing Science and Statistics, America Statistical Association, Alexandria, VA, 571–78.

—— M. KEANE, and P. RUNKLE (1992a), 'Alternative Computational Approaches to Statistical Inference in the Multinomial Probit Model', Discussion Paper, Federal Reserve Bank of Minneapolis.

—— —— —— and P. RUUD (1992b), 'Alternative Computational Approaches to Statistical Inference in the Multinomial Probit Model', Discussion Paper, University of Minnesota.

—— J. R. SLONIM, and G. ZARKIN (1992c), 'Econometric Solution Methods for Dynamic Discrete Choice Problems', Discussion Paper, University of Minnesota.

GHYSELS, E., C. GOURIÉROUX, and J. JASIAK (1994a), 'Market Time and Asset Price Movements: Theory and Estimation', Discussion Paper, CREST and CIRANO.

GHYSELS, E., L. KHALAF, and C. VODOUNOU (1994b), 'Simulation Based Inference in Moving Average Models', Discussion Paper, University of Montréal.

GOURIÉROUX, C. (1992), Modèles ARCH et applications financières, Economica, Paris; English translation, Springer Verlag, forthcoming.

—— and F. JOUNEAU (1994), 'Multivariate Distributions for Limited Dependent Variable Models', Discussion Paper, CEPREMAP.

—— and A. MONFORT (1989), Statistique et modèles econométriques, Economica, Paris; English translation, Cambridge University Press, 1995.

—— —— (1991), 'Simulation Based Econometrics in Models with Heterogeneity', Annales d'Economie et de Statistique, 20/1: 69–107.

—— —— (1993a), 'Simulation Based Inference: a Survey with Special Reference to Panel Data Models', Journal of Econometrics, 59: 5–33.

—— —— (1993b), 'Pseudo Likelihood Methods', in Handbook of Statistics, G. S. MADDALA, C. R. RAO, and H. VINOD (eds.), North-Holland, Amsterdam.

—— (1995), 'Testing, Encompassing, and Simulating Dynamic Econometric Models', Econometric Theory, 11: 195–228.

—— —— and A. TROGNON (1984a), 'Estimation and Test in Probit Models with Serial Correlation', in Alternative Approaches to Time Series Analysis, J. P. FLORENS, et al. (eds.), University St Louis, Brussels.

—— —— —— (1984b), 'Pseudo-Maximum Likelihood Methods: Theory', Econometrica, 52: 681–700.

—— —— —— (1984c), 'Pseudo-Maximum Likelihood Methods: Applications to Poisson Models', Econometrica, 52: 701–20.

—— —— A. E. RENAULT, and A. TROGNON (1987), 'Simulated Residuals', Journal of Econometrics, 34: 201–52.

—— —— —— (1991), 'Dynamic Factor Models', Discussion Paper, CREST.

—— —— —— (1993), 'Indirect Inference', Journal of Applied Econometrics, 8: 85–118.

—— E. C. RENAULT, and N. TOUZI (1994), 'Calibration by Simulation for Small Sample Bias Correction', Discussion Paper, CREST.

GREGORY, A. W., and G. W. SMITH (1991), 'Calibration as Testing Inference in Simulated Macroeconomic Models', Journal of Business and Economic Statistics, 9: 297–303.

GUARD, T. C. (1988), Introduction to Stochastic Differential Equations, Marcel Dekker, New York.

HAJIVASSILIOU, V. A. (1993a), 'A Simulation Estimation Analysis of the External Debt Crises of Developing Countries', Discussion Paper 1057, Cowles Foundation, Yale University.

—— (1993b), 'Simulation Estimation Methods for Limited Dependent Variable Models', in Handbook of Statistics, ii, G. S. MADDALA, C. R. RAO, and H. VINOD (eds.), North-Holland, Amsterdam, 519–43.

—— (1993*c*), 'Simulation for Multivariate Normal Rectangle Probabilities and their Derivatives: The Effects of Vectorization', in International Journal of Supercomputer Applications, 231–53.

—— and D. MCFADDEN (1989), 'Country Heterogeneity and External Debt Crises: Estimation by the Method of Simulated Moments', mimeo.

—— —— (1990), 'The Method for Simulated Scores for the Estimation of LDV Models with an Application to External Debt Crises', Discussion Paper 697, Cowles Foundation, Yale University.

—— and P. RUUD (1994), 'Estimation by Simulation', forthcoming in Handbook of Econometrics , iv, C. ENGLE, and D. MCFADDEN (eds.), North-Holland, Amsterdam.

—— D. MCFADDEN, and P. RUUD (1996), 'Simulation of Multivariate Normal Rectangle Probabilities', Journal of Econometrics, 72: 85–134.

HAMILTON, J. (1989), 'A New Approach to the Economic Analysis of Nonstationary Time Series and the Business Cycle', Econometrica, 57: 357–84.

HANSEN, L. (1982), 'Large Sample Properties of Generalized Method of Moments Estimators', Econometrica, 50: 1029–54.

—— and J. SCHEINKMAN (1995), 'Back to the Future: Generating Moment Implications for Continuous Time Markov Processes', Econometrica, 63(4): 767–804.

—— and K. SINGLETON (1982), 'Generalized Instrumental Variables Estimation of Nonlinear Rational Expectations Models', Econometrica, 50: 1269–86.

HARVEY, A., E. RUIZ, and N. SHEPHARD (1994), 'Multivariate Stochastic Variance Models', Review of Economic Studies, 61: 247–64.

HASTINGS, W. K. (1970),'Monte Carlo Sampling Methods Using Markov Chains and their Applications', Biometrika, 57: 97–109.

HAUSMAN, J., and D. WISE (1978), 'A Conditional Probit Model for Qualitative Choice: Discrete Decisions, Recognizing Interdependence and Heterogenous Preferences', Econometrica, 46: 403–26.

HEATON, J. (1995),'An Empirical Investigation of Asset Pricing with Temporally Dependent Reference Specifications', Econometrica, 63: 681–717.

HECKMAN, J. (1981), 'Statistical Models for Discrete Panel Data', in Structural Analysis of Discrete Data with Economic Applications, C. MANSKI and D. MCFADDEN (eds.), MIT Press, Cambridge, Mass.

HOTZ, J., and R. MILLER (1993), 'Conditional Choice Probabilities and the Estimation of Dynamic Programming Models', Review of Economic Studies, 60: 497–530.

—— and S. SANDERS (1990), 'The Estimation of Dynamic Discrete Choice Models by the Method of Simulated Moments', Discussion Paper, University of Chicago.

—— R. MILLER, S. SANDERS, and J. SMITH (1992), 'A Simulation Estimator for Dynamic Models of Discrete Choice', Discussion Paper, University of Chicago.

HULL, J., and A. WHITE (1987), 'The Pricing of Options on Assets with Stochastic Volatility', Journal of Finance, 3: 281–300.

ICHIMURA, H., and T. SCOTT-THOMPSON (1993), 'Maximum Likelihood Estimation of a Binary Choice Model with Random Coefficients of Unknown Distribution', Discussion Paper 268, University of Minnesota.

INGRAM, B. F., and B. S. LEE (1991), 'Estimation by Simulation of Time Series Models', Journal of Econometrics, 47: 197–207.

JENNRICH, R., (1969), 'Asymptotic Properties of Nonlinear Least Squares Estimators', Annals of Mathematical Statistics, 40: 633–43.

KEANE, M., and K. WOLPIN (1992), 'Solution and Estimation of Discrete Dynamic Programming Models by Simulation: Monte Carlo Evidence', Discussion Paper, University of Minnesota.

KEANE, M. P. (1990), 'Four Essays in Empirical Macro and Labor Economics', Ph.D. dissertation, Brown University.

—— (1993), 'Simulation Estimation for Panel Data Models with Limited Dependent Variable Models', in Handbook of Statistics, ii, G. S. MADDALA, C. R. RAO, and H. VINOD (eds.), North-Holland, Amsterdam, 545–70.

—— (1994), 'A Computationally Practical Simulation Estimator for Panel Data with Applications to Estimating Temporal Dependence in Employment and Wages', Econometrica, 62: 95–116.

KENNEDY, J., and J. GENTLE (1980), Statistical Computing, Marcel Dekker, New York.

KIEFER, N., and G. NEUMANN (1979), 'An Empirical Job Search Model with a Test of the Constant Reservation Wage Hypothesis', Journal of Political Economy, 87: 89–107.

KIM C. J. (1994), 'Dynamic Linear Models with Markov Switching', Journal of Econometrics, 60: 1–22.

KIM, S., and N. SHEPHARD (1994), 'Stochastic Volatility: Likelihood Inference and Comparison with ARCH Models', Discussion Paper, Nuffield College, Oxford.

KING, M., M. SENTANA, and S. WADHWANI (1990), 'A Heteroscedastic Model of Assets Returns and Risk Premia with Time Varying Volatility: an Application to Sixteen World Stock Markets', mimeo, London School of Economics.

KITAGAWA, G. (1987), 'Non Gaussian State Space Modeling of Nonstationary Time Series', Journal of the American Statistical Association, 85: 1032–41.

KOOREMAN, P., and G. RIDDER (1983), 'The Effects of Age and Unemployment Percentage on the Duration of Unemployment', European Economic Review, 20: 41–57.

LAFFONT, J. J., H. OSSARD, and Q. VUONG (1995), 'Econometrics of First-Price Auction', Econometrica, 63: 953–80.

LANCASTER, T. (1990), The Econometric Analysis of Transition Data, Cambridge University Press.

LAROQUE, G., and B. SALANIÉ (1989), 'Estimation of Multi-Market Fix-Price Models: an Application of Pseudo Maximum Likelihood Methods', Econometrica, 57: 831–60.

—— —— (1993), 'Simulation Based Estimation of Models with Lagged Latent Variables', Journal of Applied Econometrics, 8: 119–33.

—— —— (1994), 'Estimating the Canonical Disequilibrium Model: Asymptotic Theory and Finite Sample Properties', Journal of Econometrics, 62: 165–210.

LEE, L. F. (1990), 'On the Efficiency of Methods of Simulated Moments and Maximum Simulated Likelihood Estimation of Discrete Response Models', Discussion Paper 260, University of Minnesota.

—— (1995a), 'Simulation Estimation of Dynamic Switching Regression and Dynamic Disequilibrium Models: Some Monte Carlo Results', Working Paper 9512, Hong Kong University.

—— (1995b), 'Asymptotic Bias in Simulated Maximum Likelihood of Discrete Choice Models', Econometric Theory, 11: 937–83.

LERMAN, S., and C. MANSKI (1981), 'On the Use of Simulated Frequencies to Approximate Choice Probabilities', in Structural Analysis of Discrete Data with Econometric Applications, C. MANSKI and D. MCFADDEN (eds.), MIT Press, Cambridge, Mass, 305–19.

LIPPMAN, S., and J. McCALL (1976), 'The Economics of Job Search: a Survey', Economic Inquiry, 14: 155–367.

LIPSTER, R. S., and A. N. SHIRYAYEV (1977), Statistics of Random Processes, I General Theory, Springer-Verlag, Berlin.

—— —— (1978), Statistics of Random Processes, II, Applications, Springer-Verlag, Berlin.

LO, A. (1988), 'Maximum Likelihood Estimation of Generalized Ito Processes with Discretely Sampled Data', Econometric Theory, 4: 231–47.

McCULLAGH, P., and J. A. NELDER (1989), Generalized Linear Models, Chapman & Hall, London.

McFADDEN, D. (1976), 'Quantal Choice Analysis: a Survey', Annals of Economics and Social Measurement, 5: 363–90.

—— (1989), 'A Method of Simulated Moments for Estimation of Discrete Response Models without Numerical Integration', Econometrica, 57: 995–1026.

—— and P. RUUD (1987), 'Estimation of Limited Dependent Variable Models from the Regular Exponential Family by the Method of Simulated Moment', Discussion Paper, University of California at Berkeley.

—— —— (1990), 'Estimation by Simulation', Discussion Paper, MIT.

McGRATTAN, E. (1990), 'Solving the Stochastic Growth Model by Linear–Quadratic Approximation', Journal of Business and Economic Statistics, 8: 41–4.

McKINNON, J. G., and A. A. SMITH (1995), 'Approximate Bias Correction in Econometrics', Discussion Paper, Queen's University.

MAGNAC, T., J. M. ROBIN, and M. VISSER (1995), 'Analysing Incomplete Individual Employment Histories Using Indirect Inference', Journal of Applied Econometrics, 10: 153–70.

MALINVAUD, E. (1970), 'The Consistency of Nonlinear Regressions', Annals of Mathematical Statistics, 41: 956–69.

MARCET, A. (1993), 'Simulation Analysis of Dynamic Stochastic Models: Applications to Theory and Estimation', Discussion Paper 6, University of Barcelona.

MARIANO, R. S., and B. W. BROWN (1985), 'Stochastic Prediction in Dynamic Nonlinear Econometric Systems', Annales de l'INSEE, 59-60: 267–78.

MELINO, A., and S. M. TURNBULL (1990), 'Pricing Foreign Currency Options with Stochastic Volatility', Journal of Econometrics, 45: 239–65.

METROPOLIS, N., A. W. ROSENBLUTH, M. N. ROSENBLUTH, A. H. TELLER, and E. TELLER (1953), 'Equations of State Calculations by Fast Computing Machines', Journal of Chemical Physics, 21: 1087–92.

MIZON, G. E., and J.-F. RICHARD (1986), 'The Encompassing Principle and its Application to Testing non Nested Hypotheses', Econometrica, 54: 657–78.

MONFARDINI, C. (1996), 'Estimating Stochastic Volatility Models Through Indirect Inference', Discussion Paper, European Institute, Florence.

MORAN, P. (1984), 'The Monte-Carlo Evaluation of Orthant Probabilities for Multivariate Normal Distributions', Australian Journal of Statistics, 26: 39–44.

MUHLEISEN, M. (1993), 'Simulation Estimation of State Dependence Effects in Unemployment', Discussion Paper, University of Munich.

NELSON, D. (1990), 'ARCH Models as Diffusion Approximations', Journal of Econometrics, 45: 7–38.

NERLOVE, M., and T. SCHUERMANN (1992), 'Testing a Simple Joint Hypothesis of Rational and Adaptive Expectations with Business Surveys: an Exercise in Simulation Based Inference', Discussion Paper, University of Pennsylvania.

—— and M. WEEKS (1992), 'The Construction of Multivariate Probability Simulators with an Application to the Multivariate Probit Model', Discussion Paper, University of Pennsylvania.

NEWEY, H. (1982), 'Maximum Likelihood Estimation of Misspecified Models', Econometrica, 50: 1–28.

NEWEY, W. K. (1989a), 'Locally Efficient, Residual Based Estimation of Nonlinear Models', Discussion Paper, Princeton University.

—— (1989b), 'Distribution-Free Simulated Moment Estimation of Nonlinear Errors in Variables Models', Discussion Paper, MIT.

—— (1993), 'Flexible Simulated Moment Estimation of Nonlinear Errors in Variables Models', Discussion Paper 9318, MIT.

NEWEY, W. K., and K. D. WEST (1987), 'A Simple, Positive Definite Heteroscedasticity and Autocorrelation Consistent Covariance Matrix', Econometrica, 55: 703–8.

NICKELL, S. (1979), 'Estimating the Probability of Leaving Unemployment', Econometrica, 47: 1249–66.

PAKES, A., and D. POLLARD (1989), 'Simulation and the Asymptotics of Optimization Estimators', Econometrica, 57: 1027–57.

PARDOUX, E., and D. TALAY (1985), 'Discretization and Simulation of Stochastic Equations', Acta Applicandae Mathematica, 3: 23–47.

PASTORELLO, S., E. RENAULT, and N. TOUZI (1994), 'Statistical Inference for Random Variance Option Pricing', Discussion Paper, CREST.

PESARAN, H., and B. PESARAN (1993), 'A Simulation Approach to the Problem of Computing Cox's Statistic for Testing Non-Nested Models', Journal of Econometrics, 57: 377–92.

RAO, P. (1988), 'Statistical Inference from Sampled Data for Stochastic Processes', Contemporary Mathematics, 20, American Mathematical Society.

RICHARD, J.-F. (1973), Posterior and Predictive Densities for Simultaneous Equation Models, Springer-Verlag, Berlin.

—— (1991), 'Applications of Monte Carlo Simulation Techniques in Econometrics and Game Theory', Discussion Paper, Duke University.

ROBERT, C. P. (1996), Méthodes de Monte Carlo par Chaînes de Markov, CREST.

ROBINSON, P. (1982), 'On the Asymptotic Properties of Models Containing Limited Dependent Variables', Econometrica, 50: 27–41.

RUDEBUSCH, G. D. (1993), 'Uncertain Unit Root in Real GNP', The American Economic Review, 83: 264–72.

RUUD, P. (1991), 'Extensions of Estimations Methods Using the EM Algorithm', Journal of Econometrics, 49: 305–41.

SCOTT, L. (1987), 'Option Pricing when the Variance Changes Randomly: Theory, Estimation and Application', Journal of Financial and Quantitative Analysis, 22: 419–38.

SHEPHARD, N. (1993), 'Fitting Nonlinear Time Series with Applications to Stochastic Variance Models', Journal of Applied Econometrics, 8: 563–84.

—— (1994), 'Partial non-Gaussian State Space', Biometrika, 81(1): 115–31.

SMITH, A. (1990), 'Three Essays on the Solution and Estimation of Dynamic Macroeconometric Models', Ph.D. dissertation, Duke University.

—— (1993), 'Estimating Nonlinear Time Series Models Using Simulated Vector Autoregressions', Journal of Applied Econometrics, 8: 63–84.

STEIN, E. M., and J. C. STEIN (1991), 'Stock Price Distribution with Stochastic Volatility: an Analytic Approach', Review of Financial Studies, 4: 727–52.

STERN, S. (1992), 'A Method of Smoothing Simulated Moments of Probabilities in the Multinomial Probit Models', Econometrica, 60: 943–52.

THELOT, C. (1993), 'Note sur la loi logistique et l'imitation', Annales de l'INSEE, 42: 111–25.

TIERNEY, L. (1994), 'Markov Chains for Exploring Posterior Distributions (with discussion)', Annals of Statistics, 22: 1701–62.

TOUZI, N. (1994), 'A Note on Hansen–Scheinkman's Back to the Future: Generating Moment Implications for Continuous Time Markov Processes', Discussion Paper, CREST.

VAN DIJK, H. K. (1987), 'Some Advances in Bayesian Estimation Methods using Monte Carlo Integration', in Advances in Econometrics, vi, T. B. FOMBY and G. F. RHODES (eds.), JAI Press, Greenwich, CT.

VAN PRAAG, B. M.S., and J. P. HOP (1987), 'Estimation of Continuous Models on the Basis of Set-Valued Observations', Paper presented at the Econometric Society European Meeting, Copenhagen.

WHITE, H. (1982), 'Maximum Likelihood Estimation of Misspecified Models', Econometrica, 50: 1–28.

WIGGINS, J. (1987), 'Option Values under Stochastic Volatility', Journal of Financial Economics, 19: 351–72.

ZEGER, S., and R. KARIM (1991), 'Generalized Linear Models with Random Effects: a Gibbs Sampling Approach', Journal of the American Statistical Association, 86: 79–86.

ZELLNER, A., L. BAUWENS, and H. VAN DIJK (1988), 'Bayesian Specification Analysis and Estimation of Simultaneous Equation Models using Monte Carlo Methods', Journal of Econometrics, 38: 39–72.

INDEX